# Feeding Frenzy

Across Europe in Search
of the Perfect Meal

## Stuart Stevens

Ballantine Books • New York

A Ballantine Book
Published by The Ballantine Publishing Group

http://www.randomhouse.com

Library of Congress Catalog Card Number: 98-96012

ISBN: 0-345-42554-5

This edition published by arrangement with Grove/Atlantic Inc.

Cover design by Min Choi
Cover illustration by Michael Tedesco

Manufactured in the United States of America

First Ballantine Books Edition: June 1998

10 9 8 7 6 5 4 3 2 1

For
PAUL CUBETA,
who taught me how to read,
and
J. P. COSNARD,
who tried to teach me how to eat

# Feeding Frenzy

# Chapter
# One

Blame it on Rat. I do.

      She proposed the idea when we were lifting weights. It was a late Friday night in New York and we were doing what we had fallen into a lot that spring—we'd meet at the World Gym, lift, and then go eat. Rat was wearing a black one-piece suit that looked like the sort of thing bathing beauties wore on the Riviera in the twenties. There's a picture around of Zelda trying to look sexy and she's wearing something similar. Only Rat—that was her name, Rachel Kelly, but even her mom called her Rat—hers was all shiny and made from some sort of high-tech sports stretchy stuff that was supposed to do miraculous things, like make sure you never sweat or whisk the sweat away from your skin, something like that. I never could get this kind of thing straight, but Rat knew all about it. She was an ex-model who worked for a fashion designer and could explain quite movingly why some grades of wool make you look like a million dollars and others, you were better off cutting a few holes in a big plastic garbage sack and heading out the door. Call it a flair for fashion.

      I had never known anybody who worked in the fashion business. I had also never known a woman who was almost six feet tall and could bench-press more than my IQ. Not that there aren't a lot of strong women in the world these days, and most seem to find their way to the gyms of New York. I've seen women in New York health clubs that I'd trade a first-round draft pick for without even knowing what they did in the forty-yard dash. You know what I mean—BIG WOMEN. Strong women.

But Rat wasn't like them, you see. She didn't look BIG, just tall and lithe, at least until she took off the old University of Wyoming tee shirt she liked to wear, the one with the bucking horse and the slogan "Ride with Me Wyoming," and got down to just that shiny black old-fashioned bathing-suit thing and you saw her pick up seventy-five pounds of curl bar the way my high school girlfriends in Mississippi used to hoist diet sodas.

Anyway, we were working on incline presses and she put it something like this: "What if we went to Europe and ate. Ate a lot."

This surprised me. Not that she liked the idea of eating but the notion of us traveling together. Somewhere in the background there was a serious boyfriend I had always figured to be of the live-in variety. He was a lawyer, I knew, and older, a midforties guy who was a partner in one of the big white-shoe law factories. Rat had talked about how he didn't like it when she introduced herself at firm functions as "Rat" Kelly. She had tried to reassure him, she told me, by explaining to him that all his partners were way too busy thinking about how they wanted to sleep with her to worry about her name.

"I'm sure he found that very reassuring," I said.

"Not really." She frowned. "Lawyers in love." She shrugged.

"Europe?" I asked her how, as we changed weights ferociously. We liked to lift quickly, pyramiding up to a maximum and then working down. This may seem unimportant but it was a matter of great controversy in the gym, where you either believed in pyramiding or you didn't, and blows had actually been exchanged over this subject, though usually by the heavy steroid users and nobody paid much attention.

"I think we should go," she said decisively. "Just to eat." She said this last bit because I was looking sort of skeptical.

We liked to eat and did it a lot. It was really all we did together, go to restaurants and the gym, which made, I suppose, for an appallingly shallow sort of New York nineties-styled friendship. This never bothered me at all. Rat was an inspiration in the gym and a pleasure around the dinner table and neither one of us cared to ask a lot of difficult questions. The truth was, I really didn't know Rat Kelly very well at all. Later, I would think about this a lot, when it was entirely too late.

"Where?" I asked, as she slipped under the bar.

"Start in England. Work our way over to France."

France. Which made me think about the first great meal I ever had.

I thought I could remember every bite, even though it had been a whole bunch of years. I know I swore at the time I'd never forget. I'm positive we had sweet mussels, tiny little things, in a sauce of white wine, cream, and chives. There was lobster doused, oddly, with port and grilled with butter. She had a bouillabaisse and I had grilled sardines, the only time, before or since, I've ever liked the things. I can't imagine why I ordered them, but maybe the waiter insisted or maybe it was because I was excited seeing a name—*sardines*—on the menu that I actually recognized. It was, after all, my first time in France.

We were in a little restaurant on the side of a cliff in a town called Eze, wedged between Saint-Jean-Cap-Ferrat and Monte Carlo. I was nineteen, I think, and on one of the many interminable vacations that Oxford likes to provide. She was a few years older, an American, but she had lived in France for a while, which seemed very impressive and somehow important. It was late March and not far away there were almost-nude women lying on rocks they called a beach.

I swore then that before long I would come back and eat in every good restaurant in France.

Which, of course, I never did.

Instead I seemed to be drawn to countries with the worst food imaginable, places like Turkistan and Africa, where every day you woke up hoping you could avoid gustatory terror but knowing that before you slept again, horrible things would be going inside your mouth. The best strategy was simply to try to eat as little as possible. But I seemed cursed by an ever hopeful palate. "Termites? Termite larva? Could be interesting. I'll try a handful." This was never a good idea.

But France . . .

"*Stuart!*" Rat yelled. Her face was bright red as she struggled under some impossibly large weight.

I snapped out of my gustatory trance and helped her right the bar. "You are some big help. Like lifting with Carl, for Christ's sake."

Carl was the lawyer Rat called her boyfriend. And he hated gyms and exercise. That much, at least, I knew.

"What restaurants?"

"Three-stars," she said without a moment's hesitation. "Just the Michelin three-stars. The best food in the world."

"When do you want to go?" I asked.

"How about next week?"


The car started on the first crank. This made me very happy and inexplicably proud.

The dockworkers all gave exuberant thumbs-up signs, as if we had just test-fired the space shuttle. Without blowing any-one up.

The engine was about as loud as the space shuttle but with a deeper, sexier growl. In the closed belly of the cargo ship that had brought it over from America, it sounded like a wild beast anxious to escape its cage. I squeezed down gently on the accelerator.

The car leapt forward. The dockworkers applauded.

The gangplank was pitched at a ferocious angle. With my ears ringing with the growl of the V-8 engine, I put on the brakes. Nothing happened. This was not good.

The Mustang leapt down the gangplank. A pair of workers in white smocks jumped for safety. "I can't stop!" I yelled, redundantly. The top was down. That was the first thing I had done, of course. Put the top down.

I steered toward the parking lot next to the docks. It was large and empty and I drove the car in a circle, wondering what in God's name I was going to do. Like concerned physicians, dockworkers in their white coats gathered around as I drove the car in a tight circle. Or at least as tight as a 1965 Mustang would turn.

The workers yelled advice. With the engine roar and their thick accents, I had trouble understanding them. One fellow with long sideburns of the type favored by Elvis in his later years held up his hand and motioned. At first I didn't understand but then it made perfect sense. I could read his lips:

"TURN OFF THE DAMN ENGINE!"

Which I did.

It shuddered to a stop.

"What's the problem, mate?"

"The brakes don't work."

A long pause ensued while they all nodded their heads as if the X rays had come back showing particularly nasty stuff.

"Now, mate," the one with the Elvis sideburns finally offered, "you are buggered but good."


When I finally pulled into the Royal Overseas League, Rat was having tea in the garden.

"So is the car beautiful?" she wanted to know.

I groaned and sank into the uncomfortable wrought-iron chairs. With shaky hands I took a sip of her tea and realized for the first time that my hands were filthy. Rat took one of the linen napkins and wiped off my face.

"You look terrible," she said. "Was car-car naughty?"

This struck me as both a phenomenally idiotic and annoying question, rather like asking a soldier on leave from the Somme, "Was it muddy?"

A young waitress appeared over me. She seemed amused at my condition.

"Beer. I can have beer, can't I?" I asked.

"You can have all the beer we've got," she promised and scampered off.

"El Cid has problems?" Rat asked. For some reason she had always referred to the Mustang as El Cid.

I looked around the garden. A young couple dressed in white sat across from us drinking Mumm's champagne. They were maybe twenty at the most and looked at each other with a first-date longing that filled the air with sex. With their white clothes and prim haircuts, the ostentatious champagne, the two could have been period pieces of twenty, thirty, fifty years ago. They spoke in guarded conversation that never steered close to the lust that hung between them—just a little bit of English repressed desire perfectly captured for the ages.

The other tables were filled with the sort of people you'd expect to turn up at a lecture entitled "New Geographic Discoveries in Ancient Turkey," the evening's entertainment at the Royal Overseas League. Through some odd series of events involving an obscure friend, Rat and I had ended up staying at this place, where the Mountbatten lecture hall seemed to await his eminent return.

Looking out over the shaded garden just a hedge away from the lush greens of St. James's Park, I thought back to the motorway rest stop where I'd spent a lot of the hot June afternoon. It had been crowded with scores of tie-dyed Grateful Dead fans jockeying for space with the English version of Hell's Angels, mostly a polite bunch on Japanese bikes that would have been whacked to pieces with baseball bats by real bikers on Harleys in America. The bikers I'd liked more than the Deadheads. The bikers had helped me with the brakes while the Deadheads stood around the Mustang and said "Cool" a lot.

I looked over at Rat. She had a happy gleam in her eye that didn't quite figure.

"We have a little problem," I told her. "With the brakes." I started to explain how at the moment the brake system was held together with a throttle spring borrowed from the saddlebags of a well-equipped Honda rider, but it seemed too preposterous even to talk about. The Mustang, after all, had been my idea.

Sitting in New York it had seemed most important to make the trip in a very American car, and an old Mustang convertible was perfect. That way no one could think we were English—a particularly disturbing notion—or French, which would also be highly regrettable. All of my car aficionado friends assured me we could sell it at the end of the trip for a handsome profit. This was very appealing considering the dollar–to–foie gras exchange rate. Which is how I ended up on the phone to a place called Mid-American Mustang in St. Louis, buying a candy-apple red 1965 Mustang convertible I had never seen and wouldn't see, circumstances being a bit rushed, until I had arrived in Southampton that morning to drive it not so triumphantly off the boat.

For a moment Rat seemed truly worried. "But you drove it here? It made it?"

"Yes. Sort of. But we may die the first time we try to drive it."

"Oh, that's okay," she said cheerfully, standing up. "Come here, I have to show you something."

She stood up, and for the first time I saw that she was wearing a gold lamé dress that had been easy to pack because there wasn't much of it. The teenagers drinking champagne stared unhesitantly.

I followed.

She walked over to the far corner of the garden, where a little iron gate led out onto Queen's Walk and, just beyond that, St. James's Park.

She pointed to a contented-looking golden retriever tied to the fence.

"What's that?" I asked, a sense of dread cascading rapidly through my being.

"That's Henry, and he's ours!"

"Rat." I could still hear the roar of the Mustang's V-8 in my ears. In all likelihood, I had suffered permanent hearing loss. "Where did this come from?"

"I'll tell you all about it," she promised. "Isn't he adorable?"


We left the Mustang at the Overseas League and took the train to the Waterside Inn. There were three of us—me, Rat, and the Dog. That's how I thought of the creature—the Dog. Rat, of course, called it Henry. She called it Henry in quite loving tones that I'm sure would have driven Carl the Lawyer mad with jealousy. But I refused to think of the Dog as Henry. Even though Henry was a name I liked not in the least, Henry *was* a name, and any sort of name, particularly a first name like Henry, implied a sort of intimacy I had no intention of establishing with the Dog. The Dog was not going to be part of this trip, of that I was certain.

There were three of us on the train because there was no easy place to leave the Dog. This is the sort of problem that people traveling with dogs have all the time, or so I imagined,

and one good reason I did not own a dog or intend ever to travel
with the same. As far as I was concerned, man had spent thousands of years evolving to the point where it was no longer necessary to sleep and travel with animals, and I felt a certain personal
obligation not to let this progress backslide.

British Rail seems to share my canine attitudes. They have
a list of regulations that basically outline the hows and whys of
dog transport, a long list that boils down to the fact that they
prefer all dogs to schedule a session with a taxidermist before
availing themselves of the services of British Rail—an entirely
sensible position, I felt.

An Anglo-Indian rail official with a long ponytail stopped
Rat as she was strolling onto the 8:05 local to Bray-on-Thames.
He was maybe twenty-five and somehow wore his blue British
Rail uniform with a certain jauntiness, as if it were a costume he
had found in a secondhand store and he was on his way to a
party.

"That is," he observed most casually, "a dog, I believe."

"Bet your ass." Rat beamed. "Beauty, huh?"

"This is a problem, I'm afraid."

"Don't be. His name is Henry. I'm keeping him for a family that was going to take him to America for a year but found
out that he would have to be quarantined for two months and
it would have broken their heart to do that to their dog. So we
just agreed to take care of him."

"We?" I mumbled. I had heard this story before. The family had been staying at the Overseas League, and I suppose I believed Rat's story. I couldn't think of any logical reason she would
have gone out and kidnapped somebody's dog, and I knew for
a fact she hadn't brought it from New York.

"Where are you going?" the official asked. He was suddenly
staring at us both, but mostly Rat. On a late Sunday afternoon
in Paddington Station we seemed egregiously overdressed—me

in a dark double-breasted suit and she in her gold lamé something or other. Standing over six feet in her heels with Henry on a black leather leash, Rat looked like a Helmut Newton model on her way to work.

"To some restaurant called the Waterside which will probably be terribly boring but we were thinking about going out later when we came back and we were wondering if you could suggest some place fun. A club sort of place." She blurted this all at once at a stream-of-consciousness pace. It was news to me that we were planning to go out afterward. After my day wrestling with the Mustang, I wasn't even sure I could make it through dinner without falling asleep.

"You like to go to clubs?" the ponytailed train official asked.

"Is the Pope Catholic?" Rat demanded.

He concentrated on this for a moment and then smiled. "I like clubs."

"Great!" Rat made it sound like he had just told her that she had won the lottery. "Let's meet later on!"

He glanced quickly at me.

"It's okay," Rat explained. "He's not my boyfriend."

She said this with the dismissive tone of a big sister explaining the presence of a younger brother.

The conductor's face brightened—and then fell when Rat added, "My boyfriend is in New York." She paused, seeing his disappointment. "And New York is a *long* way away. We'll have lots of fun. Where should we meet?"

He hesitated for a moment, as if wondering if he were the victim of some cruel practical joke, a *Dating Game* prank.

"There is a place," he finally said, lowering his voice as if passing on state secrets, "that we could meet. It is in Soho. Manitoba Coffee Shop."

"Great! Around midnight, maybe a little later," Rat said, and then she held out her hand. "Rat Kelly."

"Vetrham. Vetrham West."

I introduced myself and we marched on board—me, Rat, and the Dog.


It was a local commuter train, with bench seats; more of an overgrown subway car than a grand long-distance express. Everyone seemed to be reading one of the London tabloids—the *Daily Mail* or *Sun*—and the headlines screeched of a fresh U.S. bombing attack on Iraq, the first for President Clinton.

"I feel better when we are bombing them," the very tall young man across from me said without a hint of a smile. He was maybe thirty and had an unfortunate haircut that seemed to involve a pair of shears and an oval bowl. With his reddish nose and angular features, he reminded me of a military recruit on his way to his first posting.

"Them?" I asked, not because I didn't understand but because I was startled and had to say something.

"Iraq," he explained, a bit exasperated. "Our Bedouin brothers. Rug merchants to the stars."

"You feel better when we're bombing them?" I asked.

"Don't you?"

It was not a subject I really had an opinion on. I had to admit that it certainly didn't *bother* me that we were bombing Iraq.

"Should have marched right into Baghdad when we had the chance. The best thing that could have happened to them. Put a Marks and Sparks right smack on Saddam Avenue. Bloody marvelous." He laughed.

"What's Marks and Sparks?" Rat asked.

"Where you didn't get that dress, I'll tell you that."

"Am I suppose to be offended?" Rat asked pleasantly, stroking Henry's head. I had to admit that Henry had taken to train travel with great equanimity, and I wondered if he was an experienced sneaker-on of trains.

"Complimented, most definitely," our friend with the bad

haircut said, smiling broadly. He arched his eyebrows and whispered urgently, "Hung 'em up by the lampposts."

"What?" I asked, startled.

"That's what Saddam did to everybody that opposed him when he came up. Those fundamentalist-type, junior-grade ayatollahs in training? Drove nails right into their heads. While their families watched."

He said this with a certain glee, eyes widening in appreciation. Rat stiffened and, I suppose, so did I.

"Nip that stuff right in the bud. Marvelous." He said this slowly, for dramatic power, no doubt. He was a great performer.

"Beautiful scarf," he observed casually to Rat. It was a long, soft thing. "That's the stuff the baby Jesus would have loved to have been swaddled in, you can bet on that."

Rat and I looked at each other. Neither of us said a word. Nor did we say anything until he got off at the next stop, South Hall.

"Mad," Rat whispered, as if she were afraid he might overhear.

"Well," I said, "he does have a point. A very upscale sort of nativity scene, but I could see it." I felt her scarf.

"Polyester," she announced petulantly. "A very fine cut of polyester."

The bleak suburbs of London rolled past, rows of block council houses. Flashes of well-tended gardens squeezed in between the rows made it only more depressing. The soft light of an English summer cast the red brick in a warm glow. These places would never look better, and on a December afternoon when it was getting dark at 3:30 and pools of ice lay in the cracked asphalt sidewalks, it would be hard to imagine a more cheerless and despairing scene.

We were heading to the Waterside Inn, about forty miles outside of London. It was a creation of the Roux brothers, the pair that had helped teach London what it was like to eat great food. I had been dreaming about their duckling cured in tea, a Roux rendition that was supposed to be extraordinarily lean and delicate, two hard things to come by in a duck.

Everyone who knew the Waterside talked about its tranquil riverfront setting and described the place as a perfect country haven. But since leaving London we had been traveling through what looked to be the set of *A Clockwork Orange*, a failed industrial landscape where despair rose like heat waves from every street.

This was when Rat decided to tell me what apparently she had been waiting to tell me since that first day in the gym.

"Stuart," she began, in an excited tone that I was learning to fear, "I've got this idea of how we should do the trip."

"Umm." I was staring at the page-three girl of the Sunday *Mail*. It always amazed me how the English could take pasty and pudgy girls of the sort you saw lounging around every corner tea shop and celebrate them as pinups. This was probably a very healthy tendency, all in all—praising the everyday instead of some unlikely ideal.

"I think we should eat in all of the Michelin three-star restaurants."

"We are," I said. "Tonight the Waterside, and tomorrow we've got reservations at La Tante Claire. That's it for England."

"No, I mean *all* the restaurants. In Europe."

I smiled, even though the Dog had begun to chew on my ankle. It was a lunatic notion.

"On consecutive days," she added.

"Rat, I *am* going to kill this dog. Or leave it at the restaurant. I'm sure some rich stockbroker will take it home to his overpriced flat."

"All the three-stars on consecutive days. England first, then Belgium, Germany, France, Italy. There are only twenty-nine."

It did have a certain appeal. "That's ridiculous," I said, which, of course, it was.

"I sort of have to."

"Have to—"

"Eat in all of them."

"This is a mandate from God?"

"Carl," she corrected. "He promised he'd pay for the whole thing if I ate in all of them on consecutive days."

"You're kidding."

She shook her head.

"I thought he didn't want you to leave New York?"

"Of course he didn't. We had this huge fight. But if I eat in all twenty-nine nonstop, he pays."

"Why?"

"He likes to challenge me. Particularly with things he thinks are sort of demeaning."

"What a delightful relationship. And why is eating in all the three-stars demeaning?"

"On consecutive days, sure it is. Who could actually enjoy that?"

"I could," I said without hesitation. Then thought about it for a moment and added, "I think."

"I think it sounds terrible," she said brightly. "But we have to do it."

"Let me ask a silly question. *Why* does Carl like to propose demeaning challenges?"

"He's a sicko, obviously. Which means that the next question is going to be, Why is he my boyfriend?"

"You're right. That is the next question."

"Look, it's not that complicated. New York City is full of strange and twisted interdependent sick kinds of relationships. Should it be that odd that I happened to find myself in one? You know what it's like for a girl to come from Wyoming to New York?"

I thought about this for a moment. "No."

"You meet the most unbelievable creeps imaginable. I could tell you first-date stories that would stop your heart with sheer horror."

We both laughed. There was something in the back of my mind that was going off like a yellow caution light, but I figured I would just worry about it later.

The Burnham stop passed by and the train thinned out and then there was more green than junkyards and brick and it began to look like the countryside England likes to advertise.

"Good," she announced. "I knew you'd like the idea. We'll leave for Brussels the day after tomorrow."

"Rat!"

"Don't worry. I'll take care of everything."

She jumped up, trailing Henry by his leash. I looked out the window and saw that we were at Bray-on-Thames.

"Dinner," Rat said. "Everything depends on dinner, right?"

I followed her and the dog out of the train.

# Chapter
# Two

When the Dog and I appeared at the front door of the Waterside, the doorman in black tie seemed startled. "You don't allow dogs, do you?" I asked hopefully.

Rat was unwinding herself from the cab we'd gotten at the station. He looked at her and seemed to be struck dumb.

"I knew it would be okay," Rat said, taking the leash from me and leading a madly tail-wagging Henry into the restaurant.

"Rat . . ."

The doorman smiled and shrugged.

We entered what looked like a small inn or pub of the sort you could find everywhere in England. It seemed odd that everyone talked about what a gorgeous place it was. The maître d' met us in the foyer, which was decorated with the usual plaques and awards. He smiled and, instead of objecting strenuously to Henry, as I had hoped, he simply took the leash from Rat, as if we had just handed him a present he had been expecting for some time.

"A retriever?" he asked and, without waiting for an answer, said, "He'll have a splendid meal."

*What about us?* I wanted to yell.

He handed the leash to a tuxedoed assistant and gestured for us to follow him into the dining room. We walked into one large open room, and then at a glance I understood why everyone called the Waterside beautiful. It wasn't the dining room—a simple, but pleasant space dominated by white—it was the way the room blended into the river, with sliding glass doors open so that the pier jutting into the river looked like an extension of the room.

On a garden bench by the pier we ordered drinks, and I felt a deep sense of well-being begin to seep into my soul. Around me was an ordered, peaceful world, a world with rules I welcomed. Over the next couple of hours I wouldn't have to deal with Mustang brakes or dogs or telephones. There was every reason to believe that pleasure was imminent. Chaos would be banished. I felt safe. Protected.

Rat, who had worked in restaurants for years between modeling jobs in her early days in New York, looked the dining room over with an appreciative eye. "Twenty, maybe twenty-two tables. Listen," she said, nodding toward the room.

Even though every table was full, except for the one waiting for us—or, at least, I hoped the empty one was waiting for us—only a low-level buzz emanated from the room. "In New York," Rat explained, "there would be three more four tops and a pair of deuces at least."

"Four tops—tables for four," she answered my confused look. "Deuces are tables for two. As in 'Check out the cute single on the station-four deuce.'"

"Right."

"I count twenty-one, no, twenty-two in the front house." She nodded toward the staff bustling around. "It's interesting how the back waiters are dressed the same as the maître d's and headwaiters. Very democratic."

There were a lot of ways I would have described the Waterside before I came to the notion of *democratic*. The crowd was Typical English Country—which is to say, a mostly unattractive bunch with too many teeth and a consistently thick subcutaneous layer of fat that probably wasn't going to be decreasing by the evening's end. But this was a little world that had been de-

signed to hold these people, and just as a basically disagreeable
piece of furniture can look inviting if surrounded by complementary pieces, the clientele seemed perfectly *appropriate*. In truth, it
would have been quite odd to walk into what was basically a
sexed-up pub on the outskirts of dreary suburban London and
find a drop-dead-gorgeous gaggle of models or a scruffy bunch
of foodie intellectuals—no matter how much fun it might have
been.

"The question is . . ." Rat pondered.

"Yes, Rat, what *is* the question?" I asked, feeling, suddenly,
preposterously good. The alcohol had no doubt played a role,
along with the soft light. A young waiter had brought us our
drinks—both of us had ordered beer. In the fading twilight of
an English summer day, it was exactly the right thing to drink,
but there were few restaurants of this sort in which you could
order beer before dinner and not have sensed the staff reacting
as if a homeless person had burst into the restaurant to announce
that he was taking over the kitchen and just wait until you tasted
his soufflé. I mean, this sort of thing simply *isn't* done.

But in England, of course, it is, all the time. Even at the
Waterside. After all, the English had been doing this for a long
time. Back in 1436, Henry VI had issued a Royal Writ hailing a
new drink "called biere" as "notable, healthy and temperate."
About 150 years later, a Dutchman named Paul Hentzner wrote
in a *A Journey into England*, which no less than Horace Walpole
translated, that "the general drink is beer, which is prepared from
barley, and is excellently well tasted, but strong and what soon
fuddles."

I was enjoying the fuddling qualities when Rat interrupted.
"The question," she said with great profundity, "is how many
people are in the kitchen?"

It was *food* I was thinking about, not staff. It was *the menu*
that had seized my attention.

Menus are tricky. They should be little windows into the soul of a restaurant, not just a list of what and how much. We turn to menus with fear and doubt, looking for the reassurance of an old friend, the insight of a trusted sage. You want to be able to talk to a menu, ask it questions and get candid, brilliant responses. Did the last people fall in love with the *Noisettes d'Agneau et ses Ris Gratinés aux Fines Herbes?* Is the *Pavé de Bar Grillé au Parfum d'Olives* simply enchanting or merely simple? Is the chef happy tonight? Is the chef here tonight? Is the food better when the chef isn't around? (This is the case more often than we like to admit, I fear.) What's left over from yesterday and what came from the market just this morning?

But, alas, most menus are stupid and, worse yet, deceptive, deceitful creatures. Experience teaches us to approach them with wary suspicion, looking for traps and deadfalls at every turn. They must be pondered and studied for hints and clues, like the trail of a wary beast determined to hide his true destination. We stare at menus in windows, desperately wanting more information. We press against the glass, hoping someone will whisper the *inside story.* Is this worth an evening of my life? Will I feel enriched, graced, or cheated and soiled, left with the bitter aftertaste of money spent and disappointment delivered?

The Waterside's menu was an appalling-*looking* document. It was the sort of thing a French restaurant in my hometown of Jackson, Mississippi—that one, really expensive place that thought so much of itself—would have considered very distinguished. *Classy.* It was four pages of sepia-toned script on a cream-colored stock. There was something about the combination of French and English I found grating, like a badly dubbed film or a starlet from Oklahoma rolling her r's and lamenting how much the Left Bank had changed. If what language is about is this thing called communication, why is it necessary to write "If a starter or crustacean is required as a Main Course there will be a charge

of 50% extra" in English but then describe those same crustaceans as "*Crabe des Iles*" or "*Tronçonnettes de Homard Poêlées Minute
au Porto Blanc?*" It's not like the English language lacks a precise
English translation for *crabe*, for Heaven's sake.

"You don't get it," Rat said, interrupting my menu rant.
"The fake French is part of the Total Restaurant Experience. It's
what people want, or think they want, when they Dine Out.
Restaurants are theater, and this is just another theatrical touch,
like the way they hand you your Playbill and escort you to your
seat—"

"Playbills are in English," I groused.

"Shut up," she said pleasantly. "Or the dimming of the lights
and those Milk Dud things they serve at intermission. It's a little
ritual of dining that if you don't know French you are supposed
to be enchanted and impressed and, of course, intimidated by
and if you do know French, you get to show off and impress
everybody else at your table. Get it?"

The maître d' appeared and gestured toward the one empty
table. He was in his midthirties with a beard and the sort of friendly
eyes that come with liking what you do.

"Tell me," Rat asked, and he gave Rat a look that made it
clear he would tell anything she wanted to know, "how large is
the kitchen staff?"

He looked at Rat inquisitively, a smile playing across his
face.

"Large? A few are quite large. You would like to see?" He
gestured toward the kitchen.

"I am *starving*," I said emphatically, realizing it for the first
time.

"How *many*?" Rat persisted as she took the chair the maître
d' held for her.

"Twenty or so. It depends . . . but basically the same as you
see here . . ." He gestured out across the dining room.

"One to one," Rat said. "I like it. You would never see that in America. Never."

Two small plates magically appeared before us. I dove right in. It was sharp and tangy and crunchy and good.

"I would say," Rat said, pausing in midbite to savor, "a tapenade with tomato mousse and greens in Dijon vinaigrette. What would you say?"

"I would say it's an olive paste on croutons with a little tomato action and I wish it were bigger."

"Exactly."

We looked up from our suddenly empty plates and smiled at each other. This was going to be fun.

"Is it my imagination," I muttered, still smiling, "or is everybody in this place staring at us?"

"Well," Rat answered, still holding her smile, "it is doubtful that ever in the history of the Waterside has a first-course freebie been devoured with such alacrity and speed."

"Alacrity and speed. That's good."

Despite how uninviting, how *boring* it looked from the outside, the menu held promise. By habit, I read the fish courses first. There were only a few items, always a good sign.

*Pavé de Bar Grillé au Parfum d'Olives*
*Dos de Saumon Poêlé aux Epices sur Croquants de Légumes,*
  *Nage de Persil*
*Chausson de Lotte Beurre de Noisettes Truffé, sur Nage de Citronelle*
*Truite au Bleu, Beurre de Nage et Peluches de Cerfeuil*

A note at the bottom read, in English, "Our Crayfish and Trout are kept in a fish tank and prepared when ordered." It reminded me of the scene in one of my favorite books, *Blue Trout and Black Truffles*, in which the author, Joseph Wechsberg, describes visiting the legendary Fernand Point's Restaurant de la Pyramide just outside Lyons.

He [Fernand Point] ushered me through a doorway and took me into a small courtyard. "I want to show you our aquarium," he said.

The aquarium consisted of two square tanks. In one I saw a couple of dozen brook trout swimming around, and in the other a number of crayfish. The water in each tank was kept fresh by a flowing faucet.

M. Mercier joined us. "Are we going to serve monsieur a trout?" he asked. "*Au bleu*, perhaps?"

"I haven't decided yet," M. Point said.

He turned to me. "So often our clients ask for what they call difficult things, with long and fancy names. People don't know that the most difficult and also the best dishes are the simple ones. What did you cook for your family on your last day off, Paul?"

"A *choucroute*," M. Mercier said.

"There you are. Here is a great chef, who can cook a chicken in champagne with truffles the like of which has never been tasted, and what does he cook for himself at home? *Choucroute*—cabbage, delicious soft ham, Alsatian sausage, and very young potatoes—and what could be better?"

He swallowed. I found myself swallowing too. My stomach was gnawing.

"But it takes experience," he said. "What looks easier than to make a *sauce béarnaise*? Butter, egg yolks, chopped shallots—nothing to it, is there? But years of practice are needed before you can do it right. Forget to watch for a single instant and it's gone, finished, lost. Everybody thinks he can fry eggs, and I suppose anybody can, but to fry them so they are soft and mellow throughout, not burned on the bottom and raw on top—that is art, my friend. Isn't that right, Paul?"

"Absolutely," said M. Mercier.

"Absolutely. Now monsieur, let us return to the salon and think seriously about lunch."

The trout sounded delightful, but I thought I knew what it would be like and the bass I could only just imagine—the tartness of the olives. But the question of the "*pavé*" preparation put me off. By all rights it should have been wonderful, but I had not had the best of days and was looking for a sure bet.

Which is how we landed on the duck: *Caneton Challandais Rôti au Jasmin et son Jus à la Cannelle* (*2 personnes*).

There was a time, call it a stage, when I had ordered duck right and left. I ordered it like a Texan would a steak, a simple, dependable choice always gratifying in a certain obvious way and hard to really screw up. But then I spent months in China and, until I learned better, I assumed I had landed in Duck Heaven. In fact, it was more of a hell, and I waded—quite literally, given the grease—my way through a succession of the most appalling fowls imaginable. I was a prisoner of my own lack of imagination, and as my own jailer, I kept serving up the canard equivalent of prison fare. Until finally it dawned on me that the gate was open and I could just walk out into freedom. That little epiphany came one February night in Beijing when it was, typically, about zero degrees and the restaurant, also typically, was only about ten degrees warmer. There were no doors, only heavy blankets that flapped in the fierce wind, and I was staring at what seemed like my hundredth duck of the winter. A beggar dashed over from the edge of the room and grabbed a slice off the serving plate in the center of the table. This happened not infrequently and was greeted by the regular patrons with the same calm disdain that a homeless beggar outside of a restaurant in New York elicits from the exiting patrons. It wasn't that anyone *liked* it, but there was a certain guilt of the well-fed at work and no one vociferously objected, including the management.

The beggar, who was a few years older than me, wore fingerless gloves, highly functional attire for keeping the hands warmish but the fingers still nimble for the quick snatch. I was wearing similar gloves, the notion of which—wearing gloves in a restaurant—would have struck me as bizarre just a few months earlier but now seemed no less odd than putting on a coat in a snowstorm. It was freezing, and the fact that you were inside dining could not obscure the looming discomforts of frozen digits.

I did not begrudge the beggar a piece of my sad pile of duck remains. He darted in, snatched, and retreated to the sidelines. We looked at each other across the restaurant, the air crowded with the smoke of the little fires heating Mongolian hot pots and the haze of bad cigarettes, and though he said not a word, I know as he bit into his largish hunk of duck, he was thinking, "This is really bad."

Across the room, I gnawed a piece of the duck, and he knew I was thinking, "Do we really have to eat this?" But we did, because this was 1987 Beijing on a February Saturday night and you had to eat something and better choices were elusive.

That was the last duck I had eaten until the Waterside one soft June evening.

Michel Roux came out when the duck was presented. He looked to be a man comfortable with his role in life: late fifties, eyes that smiled, and a gentleness that was immediately endearing. He stood to the side while one of his captains lifted the silver lid of the serving platter with the mandatory flourish. Another, more senior captain, stood ready with glistening carving knife and serving fork.

In truth, the duck looked a bit forlorn on its grand platter: a smallish fowl with shiny brown skin, a pretty piece of work with a comforting, woodsy smell but hardly a showstopper. As if to

counter this somewhat vulnerable moment, the captain immediately set to work with his elegant dismemberment. Michel Roux
smiled at the sight. "It is the carving of the duck that is most
pleasant, don't you think?" We nodded, but of course I'd never
thought about it before in my life. I was still surprised by the fact
that he was standing over our table, great white toque worn at a
jaunty angle, his apron tied with a flashy side knot. Was it Rat
that drew him out, or was it just routine graciousness and charm?

Watching the carving closely, Rat noted that the creature
looked exceptionally lean. She had a way of talking about the
fat content of a dead duck that made it sound like some great
sexy secret. The chef's eyes flared, and he immediately began to
explain that the problem with so many ducks these days is that
they are raised primarily for foie gras, hideously force-fed until
bursting. He pantomimed the force-feeding of a duck with great
vividness, cheeks bulging, eyes wide as saucers. I was impressed.
Rat giggled. This sort of feeding, he told us, was great for the liver
and the foie gras but terrible for the meat of the fowl. "So fatty!"
He shuddered. The Roux ducks were different. They were raised
solely for their meat, fed perfectly designed, balanced, low-fat
meals from birth. A super duck for the eating! A bodybuilder of
a duck! Lean, strong! Like mademoiselle!

And with a quick half bow, the chef was gone and we were
facing plates of perfectly carved, decidedly lean-looking duck.
The captain stood discretely to the side, an expectant, confident
smile on his face. I had that reassuring, quite pleasing sense of
being surrounded by professionals who were good at what they
did and loved their work. It was a pleasant, almost childlike
sensation.

The Waterside was the second of two restaurants started by
the Roux brothers to earn three stars. The other, Le Gavroche,
was the first three-star restaurant in England—but when the
Waterside opened, Michelin immediately dropped Le Gavroche

to two stars. It was understood that this was punishment for the brothers dividing their attention. In the eyes of the Michelin Gods, running two restaurants was a seductive, evil sort of thing that began to smack of franchising. One chef, one restaurant: this was the natural order of the world, and any sort of tampering could not be tolerated.

The duck did not disappoint. Somewhere underneath the strong natural flavor of the duck was a hint of tea. The flesh was moist, the skin crisp, and, yes, it was the leanest duck I'd ever tasted. Eating duck is an easy thing to regret immediately after the fact, like too many desserts or hot dogs for breakfast. It's that heavy, somehow *unclean* sensation of gustatory sin. But not the brothers Roux duck, which struck me as something of a major achievement in the grand scheme of things.

A dyspeptic motorboat passed by billowing pungent clouds of gray smoke that wafted toward the dining room. Rat and I looked at each other, giggling. It seemed everyone else chose to ignore it, as if some grievous social faux pas had been committed and by not acknowledging it, embarrassment was spared for all parties.

We adjourned to the gazebo for dessert and coffee. *Adjourned.* That's how one of the captains put it—Would you care to adjourn to the gazebo?—an old-fashioned, not incidental turn of phrase, at once both gracious and self-aggrandizing. It implied that something grand and important had occurred from which one *could* adjourn. No one *adjourned* from McDonald's. And it implied—insisted, really—that this was an evening that was occurring in acts, with a beginning, middle, and end, a participatory sort of performance piece launched by this efficient staff led by a highly decorated artistic director. There was something silly about it, of course, but all ritual had a preposterous, ludicrous quality if examined with any seriousness, from strapping into a tux for the opera to the motions of obedience at the heart of any religious service. This was a mutual conspiracy between all parties to lend grace and importance to a few hours of borrowed time.

The gazebo seemed to be a prop left over from some mad tea dance on Fire Island: red, green, and so very *frilly*. A plate of brightly colored, overdecorated petit fours was waiting on the table, like the final stage dressing just before the curtain rose.

"Cookies," Rat exclaimed, with what seemed a far inadequate description for what we were facing, "are absolutely my favorite food." She dove right in, scooping up several of the petit fours.

"Do you think those are for us?" I whispered, as if other guests were lurking about in hiding, perhaps under one of the froufrou cushions.

Rat shrugged happily just as a wild cry went up and a half dozen waiters exploded from the rear side door of the Waterside. They were carrying a laughing, kicking chef who looked to be in his early twenties. They headed straight for the water, followed by dozens of other back waiters and kitchen staff.

The captain appeared with a dessert menu and explained that this was a Waterside tradition—whenever anyone left the restaurant, on their last night they were dunked in the river. A loud splash and louder laughter punctuated his account.

"You mean like that," Rat said, helping herself to more of the petit fours.

"It's why I will be here all my life," the captain said. "I am terrified of the water."

Rat laughed.

"He's leaving," the captain explained, nodding toward the dripping young man crawling out of the river, "to go to Michel Guérard's restaurant. Do you know it?"

This was sort of like asking if we had heard of an island in the North Atlantic called Manhattan. Guérard was something of a legitimate legend, a man who had started in a little place called Pot-au-Feu that had been anointed with two stars faster than any other restaurant in Michelin history, or so they said. Now he had retreated to some remote corner of southwest France, where he ran an establishment that seemed to have an absolute lock on three stars.

"Monsieur Roux arranged it. He may be a young boy with a future. . . ." He said this proudly, with a certain wistful quality that touched on envy. The young chef in the making, perhaps a great chef in the making, walked back up toward the Waterside kitchen, soaking wet and shaking his head like a drenched Lab puppy, splashing his comrades with glee.

It was almost eleven o'clock but there was still a glint of light in the sky. The air was cool, and motorboats had been replaced with ducks, eager to feed from the crumbs sprinkled by a couple wearing matching pink pantsuits. Across the way a pair of young accountants trying to look older sipped brandy and puffed cigars, like kids imitating some notion of after-dinner sophistication.

I was glad I wasn't sitting at their table.

Of course I had forgotten about Rat's late date with the Indian train conductor, not that I had ever taken it seriously in the first place. Naturally I had assumed that it was all merely a diversion, a casual and useful flirtation that served us well, the sort of thing at which Rat was particularly skilled. On some level it probably said a lot about the way she moved through life, but I never really thought about that sort of thing with Rat. At least not at this stage. Mostly it was just Rat being Rat, and having decided I liked Rat from about the first time we'd encountered each other at the dumbbell rack, I hadn't really rethought the Rat equation.

But after stashing Henry back at the Royal Overseas League—Lionel, the night doorman, thought he was delightful;

England seemed to be populated with an appalling collection of dog lovers—Rat insisted we head out to meet her conductor date. "You go," I said. "I don't think it was my gold lamé dress that caught his eye and, anyway, I'm exhausted. *You* weren't out on the bypass this afternoon getting advice from a bunch of Dead-heads on fixing Mustang brakes."

But Rat wouldn't hear of it. She insisted I tag along, finally appealing to my latent Southern upbringing by pointing out that it would be incredibly rude to stand the young man up and in-credibly dangerous if she went out to deepest darkest Soho on her own. Not for a second did I think she really believed either one, but this didn't negate the effectiveness of the ploy.

The Manitoba Coffee Shop was in the heart of Soho in a warren of Malaysian noodle houses, record stores, and sex shops. It was a clean, well-lighted space staffed by a pair of long-haired Canadians, both attractive and freshly scrubbed, one male, one female. Buried in a neighborhood with an intensely commercial interest in appearing scruffily hip, the coffee shop carved out a peaceful haven of order, a not un-Canadian sort of image.

But waiting for Rat's erstwhile friend to appear, I started wondering why the Manitoba *Coffee Shop?* What was it about the mountains or Great Plains of Canada that had even the remotest connection with coffee? Across the street was a stand selling Rocky Mountain Ice Cream. *Rocky Mountain Ice Cream?* I'd spent years, off and on, around the Rockies and never stumbled across a thriv-ing indigenous ice cream culture. And though I'd never been to Manitoba, it seemed a pretty sure bet that there was not a hidden colony of rabid coffee growers or drinkers.

I thought about this over what I had to admit was a terrific French roast the Canadians turned out. It wasn't really that complicated, I suppose. We were used to the notion of *place* being used to sell food. At its most basic, that's really what that magi-cal phrase *French food* was about, like *Georgia* peaches, *Swiss* cheese, *North Carolina* pit barbecue, *Bresse* chicken, *Polish* sausage, *New Zealand* lamb.

At some point these labels had actually indicated a uniqueness of style or quality, a gustatory idiosyncrasy of a region. Now they were mostly generic labels, of course, descriptive shorthand. Could anyone really pick a Georgia peach in a blind tasting, Swiss cheese from the Jura versus that from Vermont? (Actually, probably so, given our crazy FDA regulations meant to protect us from tasty cheeses.) But Polish sausage?

Somewhere along the line, place became less about describing a point of gustatory origin and more about evoking an image. Which was, of course, what most advertising had been about for decades, if not centuries. The Marlboro Man portrayed an image, not a taste. "Chevrolet—the Heartbeat of America" told us what we would *feel* in a Chevy—connected, inspired, patriotic— not why or how one car could do a better job of getting us from point A to point B. And just as cigarettes became about image and cars about emotion, so the selling of food was increasingly disconnected with any relevance to its essence as a nurturing, life-sustaining element.

Rocky Mountain ice cream? I *could* picture that. I couldn't *taste* the name, not like, say, butter praline, but I could visualize a feeling—cool, clean, frosty, and fun. The Manitoba Coffee Shop—a clean well-lighted space, sane, safe. Like Canada, no?

I looked up from my coffee and realized Rat had disappeared. It had been a long day, and I wondered for a moment if I had fallen asleep at the Manitoba counter dreaming about Polish sausage and Canadian cleanliness. Then I spotted her through the window, standing in front of a brightly lit SEX SHOP sign across the street. She gestured for me to join her.

She pulled me in by the arm. "They have the most amazing stuff," she said. We walked through a beaded curtain into the sex shop. It was clean and intricately organized, with bold signs designating every category of sexual pursuit imaginable. The inventory was impressive.

"May I help you?" A man somewhere in his thirties was perched behind the counter. He had short blond hair and wore tortoiseshell glasses. His voice had a trace of public school in its measured richness, and were it not for his black leather shorts and sleeveless leather vest, he would have cast a distinctly academic presence. As it was, he resembled a professor of erotica at some mad Sexual University of Soho.

"Doesn't this get awfully hot?" Rat asked. She was standing in front of a full-length latex bodysuit complete with hood.

The gentleman behind the counter arched an eyebrow inquisitively and answered with a question. "Do you think that might be enjoyable?"

Rat appeared flustered, a rare state.

"Being hot?"

"Well," the clerk said, coming from around the counter to join Rat in front of the latex outfit, "wouldn't it be a very special sort of clammy, confining, possibly exciting kind of hot? Not just your everyday walk-in-the-midday-sun kind of hot."

Rat laughed. The clerk peered at her inquisitively, with the hint of a pleased smile, like a teacher who was enjoying jousting with a favorite pupil.

"It would be just the thing for tonight," the clerk said.

"Tonight?" I asked. I had been standing off to the side, pretending to admire the extensive collection of gleaming handcuffs.

"Well," he said, lowering his voice, "this is the ball of the year tonight, isn't that right?"

"If you say so," Rat answered. She reached out and fingered the sleeve of the bodysuit, her fashion background rising forward.

"The finest latex," the clerk said quite proudly. "Made in France by hand. Not like those cheap Taiwan imports. Like wearing a cheap raincoat, those are."

"I can imagine," Rat said.

"Tailored this is. Would you like to try it on?"

Rat ignored the invitation. "Tell me about the ball," she said.

"Well." He lowered his voice again to a conspiratorial level and glanced over his shoulder. There was one other couple, a pair of long-haired rockers with brightly dyed hair, browsing in the aisle. "It's the biggest scene party of the year."

"Scene?"

Our professorial clerk looked pained, as if we'd misconjugated basic verbs.

"The S-and-M scene. I promise you this will be the hottest party of the year. A couple of hundred of the major players around England."

"Where is it?" Rat asked. She was now looking at the selection of edible underwear, arranged by flavor.

"I don't know," he said. "No one does." He pronounced this with great mystery. Clearly this had been the punch line he had been hoping to deliver.

Rat and I looked at each other and waited. I wondered if Rat's conductor friend was expecting us across the street.

The Professor of Sex looked at his watch. "In a quarter of an hour someone will call with the location. It's always done that way, to keep the party from getting busted."

"They call *everyone?*" I asked. This struck me as quite an impressive organizational feat.

"What time does this thing start anyway?" Rat wondered. It was almost one A.M.

He shrugged. "About two usually." He smiled. "Would you like to go?"

"But what would we wear?" Rat asked. She was joking— or at least I think she was joking—but our friend took her most seriously and immediately threw himself into solving this dilemma. He went through the store pointing out several outfits that seemed to be largely constructed of vinyl, latex, or leather, everything from diaperlike loincloths to vinyl tuxedos. "Particularly handy for those messy dinner parties," Rat pointed out. "Just step into the shower and hose everything down."

"Will a lot of people be at this thing?" I asked.

"Maybe two hundred. But it's not just the number. It's the *quality*. You know, in England we do this sort of thing in great form. It's one of our *traditions*. Some of our greatest men have been deeply involved in the lifestyle."

He didn't wait for us to ask for names.

"The great poet Shelley—"

"Shelley?" I asked skeptically.

"Oscar Wilde," he continued, "Anthony Burgess, George Orwell. Some say Lord Mountbatten. Just to name a few."

"Can't we just go to this party without one of these . . . costumes?" Rat asked.

A look of genuine sympathy crossed his face. "You just wouldn't feel comfortable, would you? It would be odd. Unpleasant. No. It just can't be done."

"Not proper?" I asked, trying to lay in a bit of irony at the notion that it was improper not to wear a latex diaper to a party.

"That's it!" he cried, delighted that I had finally understood.

The telephone rang. The clerk pounced on it, uttered a few cryptic affirmations, and signed off with a hearty "Jolly good."

"Now," he said, "what are you two going to wear to the ball?"

Rat and I heard this just as we were slipping out the door.

Across the street at the Manitoba Coffee Shop there was no sign of Rat's Indian conductor friend. We waited a few minutes and then even Rat conceded she was tired.

Henry was waiting patiently when we returned to the Overseas League.

* * *

"I can't believe the brakes aren't working!" Mike shouted over the transatlantic line. "My man drove that thing to the boat in Newark all the way from St. Louis! If the brakes weren't working, he'd sure as damn well know it!"

The logic of this was irrefutable.

It was early afternoon in London, breakfast time in St. Louis. I was on the phone with Mike from Mid-American Mustang, and neither one of us was very happy. Mike hated the idea that one of his prize Mustangs had come up lame, and I hated the reality that every time I got behind the wheel of the car a near-death experience loomed large.

Mike and I were very close, a bond forged through lengthy conversations that bordered on phone sex about the unique joys of Mustangs. We had never met, but this minor matter was far overshadowed by the Brotherhood of Mustangs.

Mike was the owner of Mid-American Mustang, and his entire life revolved quite happily around Mustangs. "You got to believe in something," Mike had said when I'd asked him how long he had been Pony car preoccupied, "and I believe in Mustangs."

Though Mike accepted me with open arms into the Mustang Cult, in truth I was a pale pretender. Not that I hadn't fallen in love with the cars when they first hit the streets; in fact, they were the first—and one of the very few—cars I had ever actually admired with twinges of automotive lust. But of course just *admiring* Mustangs meant nothing. To *really* belong, you had to *worship* Mustangs, live, breathe, and die Mustangs.

When a French friend living in New York had suggested I import a classic American car to France, promising it could be sold for Big Bucks, I immediately liked the concept. It had all the trappings of an enjoyable scam—buying low and selling high, tricking innocent locals, simplicity of execution, and so on.

The idea was so appealing, I didn't stop to think that the fellow recommending it was a completely untrustworthy flake who had latched onto a half dozen get-rich-quick schemes with no apparent success. I instantly decided it was a great idea and never considered importing any car other than a vintage Mustang.

But that was the easy part. With a little research in mind, I headed to my favorite newsstand in Manhattan to see if there were any relevant car magazines. I was envisioning something along the lines of a *Consumer Report for Vintage Cars*, but what I stumbled into was a whole obsessive world of Mustang Mania. There were no less than four national magazines dedicated to nothing but Mustangs. And we're not talking skimpy little black-and-white newsletters. These were posh, four-color, eye-popping productions with names like *Pony World* and *Mustang Life*. Big-Time Stuff. Marveling at my discovery, I peered wide-eyed into this world, trying to determine which publication held the True Secrets. In the end, of course, I bought them all, along with a handful of other, more general-interest classic-car publications like the *Robb Report*, a brown-paper journal that had a strangely official look.

I read them cover to cover. Without fully realizing the consequences, I had stumbled into a fascinating, complex Alternative Universe, complete with its own language, unique values, rituals, even currency. A proposition like "Virgin pony int., 65 and a half, top down delight, triple A show winner, for cherry Mach original, 67 only, please" brimmed with meaning and opportunity that verged on the evangelical.

Very quickly I found myself on the phone talking with potential sellers who seemed eager to spend hours describing not only the specific joys of their particular car but the broader implications of this very thriving cult. These were people who just liked to talk Mustang. They were good at it, enjoyed it, and could and would do it for hours.

As I was swimming in this sea of Mustang possibilities, a friend—and multiple Mustang owner—recommended I simplify things by turning over my fate to Mike of Mid-American Mustang. This proved to be a wonderful suggestion. "I've got just what you need," Mike said within minutes of our first conversation, right after I explained that I was looking for a convertible, 1965 or 1966 only (before they changed the lights and side grilles, of course, and went to more of a muscle-car look), and V-8 (for obvious reasons). I didn't want a show-class-quality all-original virgin, nor did I really care about the pony interior, mainly because it would propel the price upward without, or so I was told, increasing the value proportionally for that nice French investment banker or dentist, somebody who had seen *A Man and a Woman* a dozen times and, I hoped, would find the machine irresistible.

And so it came to pass that I purchased, sight unseen, a 1965 Candy Apple Red (an original color, naturally) Mustang convertible, which Mike agreed to deliver directly to the boat in Newark.

The very same Mustang that now sat outside the Royal Overseas League like some kind of flamboyant death-trap flower that attracts prey by its bright colors only to snuff out all life for those who dare to land within.

While I sat in the Overseas League on the phone, Mike paced back and forth in his showroom; I knew he was pacing because he told me, as in, "I'm so goddamn upset I'm walking my ass off up and down." In the distance I could hear his feet striking the hard linoleum of his showroom. Mike wanted a detailed analysis of the Mustang ills. This, I promised him, was not complicated. "The brakes don't work," I told him, which is something I seemed to have been saying for days.

"Yeah, yeah, yeah, but *how* do they not work?"

"I put my foot on the brake pad and nothing happens. That's how they don't work."

"You've got to be more technical, son!" Mike yelled.

I had the feeling that I was trapped in the middle of one of those airplane disaster films and I was the well-meaning but hopelessly inept passenger—say, a salesman from Des Moines—who had ended up behind the controls after the pilot and co-pilot had both been shot by a terrorist or at least rendered helpless by food poisoning from the off-brand shrimp cocktail. The veteran pilot on the other end of the radio was our only link to possible survival.

My role was clear: swallow my rising panic and try to let the Big Guy on the line talk us to safety. "Well," I said, trying to think of a more *technical* way to describe the fact that the brakes were a life-threatening disaster, "when you push down on the brake, it goes down and sometimes it will stop the car, but the brake never pops back to its original position. You have to lift it off the floor by hand."

"Now we're getting someplace!" Mike crowed.

"We are?"

"Anybody on that ship real fat?"

"The ship that brought the car over from Newark?" I asked.

"That ship," Mike sighed. This was like the moment when the passenger-pilot asked some incredibly stupid question, like "What's this little switch that says, 'Fuel pump off'?"

I had to admit that I had been so excited to see the car, and then so preoccupied by the possibilities of crashing and burning in the brakeless wonder, that I hadn't really taken the time to appreciate the relative weight of the various crew members.

"I tell you what I think happened," Mike pronounced, sounding like a detective closing fast on his prey. "I think some fat-ass dockworker slammed his big feet down on the brake so damn hard it shattered the brake drum. *I could kill him!*" Mike shouted, and had the guilty dockworker been standing right in front of Mike, even if the heavy-footed fellow had weighed in at over three hundred pounds (or however many stone that works out to be), I would have put my money on Mike to teach the clumsy oaf a thing or two about how to treat a 1965 classic with love and respect. "How could he do this to our beautiful car?" Mike cried, with all the genuine grief of a man learning a loved one had been kidnapped and tortured by fiendish experts.

"Mike, Mike, *please*," I pleaded. "What am I going to do?"

"I made a few calls," Mike said, resuming his calm pilot-in-control voice, "and I found a Ford dealership—"

"Mike . . ." I sighed. There were Ford dealerships all over England. But they were full of people who thought an Opel was an efficient design and considered a Taurus an interesting example of American creativity. These people knew *nothing* about a 1965 Mustang.

"With an American mechanic," Mike continued, still calm. "He's supposed to be good."

"A real American?" I asked, as if there had recently been a rash of impostors roaming the British Isles.

"From Kentucky," Mike assured me. We both took this as a good sign. There were a lot of Mustang freaks in Kentucky—just take a look at any issue of *Pony Talk* magazine.


His name was Ray and I could barely understand him. The accent was Harlan County, Kentucky, sorted through twenty years of suburban, working-class England. He was a tall fellow with long, bushy sideburns wearing a white smock with "Ray" in a delicate, silly red script over his heart. The smock ended just above his clunky motorcycle boots with a glimpse of tight black jeans tucked into the boots. The total effect was of an aging rockabilly star pretending to be a mad scientist.

He grinned and held out a big, rough hand that felt like a paving stone. A few joints were missing from the tips of his fingers.

"Had one," he said right off the bat, or at least I think that's what he said as he walked around the Mustang with a grin that made him look a lot younger. "Not like this, mind you. Had me a Cobra. Fastback. Never got so many girls in all my life." He paused, as if thinking about it. "Had to be the car. Couldn't have been me, 'eh?"

The Eastgate Ford manager—Nigel was his name—smiled an embarrassed smile and shot me an apologetic look. Nigel's last name was Lombardo, and he looked to have escaped from a fashion magazine, a preposterously handsome fellow of about thirty. I wondered if Ray's comment had something to do with the reputation Nigel might have as a ladies' man. Or maybe Nigel was gay. Or maybe Ray was just talking.

As befitted his position as Resident Master American Mechanic, Ray had an assistant, a young Pakistani who also wore a white smock, though not as white as Ray's. His scripted name tag read "Ernest," and I was dying to ask him if that was his real name or if he had just inherited it from the real Ernest, who had since moved on to greater glory. It appeared I would never learn his real name from Ray, who treated his assistant like a famous heart surgeon would a fledgling nurse, a strictly as-needed, performance-driven sort of relationship.

"Creeper," Ray barked, and for a moment I thought he was talking about his assistant, but then the young Pakistani rolled into place a high-tech looking board on wheels and Ray lowered himself faceup onto the board. He waved off his assistant, who stood at the ready to roll his mentor forward, and, grabbing the bright chrome bumper—the sort of bumper you would never see again on a car, a bumper that cut through the air like a proud battering ram—he pulled himself solemnly under the Mustang.

"He is our best," Nigel whispered. "You've really heard of

him in America, huh?" he asked, still impressed that I had called in advance to confirm that the American—or the once American—was still an Eastgate Ford employee.

"*Very* famous," I confirmed. Why not? There was something appealing about increasing the Legend of Ray.

The rockabilly mechanic stayed under the car for a long time. Every few minutes he would bark out a command for a new tool, his assistant always at the ready.

Like an expectant father waiting outside the delivery room, I decided to take a walk to ease the tension. Nigel looked at me with terribly sincere conviction and held up his crossed fingers. His concern was touching. I wanted to tell him not to worry, that if Ray failed I was the one who was doomed to immolation on the motorway, not him. But I let it go with a reassuring pat on the back and headed for the door.

Outside, I had two missions: get something to eat and find a place to make an extra set of Mustang keys, an optimistic sort of gesture implying that I might actually get to drive the thing someday. I stopped a strolling policeman and asked him where I might be able to get something to eat.

"What kind of place?" he demanded.

I shrugged. "It doesn't matter. I just want to get a salad or something."

"A salad?" he asked, in highly suspicious tones, as if I had inquired about the best place to purchase a Stinger surface-to-air missile. "A salad," he repeated, stunned. He thought for a moment and then asked, "Why?"

I wanted to stick my face right in front of his nose and scream, "Because I'm an alien from another galaxy and if I don't get a salad at least once a day, I have no choice but to rip out the heart of any passing policeman and eat it before his dying eyes. Any more questions?"

Instead, I sighed and asked if there was any place around that I might be able to get some fruit. Nothing exotic. Just an apple. An apple would do just fine.

"An apple?" he stared at me. "What *kind* of apple?"

"Look," I asked, changing tacks, "where do *you* like to eat?"

"Try down the street to the left, bang-up stand. Eat there every day."

So I did.

It wasn't hard to find—a little white shack next to a BP gas station with a very large, if a bit faded, pink ice cream cone melting into a bold sign declaring SNACKS! The hand-painted menu was intoxicating:

*Savoy*
*Samosa*
*Russian Salad*
*Fried Eels*
*Spring Onion and Fennel Salad*
*Fried Lamb Cutlet*
*Tuna*

"What's a savoy?" I asked.

"It's a hot dog," the proprietor answered, looking up from his *Penthouse Magazine*. He was dark complexioned, and I assumed him to be Indian.

"Oh. And what's a samosa?"

"Some kind of Indian thing, I think." He shrugged.

"You're not Indian?"

The question didn't offend him, but it clearly was a surprise.

"I'm Malaysian," he explained, and though he continued to smile I felt somehow I'd inadvertently insulted him by failing to recognize his heritage.

"I've never been to Malaysia," I said, by way of trying to explain that it was unlikely I would have recognized *any* Malaysian.

"It is a very beautiful country," he answered sadly, and then I felt *really* bad, because now I'd reminded him of his faraway homeland. This was taking a turn for the worse.

"I'd love to go," I blurted, though the thought had never crossed my mind. "I've been looking forward to it for years."

"The British were there, you know," he said.

"The British *were* everywhere," I responded, and this seemed to please him a great deal.

"Now look what they have," he chuckled, gesturing down the dilapidated street. "An empire once, and now this."

I started to agree, but it hardly seemed politic to illustrate the decay of the British Empire based on the bleakness of his own neighborhood.

We smiled awkwardly at each other for a moment and then I asked him for an ice cream cone and a hot dog.

"I don't have ice cream," he said cheerfully, and had I not already spent the last ten minutes insulting his national origins and hurling him into a tailspin of diaspora grief, I would surely have asked in no uncertain tones why it was if he didn't have ice cream that a giant pink ice cream cone was melting just above his head?

But instead I took my sad-looking hot dog and headed down the street to the locksmith.

There were a half dozen stores within sight that specialized in locks and security equipment. It seemed each one was crowded. While waiting in line at B. C. Smiths Locks, I asked the fellow ahead of me in line about the abundance of security stores. He answered with a question.

"Why are *you* here," he said.

"I need an extra set of keys to my car," I told him.

"What kind of car?" he demanded with something of a scowl.

"A Mustang."

He was tall, about six foot five, and wore a turban. He had a beard, and I tried to remember if that meant he was a Sikh or a Hindu. But after insulting the Malaysian, I certainly had no intention of asking.

"Ah," he said, "the Mustang." He smiled at the thought. "It is a beautiful car."

I agreed, wondering if he was another rabid member of the Mustang underground. He probably had a life's subscription to *Pony Car News* and talked to Mike at Mid-American Mustang on a regular basis.

This was something I was about to ask when he leaned over and whispered, "I am here for the exploding mailboxes."

I nodded understandably. An exploding mailbox? Of course.

"Are they expensive?" I asked.

He scowled intensely. "Dear!" he hissed. "Very dear!"

Up ahead, an elderly woman with hair the shade of bright yellow prescribed by law for New York taxicabs was waving an advertisement for canisters of pepper-gas self-defense units. She could not understand why Smiths did not sell this sort of thing.

"It's the law, isn't it?" the equally elderly locksmith kept repeating.

His young assistant, perhaps a son or nephew, smirked and pulled out from behind the counter a piece of lead pipe wrapped in tape. "Knock 'em with this, gets their attention, now doesn't it?"

"That's fine for you, all strong like you are, but what about me? I need this, don't I?"

She waved the advertisement torn from some magazine—

a *Soldier of Fortune* for pensioners?—and I saw that it featured an elderly woman not unlike herself reducing a gang of huge thugs to writhing helplessness with her vial of "PARALYZER PEPPER SPRAY."

"It's better in America," I said. "We just all carry guns."

My turbaned neighbor agreed enthusiastically. "Shoot them all first, ask questions later, it is best policy." He looked at me for a moment hesitantly and then leaned down and whispered, "You have gun you would sell?"

"Why do you need a gun?" I asked. "Can't you just use an exploding mailbox?" I was still puzzled by the concept of a booby-trapped mailbox.

"That is not funny," he lectured suddenly, waving his finger. "Four times they explode my post! Four times."

"Oh," I said, "I thought you were *buying* an exploding mailbox."

"Why do I buy when I have one exploding four times? Four times!"

"Good point. What we do in America, we get a rattlesnake and put it in the mailbox. Just a little present waiting for mischief makers."

His eyes brightened. "Clever. Very clever. Very American."

"Very," I agreed.

"I have a cousin, he has cobras."

"That ought to do the job."

He moved up to the counter and ordered a large locking mailbox. Very large, he told the clerk. The cobra is a large snake, he added, laughing.

Later, when I was walking back to the Eastgate Ford, he darted out of a dry-cleaning store and whispered, "One technical question, please. How do you stop the cobra from striking the post delivery man?"

It was a good question. I thought about it for a moment and asked, "They come at night, right? The mailbox exploders."

He nodded, hatred flashing in his eyes.

"So, just put the cobra in every night and take it out in the morning."

"Yes!" he exclaimed. "They will think Boxing Day comes early, no?"

He seemed delighted at the idea.

Outside Eastgate Ford a group of workers were gathered around a co-worker reading from the *Daily Mail*.

"How's the war going?" I asked good-naturedly as I passed the men, wondering if the U.S. had launched more missiles against Iraq.

"You've seen this, have you?" one of the men asked. He waved the paper angrily.

"Bomb 'em back to the Stone Age," I said, in what seemed like a proper macho show of solidarity.

A cheer went up from the men. I seemed to have struck a chord. Maybe, I thought, they are all Falklands veterans who liked the idea of the U.S. bombing Iraq on a regular basis.

"Bloody bombs, that's what they need, ain't it?" one shouted.

"Look at this mate, just look!" The worker who had been reading thrust his copy of the *Daily Mail* under my nose. "Pirates! Bloody pirates!"

I stopped and focused on the screaming headlines that seemed a foot high.

**PINT SCANDAL!!!!**

"Can you believe it? Huh? Unbelievable, that's what I say it is!"

The *Daily Mail*'s crack investigative squad had apparently just completed a lengthy undercover investigation of pubs and discovered that bartenders were routinely shortchanging customers, delivering less than a full pint for the price of a pint. Trick glasses that *looked* like a pint but were actually short of a pint seemed to be the culprit.

48        Stuart Stevens

At the bottom of the page was a tiny box, "U.S. BOMBS IRAQ, details on page 13."

"Unbelievable," I agreed.

As soon as I stepped inside the hangar-sized garage space, I knew something was wrong. The scene was reminiscent of the obligatory medical-drama moment when the exhausted surgeon walks out of the operating room to face the anxious family. He peels off his surgical mask and shakes his head wearily and his eyes say it all, those eyes that have seen too much . . . and then he says—he always says—"We did everything we could."

And so it was with Ray. Except instead of looking exhausted, he looked mostly angry. His assistant looked down in humiliation and Nigel, the improbably handsome manager, looked at me and shrugged.

"Buggered," Ray spat. "Just plain buggered. What you got, mate, is a busted-up brake cylinder. About the only damn thing on this baby I couldn't fix. Can't fix it, got to replace it. All there is to it."

"Can I drive it?" I asked, feeling like the patient who stoically inquires, "How long do I have?"

"You can stand on your naked in Piccadilly Circus in January," Ray answered immediately. "Both ain't a good idea."

"Is there anything you can—"

Ray interrupted. "Put a good throttle spring on the brake pedal, that should pull the brake back up."

"Madness!" Nigel whispered, but his eyes showed a certain morbid fascination, like hearing about a really gruesome crime of passion. "She cut his *what* off?"

"Where you planning on driving this thing?" Ray asked, wiping his hands on the rag offered by his ever-attentive assistant.

"Brussels," I said. "Then France, Germany, and Italy."

"What for?" he demanded. Now he sounded just like a hot-rod-loving kid from Harlan County, Kentucky. *What you want to go to Europe for anyways?*

"Eat," I answered.

"You can't eat here, or what?"

I shrugged.

"It's a damn shame," Ray said, shaking his head.

"What?"

"Wrecking a car like this for some goddamn meal."

"I wasn't planning on wrecking it," I told him.

"You weren't planning on not having brakes, now were you?"

Ray had a point. I thought about it driving back to the Royal Overseas League, nursing the brake all the way. The new throttle spring was an improvement, and I felt like I was about to die only two or three times.

# Chapter
# Three

At least Rat didn't bring the Dog.

We argued about this, of course. Delighted by how popular Henry had been at the Waterside, Rat got it into her head that it would be a cruel injustice to the staff of La Tante Claire if we neglected to bring the charming animal. When I insisted that they would somehow manage to overcome their disappointment, Rat accused me of being afraid that Henry might embarrass me in front of Véronique.

This I found a particularly annoying remark, mostly because it was absolutely true.

Véronique! She was the irresistibly sexy voice on the other end of the phone at La Tante Claire, the woman who could make directions to the restaurant sound like an invitation to a seduction, the woman who declared, "We are looking forward to seeing you this evening very much," and almost made me blush.

Given how much I was looking forward to meeting Véronique—and dinner didn't sound bad as well—I insisted we leave the Mustang moored at the Overseas League. Rat, who had taken a great and immediate liking to the car, thought this was excessively cautious and boring, two great sins in her book of values. I insisted. She pouted and talked about staying home with the Dog.

Which was fine with me. Until I started thinking about eating alone, an activity I abhorred, and lured Rat to the plate by reminding her of how much it would annoy Carl, her lawyer boyfriend looming in the background. This notion proved irresistible to Rat, so we found ourselves in the back of a British taxi rumbling past the playing fields along Royal Hospital Road to La Tante Claire.

The restaurant was an unimposing little storefront with simple charm. The door opened to a small anteroom with a fake skylight of Victorian cut glass. It was an unfortunate touch, but not very important.

The maître d' was a sizable fellow in the mandatory tux. His head seemed a bit large for his body, and he had a friendly face with distinctly rabbitlike features: large, overly exposed teeth and a turned-up nose pointing to a shock of gray-brown hair. He smiled, a curious look in his eyes. "Welcome," he said and seemed to mean it. "A glass of champagne, perhaps?"

The anteroom opened up to a small sitting area, which in turn opened to the dining room. A serious-looking woman in black stood behind a waist-high counter calculating bills that the wait staff delivered on silver trays. She wore glasses and radiated the stern competence of a very exacting math teacher.

In the small space decorated with modern line drawings and enough flowers to make any New York East Side restaurant content, I found myself missing the open expanse of the Waterside.

"Mr. Stevens?" I turned from peering into the dining room to face the woman who had been standing behind the counter. "Would you care to be seated?" She was friendly and warm but still quite a formidable figure.

We followed her to the table, and as we were sitting down, Rat held out her hand. "You must be Véronique."

She nodded, not surprised, as if assuming that we would know her name.

"You are . . . ?" she asked pleasantly.

"Rat." She answered Véronique's puzzled frown with a spelling lesson. "R-A-T. Rat Kelly. I'm starving. What's good?"

Rat's directness startled her, but she recovered. "The sea bass with consommé is divine."

"You got it," Rat said.

Véronique stared for a moment, a wondering smile playing across her face. "Yes," she answered eventually. "We do have it, of course."

Rat laughed. "I like that," she said.

The friendly captain who looked like a rabbit appeared with menus. His presence seemed to release Véronique from having to deal with these obviously dysfunctional and disturbed Americans.

"There are many wonderful choices before you," the captain proclaimed, which struck me as fairly profound for maître d' small talk. I dove into the menu and immediately came away with a few easy choices. The *Consommé de homard aux épices et raviolis* sounded perfect as a starter, followed with the *Filet d'agneau rôti en croûte d'herbes jus à l'huile d'olive*. I was suddenly very, very hungry, and meat seemed important.

Rat ordered—for the second time, in her mind—the sea bass. She was consumed by the thick wine list, hunting for the perfect Margaux. While in the taxi she had announced, apropos of nothing, that we should order only Margauxs for the rest of the trip. It was not a subject about which I had strong opinions, but she announced it as if she had been pondering it for months.

"A big wine," Rat told the captain, who seemed quite content to stand alongside Rat for the entire evening.

"The Château Dauzac," he suggested. "It has a lot of personality, I think."

"Bet your life. Go for it."

He nodded and collected the menus and wine list.

"Bet your life," he murmured, smiling.

I realized I was excited. This was always a special moment—
when you're hungry, have ordered, and have every reason to
believe that you are about to have a wonderful meal. It is the
Spring Training of dining, when all is possible, every menu item
a potential champion, and hope dances undaunted by reality.
Eating at a new, highly recommended restaurant is like a Very
Important Blind Date, a contract with uncertainty you enter into
with great expectation battling the cynicism of experience. You
sit waiting, wondering about the upcoming moments of revela-
tion. Somewhere in the back of your head is the dour warning
that disappointment is inevitable, but you don't really believe
it or you wouldn't be there. The best eaters are always optimists.

It was right after the last ravioli was disappearing that he
appeared in the entranceway to the room. He stood surveying
the room in a felt fedora and black cape, which he ceremoni-
ously tossed over his shoulder with a practiced fling. His beard
was full and impressive, and though it hid most of his face, I figured him to be somewhere in his late thirties.

He was, I was certain, a count, or at least a viscount, or
maybe a duke. Years ago in England, when I had encountered
eighteen-year-old royalty and minor royalty, I had always wondered what happened to these kids when they grew up, how they
ended up. Clearly this is how they did.

Next to him was a young woman, younger by about ten
years, dressed in a black miniskirt and some kind of fur coat. They
both seemed to be prepared for a different climate and I wondered if a sudden cold front had moved across London in the
last few minutes. Or perhaps they were returning from a costume
ball with a fall theme, say Halloween at the Opera.

The entrées arrived, brought in tandem while the captain

hovered watchfully in the background. The servers paused for a moment then, in perfect synchrony, lifted the simple silver covers.

Aroma flooded the table, a rich blend of the veal stock and bass, the olives and wild mushrooms of the lamb with the clean, woodsy smell of the herbs crusted around the lamb, and supporting it all like a solid earth floor was the Château Dauzac decanted in a simple glass pitcher at the edge of the table. I was seized with a desperate urge to eat both plates at once, first a few bites of the sea bass, then the lamb.

So I did. Rat slapped my hand and told me to behave— and then she stabbed across the table for my lamb. It was a very Rat moment; she was definitely a cross-table stabber at heart.

The room was full but not oppressively crowded in a New York–restaurant sort of way. In the far corner, a table of Americans were talking about the events of the day at Wimbledon. There was the mandatory cluster of youngish British investment bankers—all men, all dateless. It was an inconceivably depressing notion to me—going out to eat with a group of men.

The bankers kept looking at a pair of attractive Japanese women dining alone. Their outfits made staring quite excusable. Rat was certain they had just returned from a shopping spree at the designer Vivienne Westwood's showroom. They were both wearing platform shoes and big wacky hats, weird Cat in the Hat concoctions that would have made Dr. Seuss quite proud. When one of the women stood up, I was certain that her hat and shoes, if placed one on top of the other, would have been as tall as the woman. I felt like applauding.

Rat and I continued eating off each other's plate, alternating bites of the sea bass with the extraordinarily tender lamb, which had a light, crunchy crust of herbs. It was overwhelmingly gratifying, the tastes enhanced by the basic naughtiness of sitting in this three-star restaurant and munching off shared plates. It reminded me of what Laurie Colwin had written about the forbidden pleasures of eating alone in her classic essay "Alone in the Kitchen with an Eggplant": "People lie when you ask them what they eat when they are alone. A salad, they tell you. But when you persist, they confess to peanut butter and bacon sandwiches deep-fried and eaten with hot sauce, or spaghetti with butter and grape jam." Stolen pleasures.

We were getting down to the last bites when a strange sound began to emanate off to my side. As a confirmed restaurant voyeur, I was immediately intrigued, the more so when Rat, who had a clear view of the source of the sound, began to giggle with a certain maniacal glee. I tried to look scoldingly at her, but I knew it would have no effect. With studied casualness, I looked to my left and saw a most unusual sight: a man was asleep at the table—sound asleep, head cradled in his arms, snoring.

The Napping Diner was the bearded, cloaked man who had entered so dramatically. His companion—wife, girlfriend, sister?—stared resolutely ahead, toying with her salmon ravioli. She and Rat exchanged bemused grins, as if mutually confirming that men are indeed odd creatures.

"He's tired," the sleeping man's companion said, a bit unnecessarily. Was she concerned that we might think that he was sleeping because he was overly rested? Or perhaps she was interested in ruling out narcolepsy as a possible explanation. "He never sleeps at night," she continued softly, as if we had asked for further clarification. Technically, this was clearly inaccurate, as it was about ten o'clock and he seemed to have overcome any antisleeping tendencies with dramatic success. "Demons," she whispered.

"I beg your pardon?" I blurted. By now I had given up any pretense of ignoring the snores and was staring at the table as if it were opening night and the curtain had just gone up.

"The demons come at night," she said, nodding her head seriously.

This was just really quite wonderful. Of all the subjects that one might imagine discussing in casual conversation, the psychic trauma of a fellow diner possessed with demons was exceedingly unlikely. The usual subjects tended to run more along the lines of the difficulty getting truly rare salmon, rude limo drivers, and the decline in quality of Cuban tobacco. Haunted by demons? Spectacular!

Suddenly the sleeping head shot up and the bearded face stared directly at us. "Dessert!" he announced in a very distinct American accent. A Boston accent, I thought. "We must order dessert immediately!" Then, as we continued to stare in surprise, he turned to his companion and asked, "Why are these people staring at me?"

Rat and I instantly jerked our heads back around to face each other, like schoolchildren caught cheating on exams.

He summoned one of the hovering waiters and I had a terrible premonition that he would demand that Rat and I be evicted for staring.

"The entrées haven't arrived yet dear, have they?" his companion said gently. She was English.

"Don't you feel like a soufflé?" he demanded, as if questioning her sanity.

"Of course." She answered promptly. This was something she seemed accustomed to, answering promptly.

The waiter stood in front of him, awaiting instruction.

"Soufflés," he said.

"Of course, sir. Two?"

He thought about this for a moment, as if he were trying to calculate the number of people who might be joining him for dessert.

"Yes," he finally answered. "Two should do it, I think."

"Very good, sir," the waiter responded.

"For now," the man added, just as the waiter was turning his back.

"As many as you like, sir," he said, trying to hide a smile.

A soup course arrived for the newly awakened diner and his companion. Shaking his head as if to clear it, the transplanted Bostonian—I was sure he was from Boston—grasped the bowl with both hands, thrust his head just inches from the surface, and inhaled deeply. His gratified sigh could be heard across the room, though it was not a huge room, perhaps thirty or forty seats at most. He then lifted the bowl and swept it upward to his mouth, slurping loudly.

The captain approached, the tall fellow with the friendly bunny face, and though I was certain he intended to scold, he inquired—in French—if the lobster bisque was good. The Bostonian answered in superb, unaccented French that it was a delight as always. They chatted on; obviously old acquaintances, about the upcoming Tour de France.

I wondered if perhaps the man was French and had learned English from someone with a heavy Boston accent. It was all very puzzling.

"Why didn't we order soufflés?" Rat whispered across the table. The remains—not much—of our lamb and bass had been swept away and we were facing charming hand cards listing desserts, with a notation under the soufflé—a chocolate-raspberry concoction—that it required a half hour of preparation and should be ordered in advance.

"You could eat a soufflé now?"

"I can *always* eat a soufflé. What's life without challenge, anyway?"

Rat ordered a soufflé and I declined, having reached that moment when another bite would plunge me into a gluttonous abyss. Clearly I was a guy who believed in moderation—after all,

I was only planning to eat in every three-star restaurant in Europe. On consecutive days.

When the captain drifted by I caught his eye. Of course I was dying to ask him about the French Bostonian with narcolepsy but it seemed a bit obvious with the topic of discussion seated just a few feet away. Instead, I congratulated him on La Tante Claire's third star, which had been awarded the previous year.

"Thank God," he sighed, and it was such a natural, heartfelt response that I had to laugh. And so did he. "When we first came here," he continued, with great enthusiasm, "this place was called the Railway Carriage. It was narrow and dark and only sat a handful of people. Now, to win your third star, that is a great insurance policy. The best insurance policy in the world."

He said it without a hint of smugness but more with the gratitude a hardworking farmer might express for good crop prices. *We've worked hard. Very hard. We've earned this.* And always the knowledge not far from the surface: *This could go away any minute. Today. Tomorrow. Next year.*

In many ways the Gods of Michelin behaved not unlike the Weather Gods of agricultural life. Both were aloof forces that operated from on high with inexplicable capriciousness. Their whims could bring great prosperity or total financial ruin with little warning. Farmers who have blown their brains out after a crop-killing hailstorm or flood are really no different than the chefs who have been driven mad by the loss of a Michelin star. When Alain Zick learned that his Paris restaurant Relais des Porquerolles had not moved from one star to two but instead had actually lost its sole star, he did not take the news lightly. After appeals to Michelin failed—they always do—he fell into a depression and took a gun to his head a few months later.

"To get a third star is always . . ." he paused, searching for words.

"A nightmare of difficulty," Rat suggested.

He thought about this for a moment, hinting at a smile.

"A nightmare. Yes." He laughed loudly with great enthusiasm.

Across the way, the French Bostonian clucked his tongue and said in a loud, good-natured voice something about the restaurant becoming too noisy. I looked over and he was pouring Tabasco sauce on a piece of sea bass. He caught my eye and held out the bottle. When, startled, I declined, he screwed the lid back on the small bottle and tucked it away in his suit jacket.

"But to receive three stars in England . . ." He rolled his eyes. "The French . . ." He paused for clarification, then added a bit unnecessarily, "I am French. The French are not quick to believe the English can produce great food."

"But if you're French and the chefs are French . . ."

He shook his head. "We French do not like to believe great food can be produced *in* England."

"It's in the water, you mean," Rat said.

He puzzled over this. "It's not the water, it's the ingredients."

Rat started to explain but let it pass. We were floating on a wave of postmeal bliss that made everything seem right with the world. It had been a nearly perfect meal, all the more shocking, of course, and ultimately gratifying because it was just a short cab ride from Piccadilly Circus. To eat spectacularly in England still seemed like a naughty, purloined pleasure, like having great fun at a funeral.

"To reproduce French cooking in England with any success at all it is best, I think," Elizabeth David wrote, "to go for dishes with less resounding reputations and less specialized ingredients." But this evening we had enjoyed a spectacular *filet d'agneau rôti en croute d'herbes jus à l'huile d'olive* and a *consommé de homard aux épices et raviolis*, dishes that were composed of almost no homegrown English ingredients, the lamb excepted. In truth, our meal was a testament as much to the efficiency of modern transportation as to culinary skill.

The notion of the English straining to prepare French food drove Elizabeth David absolutely mad. "Because some local speciality has caught the imagination of tourists, it has, today, almost automatically come to be accepted as a great dish. Overestimation of the merits of a dish which relies purely on local conditions and ingredients for its charm will, in the end, kill it stone-dead. Take, say, from a salade niçoise the little pungent black olives of Provence, the fruity oil in the dressing, the sweet, ripe southern tomatoes, the capers and the brined anchovies which are all characteristic products of the region, and what is left? Little more than an English mixed salad."

She wrote that in 1969, but now it is possible to have any and all of those ingredients quite fresh on a chef's counter anywhere in the world. It is just a matter of expense and trouble.

In America, there seem to be two competing forces. First, there is the negative pull of mass-produced food tugging everything down to a tasteless mediocrity. Waverly Root and Richard De Rochemont sum it up this way in *Eating in America*: "Very little in the history of the United States from 1776 to our times presages the confusion and near-collapse from which mid-century on has overtaken American eating. Were it possible to envisage in one great glob the totality of what is now eaten in a single day by our fellow-citizens, whether at home, in institutions, in fast-food joints or in expensive restaurants, and to judge it in the light of what the country has produced in the past, and what it might produce again, the word 'garbage' would rise inevitably to mind and gorge."

John and Karen Hess, in their brilliant attack on American food, *The Taste of America*, lay much of the blame on the rise of mechanized farming and the spread of huge agricultural corporations.

The taste of the seasons is gone; it has been replaced by "carrying quality." More and more of the produce grown in those far-off factories of the soil is harvested by machine. It is bred for rough handling, which it gets. A chemical is sprayed on trees to force all the fruit to "ripen"—that is, change color—at once, in time for a monster harvester to strike the tree and catch the fruit in its canvas maw. Tomatoes are picked hard and green and gassed with ethylene in trucks or in chambers at the market, whereupon they turn a sort of neon red. Of course, they taste like nothing at all, but the taste of real tomatoes has so far faded from memory that, even for local markets, farmers now pick tomatoes that are just turning pink. This avoids the spoilage that occurred when they used to pick tomatoes red-ripe.

This "garbaging" of food seems to be at war with the other force, which is driven by ever-growing numbers of crazed foodies who find it a personal insult that every chain grocery store in America doesn't sell fresh radicchio. These are people who have given up pretending that food hasn't taken an inordinate place in their lives or that they aren't hopeless snobs when it comes to restaurants.

People like Rat and me, in other words. Which was probably the main reason we found it hard not to live in New York. One of my heroes, Calvin Trillin, wrote in *American Fried*, that he had "finally found the short answer [he] had been looking for" as to why he lived in New York. He was graced with this epiphany when he returned to New York from a trip to Santa Fe: "We happened to walk by a Chinese restaurant on Irving Place and we realized we had forgotten about it. I don't mean we had forgotten its name or its exact address; we had forgotten its existence." This in spite of the fact that Trillin and his wife,

Alice, had enjoyed "a spectacular meal there, including a dish that came close to being the Great Dried Beef in the Sky."

For an eater like Trillin, the implications were profound.

"'This is why we live here,' I said to Alice. 'Where else could you *forget* a restaurant like this?' Now when someone asks me why my family and I choose to live in New York, I don't have to launch into all sorts of complicated and fuzzy explanations. I just say, 'We're big eaters.'"

And so, for better for worse, were Rat and I.

# Chapter
# Four

I t suddenly became clear: we were going into the water. There was nothing I could do.

Our fate had been sealed by the brakes. By the schedule I'd misread and the doorman I liked. And the Dog. But I couldn't totally blame the Dog, as much as I wanted to. Which I did, of course, quite a bit.

I had woken up in a preposterously good mood. This was clearly my first mistake.

But why not a good mood? We had eaten spectacularly well the night before, and ahead of us stretched what promised to be a historic stint of indulgent gastronomic bliss. It was a beautiful sunny day. Awaiting me in Brussels was a new brake cylinder for the Mustang. At least, Mike had *promised* me that a new brake cylinder was on its way. There were reasons, all in all, to feel hopeful about life.

And I tend to be a hopeful sort of fellow.

It was a clear, bright day with just a touch of morning coolness, the sort of English day that feels like spring, all the more to be savored because it comes in June and everyone knows there's only a few weeks until the sidewalks start melting in the heat.

I found the night clerk standing in the front door admiring the red Mustang, which was parked between a newish Jaguar and an older Bentley. "Take the red one any day of the week," he announced. "Now that's an automobile that looks like an automobile, isn't it?"

There was no doubt the 1965 red Mustang convertible did cut an impressive figure in the drive. It gleamed in the sun, the red fins and spectacular Mustang side cuts lending an elegance to the crouched muscle-car mass. It was American. It was Grand.

And a death trap without brakes.

I didn't try to explain that the beauty he was admiring and the eight-cylinder power he longed for was actually rotting within, like a top athlete being devoured by a cancer. All looked normal and impressive from the outside, but within, disaster lurked. No, I simply nodded, wishing with great intensity that either the Jaguar or the Bentley were in fact his to trade. For a moment I wondered if I might be able to pull off the switch, talk him into swapping the Mustang for one of the other cars. "Come on, you know they"—they being the other owners, of course—"will love it! Positively delighted to learn that their boring Jaguar or Bentley has been transformed into this sleek American sex machine! They will love you for life, tip you to the stars!"

Truth is, the fellow was so accommodating and so excited about the Mustang that I might actually have been able to pull it off. But I knew his life would be ruined the first time the Jaguar or Bentley owner cranked the Mustang, hearing its astounding rumble, and then tried to ease off into London traffic only to discover that the operation of the brakes required the use of three or four feet at once, and well-trained, nimble, soccer-star-quality feet at that. The *Daily Mail* would love it:

MUSTANG CHARLIE! DOORMAN TRADES JAG FOR PONY!
The estate of Lord Smithereens has called for the immediate arrest of Charles Lettuce, the doorman of the Royal Overseas League who traded Lord Smithereens's 1995 Jaguar XJS coupe for a 1965 Ford Mustang convertible. The doorman was quoted as telling bystanders, "It was such a

swell-looking machine, I couldn't know the brakes didn't work, could I?"

Also sought for questioning was Mr. Stuart Stevens, an American who was believed to be the owner of the Mustang, which was completely demolished when Lord Smithereens was unable to stop as approaching the rear of a six-ton fuel-delivery lorry, which erupted in flames, sending a giant fireball hurtling into the morning sky over London. Mr. Stevens was last seen rapidly leaving the Royal Overseas League on foot, followed by a dog. The ownership of the dog, like the Mustang, is still under examination by the authorities.

No, I couldn't do that to the Mustang-loving Charles, who had also been good enough to find a place for Henry, Rat's wretched dog, to sleep. It would have been a clear violation of the brotherhood of the Pony, that invisible but unbreakable bond linking all true believers worshiping at the Mustang altar.

"Fell in love with the car in the States, I did," Charles explained, as we stood together in the morning sun of that spectacular June day.

I asked, as ritual demanded, where he had been in the United States.

"North Dakota," he said almost reverently.

"And?"

"North Dakota, that was my trip, wasn't it?"

"Only North Dakota?"

"Well, there was New York too, but only to change planes. An uncle I've got in North Dakota."

I started to offer my condolences.

"Grand place, it is," Charles proclaimed. "The most friendly people in the world, I believe."

"Friendly?" I asked, startled. I could have imagined a lot of adjectives to describe North Dakotans—*stoic* leading the list, followed probably by *durable*—but *friendly* would not have been on the list. Warm and cozy, a friendly place, that's North Dakota?

"The English are such a bombastic people, aren't we?" Charles said. "Not that way in North Dakota, is it?"

No, I quickly agreed, North Dakotans are rarely accused of being *bombastic*. Bombastic. What a great word.

"A man just can't see enough sky here in London, can you?" Charles squinted into the distance toward St. James's Park, sounding like a character from a Zane Grey novel.

"Well," I admitted, "it's not Fargo."

"Ah, Fargo . . ." He hit a wistful note, the way people talked about Paris in the twenties.

"How would you like a dog?" I asked. "Dogs are very big in North Dakota," I promised.

Rat emerged from the Overseas League doorway. She immediately began to thank Charles profusely for taking care of her wonderful dog. He was quite touched.

"How long have you had him?" Charles asked.

"Almost two days!" Rat proclaimed with great sincerity.

Charles nodded, obviously once again startled by the American generosity of spirit. To love a dog so, after only two days! In the background, I could hear Henry barking, as if he knew we were talking about him. I wondered how likely it might be that he would gnaw through his leash to dash around the corner and, with any luck at all, be crushed by one of the delivery lorries plying luxury goods to the shops of St. James.

When we drove out of the parking lot, Charles was still standing in the doorway, hands on his hips, staring out across the London sky waiting for the wind to blow off the prairie.

Unfortunately, my view in the rearview mirror of this heroic figure was partially obscured by a mass of fur. Henry fur. This was because Henry was in the rear seat instead of lounging inside the Royal Overseas League, where I so desperately wanted to ditch him. What made it all the more annoying is that our Western doorman friend was quite willing to take Henry off our hands, was even excited about the notion.

"He's a good animal," he had observed with a certain solemn judgment. That's how they talked out on the prairie— *animal*. A man didn't have *pets*, he kept *animals*. I figured he would have Henry out there in St. James's Park helping to herd sheep or at least retrieving a downed bird or two. It would be a great life, or so I tried to convince Rat.

But she was adamant. She was crazy, in fact, at the idea of abandoning—her description—poor Henry, as if the damn dog was a childhood pet and not just some stray that had wandered into her life in the last day or so. When I reminded her of this simple fact, she reacted with fierce outrage, as if I had gratuitously brought up the fact that her parents had abandoned her in a Dumpster and she had been raised by alley cats. Mean alley cats.

So Henry was in the back seat as we headed to Dover. We were already late, or at least I *thought* we were late. Somehow I believed that there were only two ferries a day, a ridiculous concept, in retrospect, but one I had gotten into my head by misreading a schedule I'd found at the Overseas League. I think it dated from around 1941, when service was limited due to circumstances beyond anyone's control. You wouldn't think it was difficult, getting a correct schedule for what is probably the busiest ferry in the world. But somehow I was convinced that if we missed the 12:04 departure, we'd have to wait around Dover all day until the evening ferry.

Henry was a problem. A problem that extended beyond the realities of his general existence, which is to say beyond the fact that he was in the back seat and blocking my view, not to mention the sloppy licks on the neck and the hot Henry dog breath on my neck. Henry was a problem because he didn't have a passport. Or papers of any sort. The only way Henry was going to get to France was as a stowaway. Which meant that Rat and I had to go into the dog-smuggling business.

In a 1965 Ford Mustang convertible, there is only one place to hide a largish dog of golden retriever heritage—the trunk. So Rat and I had to stop on the outskirts of Dover and try to convince Henry that he would really enjoy crawling into the trunk of the Mustang. This was not easy. Henry did not like the idea one bit.

It was not a pretty picture—Rat and I pushing and pulling poor Henry toward the trunk. We were parked along the motorway in a rest area that appeared to have been recently bombed. The asphalt was cratered and sticky in the hot sun. Huge double lorries—*articulated* lorries the English called them, a description that implies more intelligence than these brutes merit—hurtled by on the motorway, making the ground tremble and shaking the car with blasts of hot air. Henry started howling.

"We can't put him in the trunk!" Rat wailed. "This is terrible!"

"Dogs love enclosed spaces! It'll be cozy!"

"That's cats!" Rat screamed. "Cats like to be cozy! Dogs roam! They hunt! You ever hear of an English sheep cat?"

An ancient Morris Minor pulled into the battered rest area. An elderly man wearing some kind of uniform leaned out of the car and bellowed, "*What are you doing to that animal!*"

He jumped out, unwinding himself from the tiny car with surprising ease, and strode menacingly toward us. He had to be in his late seventies, a tall, trim, and very fit looking fellow, and as I stared in surprise I realized he was wearing a Boy Scout uniform.

"Tell this woman dogs like to be cozy!" I shouted at the stranger.

"Are you mad?" he demanded.

"Mad? Mad?" I was in no mood to be judged. "At least I'm not driving around in a Boy Scout uniform!"

"*Let that dog go!*" he shouted, advancing with great deliberation.

"Hey, pal, *I* was an Eagle Scout! Merit badge in animals!" I knew that wasn't the precise name of the badge, but I couldn't think of it at the moment and, anyway, it was a lie. I'd never earned a single merit badge dealing with animals. Camping, ropes, and marksmanship, that was more my line.

"We have to smuggle him to France!" Rat finally explained.

"Belgium," I corrected. "Well, France first but then Belgium."

He stopped his advance and stared at us like we were lunatics, which seemed, under the circumstances, to be entirely understandable. Henry, meanwhile, delighted now that he was no longer being stuffed into the trunk of a 1965 Mustang, plopped himself down to watch the debate.

"You're trying to put that animal in the trunk to *smuggle* it into France, is that it?" the aging Boy Scout asked.

"Yes!" we both shouted.

"Madness," he muttered. "What, is he carrying drugs or something, is that it?"

Rat and I looked at each other. Drugs?

"Is the dog carrying drugs?" Rat asked slowly, trying to comprehend.

"Made him swallow some, did you?"

"Who the hell do you think you are?" I demanded. I was sick of this drive-by Samaritan, and we were wasting time.

"If you want to take that animal to France on the ferry— and he's not transporting contraband"—he said this with great skepticism—"then I advise you to put him on the back seat and drive onto the ferry."

"He doesn't have any papers," Rat explained.

The man started to laugh. "In America, do dogs require passports?"

This guy was really getting on my nerves.

"He doesn't need any papers?" Rat asked, surprised. "No shots or anything?"

"Not since about 1956, if my memory serves me well."

Rat and I looked at each other. I couldn't remember exactly *why* I thought we needed papers. Years earlier, when living in Switzerland, I'd brought a cat from America, and it had required immense documentation. But that had been Switzerland.

"Let's go," I muttered.

"Get in the back, Henry!" Rat cooed. "We're going to France!"

We left the old scout in the rest area, staring at the disappearing fins of the Mustang.

We reached the ferry just as they were pulling up the ramp. Seized by the irrational obsession that comes with speeding down a highway for hours to beat a deadline, I accelerated madly, hurtling the Mustang onto the ship past startled dockworkers.

For about three seconds I felt quite proud of myself.

But then we crested the ramp, and I realized we were going entirely too fast. Particularly for a car with seriously ill brakes.

Rat said nothing. While others might have shouted silly imperatives like "*Stop!*" or "*Slow down!*" or even a simple "*No!*" she said nothing. Instead, she reached over and turned the ignition off.

Which caused me to yell "Rat!" but almost instantly I knew she had done the right thing. The car's momentum seem to halve, and since the Mustang had no power steering—and certainly not power brakes—I didn't suddenly find myself with a car I couldn't steer, as I had assumed as soon as the throaty roar of the V-8 died. Instead we appeared to be floating, accompanied only by the squeal of the tires as the car shuddered around the sharp turn from the ramp into the ship's hold.

A ferry worker in orange coveralls leapt out of our way as we plunged from the bright outer deck to the dark hold. A sudden inspiration struck me: *the emergency brake!* Almost blind in the dark hole, I fumbled around and found the brake with my left hand and pulled it with such fierceness that I was terrified it was going to come off in my hand. With both feet, I pumped and pulled the brakes like some kind of mad tap dancer. As my eyes adjusted to the dark, I realized that we were rolling to a stop a few feet from an old Volvo station wagon with Swedish plates. A young couple in shorts and Birkenstocks stood by the car, staring at us, eyes as wide as dinner plates.

The ferry worker approached. Inexplicably, he was American. "Cool," he said. "Came gliding around that turn just like a big Stealth bomber." He waved his hand through the air like a plane.

As we were walking up the metal stairs to the deck, I looked down and saw the Swedish couple standing by their car in apparent shock, like George Segal sculptures.

"Did you see that?" the ferry worker asked them, still excited. "Just like a Stealth bomber . . ."

Two hours later we were in France and I was feeling much better about life. Mostly this was because I did not have that gnawing sensation that a near-death experience—or worse —lurked around every bend. Truth was, there weren't many bends—the road from Calais to Brussels is flat and boring, which is exactly what I wanted. I rejoiced in the long straightaways. I celebrated the lack of twists and turns and the overwhelming *flatness* of it all.

On the ferry, I'd been reading Edith Wharton's *A Motorflight Through France*, which had just been reprinted. Truth was, I hadn't read a word of Edith Wharton since high school, but I loved the title—*A Motor-flight Through France*—and the opening was irresistible:

> The motor-car has restored the romance of travel.
>      Freeing us from all the compulsions and contacts of the railway, the bondage to fixed hours and the beaten track, the approach to each town through the area of ugliness and desolation created by the railway itself, it has given us back the wonder, the adventure and the novelty which enlivened the way of our posting grandparents.

After the claustrophobia of England—a state of mind as much as geography, I admit, but still a reality—the land seemed open and empty, accented by bursts of sunflowers and unhurried green fields that seem to stretch much further than you'd think they could in a small country like Belgium.

And Belgium is where we were in a matter of minutes. The Mustang was delighted to be able to do what it did best—drive straight at a rapid, very loud rate. Henry lay on the back seat, appearing delighted not to be jammed into the Mustang's bad idea of a trunk.

And then we reached Brussels.

I expected a simple little provincial capital and found the most diabolically difficult city I'd ever encountered. Diabolical to drive, that is. A nightmare, pure and simple.

It was the tunnels, of course.

It had all the characteristics of most urban planning, from the pedestrian malls that helped kill the American downtown in the '70s and '80s to ridiculous edifices like Paris's Pompidou Center: fundamentally silly notions that were intended more to impress other urban designers than to improve the quality of life.

As some sort of man-made anti-invasion defense, the tunnels would have worked ingeniously—sinister, hideous diversions intended to swallow whole tank divisions and spit them up miles from their intended destination. A much more elaborate and effective tactic of confusion than the English mislabeling train stations when the German invasion loomed or the Soviet insistence on narrow-gauge train tracks to ward off attack. Of course, that presumed the Belgians must actually have been willing to fight instead of rolling over and playing dead—a trait they have seldom evidenced this century.

The tunnels: simply put, they are a maze of buried highways and bypasses and connectors that burrow under Brussels like some elaborate mole den. The experience is excruciatingly annoying: you will be driving along, map on lap, reading the signs quite nicely, thank you, and without warning, the road disappears into a tunnel, swallowed by the earth. Where once there was light, now there is only darkness. All signs vanish as, naturally, do any helpful landmarks. You find yourself in a terribly confusing labyrinth of intersecting passageways, all poorly marked, if at all, until finally you are so desperate to see the sun—if, indeed, the sun has not long since set in the hours you have been hurled about underground—that you frantically look for an exit—any exit—that will burp you back into fresh air. So, once reunited with the sky and, if not earth, at least above-ground concrete (which has never looked better), you emerge in a distant corner of the city, hopelessly lost, traumatized, and most likely out of gas.

In a convertible, the frenzied roar of the tunnels was deafening and deeply confusing, a most horrific combination only a little more pleasant than running a road rally through an artillery barrage. Me, I love to drive in New York City and have no hesitancy rubbing fenders with the meanest drivers in the world; in Los Angeles, I actually find freeway driving exhilarating, even with the random sniper or two. So what if you're headed for the beach and have to dodge a few rounds of incoming fire? If Americans were bothered by that sort of thing, nobody would have moved out West in the first place.

But this Brussels tunnel roulette, this was a horror. Had I been carrying a small nuclear device, I would have gladly detonated it just for the satisfaction of thinking about the mushroom cloud arising from the tunnels. Lacking even the most petite of nuclear armament, I longed for a tanker truck into which to crash. The fireball would have been quite satisfying.

Finally we washed up miles from our downtown destination of restaurant—Comme Chez Soi—and hotel. We emerged in a pleasant, leafy suburb, and only with the greatest restraint did I resist the urge to get out and kiss a tree.

"Can you recommend a hotel?" I asked an elderly woman walking her tiny Pekingese pup. We had pulled over next to the sidewalk and Rat had a firm grip on Henry, who was eyeing the Pekingese like a luscious appetizer. Devouring someone's dog is not, all things being equal, the absolute best way to elicit help.

"You have a problem," she said.

Immediately I felt like strangling the woman. A problem? A *problem*? Just because I'm riding around in a car with no brakes in a city with man-eating tunnels and I've got a dog on the back seat who is just dying to eat *your* silly little dog and, besides, I'm about to be late for dinner at Comme Chez Soi, you think I've got a problem? PROBLEM?!

Several other pedestrians stopped and stared, and I wondered if they could read my mind and were gathering to defend this poor woman and her soon-to-die dog. They all shook their heads and clucked their tongues disapprovingly.

"What the hell?" I finally demanded.

A young boy pointed underneath the car. Hoping, perhaps, that I had run over the twin of the annoying Pekingese, I scrambled out of the Mustang and joined the growing crowd staring at the car.

The woman was right. We had a problem.

A little geyser of fluid was shooting from the car's underside innards, a bright pink stream that looked as if a minor artery had been nicked. Muttering Mustang curses, I peered inside at the dashboard and noticed for the first time that the temperature gauge was pushing into the red.

I groaned. All I wanted to do was find a hotel and go eat in what was supposed to be the best restaurant in Belgium. Was that such an outrageous notion? What had I done to deserve such torture by the Tunnel Demons and the Automotive Devils?

Henry started growling at the Pekingese, who then began to bark incessantly in a high, yapping voice. A vision danced in my head: Henry leaping from the back seat and doing battle with the yapper. All very satisfying, except that Henry's most damaging behavior would probably have been a few overaggressive licks of his long retriever tongue. Despite his low growlings—clearly intended just to impress the crowd—Henry had the look about him of a canine who would run several miles out of his way to avoid the mildest of confrontations. No killer dog, this.

"Is there a hotel nearby?" Rat asked in her most charming voice, a voice that was, I knew from experience, very difficult to resist.

There were now perhaps a dozen people gathered around the Mustang, as if conspiring to prove that, yes, just as rumored, Brussels was THE MOST BORING CITY IN EUROPE! If an old Mustang with a leaky radiator hose was this fascinating, my God, what would they do if something Really Exciting happened—say, a fender-bender car wreck. It would paralyze the town! All commerce would stop! Tens of thousands would turn out for a firsthand look! Amazing!

A middle-aged man in a tan suit and straw boater who

looked to have escaped from a Cézanne painting pointed down
the leafy street and said there was a hotel—a small place, simple
but pleasant—down the road a kilometer and to the right on the
Avenue Winston Churchill. I liked this. It was easy to remember.

As if to prove there was still life in the Mustang, I revved
the engine and popped the clutch, leaving the collection of
good, simple, and boring-to-death Brussels residents staring in
puzzlement, and spreading trail of pink antifreeze behind us like
blood.

It was not a simple matter finding the hotel, though thank
God no more tunnels emerged to hurl us into the darkness. It
was not easy to find because we did not have a name or address
and the Hôtel Les Tourelles did not look in the least like a hotel.
Surely there had to be a mistake. We were in a residential neighborhood, a place of houses and occasional restaurants, an apartment building or two. Was it possible there was a hotel here?

It also did not help matters that the Mustang had taken to
smoking and making the odd groaning sounds of an old, overheated car, the temperature gauge long buried in the red. We had
the sense that if we did not find this place *right now* we would
be doomed to sleeping in the car—which, after the engine had
melted, might be a good use for the relic. We could turn it into
the smallest—but most charming—hotel in all of Brussels. Why
not? People pay to sleep in old railway cars all the time. Why not
a Mustang? After all, is there a more notorious back seat in all of
automotive history?

Rat spotted it somehow—a small, altogether too elegant
brass plaque discretely noting HÔTEL LES TOURELLES. It was, in its
own way, a quietly flamboyant building for the neighborhood,
a large stone house with twin towers circling skyward. It was
eccentric and immediately likable. I felt the best I had since being
swallowed by the first tunnel.

Relaxing, we pulled into the driveway to turn around and park on the street—and heard a terrible scrape, like a million fingernails dragging across a blackboard. Rat and I looked at each other and suddenly I realized that she was tired. Very tired. Henry did not stir, as if he sensed any misbehavior on his part would meet with severe repercussions.

"Maybe you better get out of the car," I said to Rat. "To make it lighter," I explained.

"Then maybe *you* should get out," she answered, smiling just a touch to take the edge off.

She was right, which was annoying. I really did not want to move.

But I did, and as I watched and tried to elevate the car with brain waves, Rat shifted seats and eased the car slowly backward toward the street. As soon as the car moved, I saw the large pool of bright red fluid. Returning to the street the car scraped less onerously, but it was too late.

"It's not shifting too well," Rat said, and I knew that the red fluid spreading across the driveway, mixing with the antifreeze from the leaky radiator hose, was transmission fluid; the odds were, the Mustang would need a lot more than just new brakes to make it across Europe.

# Chapter
# Five

Rat refused to eat. At least, she refused to eat with me.
Not that I took it personally. I chose to believe that it simply had been a rather trying day, what with her poor dog almost getting stuffed in the trunk, the near plunge into the English Channel, the Tunnels from Hell, and then the terrible blows to the Mustang, and that the thought of sitting down to a two- or three-hour meal was just too much.

That's the way I chose to look at it. The other obvious conclusion was that she was sick to death of me and would have rather eaten roadkill than spend the evening together.

Me, I felt a deep need to eat. A *lust* to devour exquisite food. It seemed the best way to wash the taste of the day from my mouth—and a very convenient way not to think about what in God's name we were going to do with a wounded Mustang in the middle of Brussels.

So I called Claire.

She was the friend of a friend, an early-thirties French woman who'd moved to Brussels last year from New York. She was reported to be smart, good-looking, and funny. I liked all three. She also loved to eat. This was a claim she made herself when I called her up out of the blue and asked her if she was hungry.

"I am always hungry," she announced. "I have eaten three hot dogs at the Papaya King and walked away hungry."

This she said with the appropriate level of pride. The
Papaya King, on the corner of Eighty-sixth Street and Third
Avenue, made a legendary hot dog. Lou Reed had written about
the King's dogs. Three dogs and still hungry?

*Formidable*.

She arrived in front of the Hôtel Les Tourelles in a tiny
Renault: a petite, attractive woman who seemed to vibrate with
energy. "You saw the new study?" she asked as soon as I squeezed
inside the little white car.

"Study?"

She bolted off before the door shut, thrusting a newspaper
into my hand. "Front-page news here. A new study shows that
Belgians sleep more than any other Europeans!"

She laughed heartily with a certain manic edge.

"And . . ." She paused for dramatic effect, turning to fix me
with a bright stare. "Also the number-one collectors of toy trains."

"I see . . ." I murmured, wishing she would quit looking at
me and watch the road. We had turned off the Avenue Winston Churchill toward the Avenue Louise and downtown.
Smiling wanly, I nodded torward the road, suppressing my urge
to scream *Look where the hell you're going!*

A tunnel loomed ahead.

"Oh, dear . . ." Claire said brightly.

"You must have mastered these tunnels," I said confidently.

She laughed. "I am perpetually lost! And it is impossible
to ask directions!"

"Ummm?" If Claire was going to avoid the tunnel she
would have to veer to the far-right lane of the boulevard. At the
moment she was splitting the difference, half of the car headed
*for* the tunnel, half headed toward the right lane. I wondered if
she was taking a Ouija board approach, waiting for the car to steer
itself, magically choosing a direction.

"Claire?" I said. The tunnel was getting very close.

She laughed. "What should we do?" Her French accent made it sound quite cinematic, "*What should zee do?*"

"Well . . ." I hesitated, looking frantically around the Renault for a map.

"Maybe halfway?" she laughed.

"TURN RIGHT!" I finally shouted, causing her to jump in her seat.

"Wow!"

She jerked the wheel of the Renault to the far right, hurtling us away from the tunnel, the front wheel thumping over the curb onto the sidewalk. Pedestrians scattered like frightened quail.

"Should we ask directions?" I ventured, staring at a map I'd found crumpled in a door panel of the Renault. Like every map I'd seen of Brussels, it was incomprehensible.

"No!" Claire shouted. "It is very dangerous." She said this while once again establishing intense eye contact. The car weaved across the Avenue Louise.

"Dangerous?" I gasped, beginning to weigh the odds of survival if I opened the car door and rolled out versus staying inside. I made sure the door was unlocked.

"You can cut this city with a knife! There is the Dutch-speaking and the French-speaking. They hate each other!"

"Okay. I think we turn right here," I suggested. Comme Chez Soi was in the central part of the city and Rue de la Régence, if I was reading the map at all correctly, led there.

"You hear terrible stories, you know," she said confidentially.

"How terrible?" I asked. It was hard to imagine a city of world-class sleepers and toy-train collectors as having a murderous alter ego.

"There!" she shouted, jerking the car through two lanes of traffic to stop in a small parking lot. I looked around, expecting to see some dramatic examples of French-Belgian seeth-

ing hatred, a good knife fight or at least some vicious nation-
alistic graffiti.

"Where?"

She pointed ahead to an Art Deco sign that read Comme
Chez Soi.

"That was easy," she announced happily as we climbed out
of the Renault.

It felt like an Art Nouveau café: the design lush and fussy
but informal, more like a place people came to have a good time
than a Culinary Temple. This I liked. And when I ordered a beer,
the captain seemed to smile a bit, as if to say, *Yes, it is a hot June
day and I'd like a beer myself.*

There were flowers everywhere, but not cute or overdone
arrangements, mostly just huge sunflowers wrapped in the sweeping curves of a beautiful Art Nouveau vase of colored glass. The
menu announced, "Since 1926, three generations of tradition
and innovation."

And so the menu reflected, though it leaned too heavily
on the tradition part of the equation for my taste. Still, there were
some interesting stuff going on: *Les escalopes de foie de canard au
Porto et au gingembre* and *La canette de Barbarie grillée au miel
d'acacia.* The idea of a port and ginger sauce on duck liver I found
interesting, though it wasn't what I really wanted to eat, and I
liked the notion of eating acacia honey on just about anything.

We didn't pray over the menu. I suddenly realized I was
starving and Claire was too busy talking to ponder the possibilities for hours, so we dived in and ordered within minutes. I did
the typical casual-diner thing and ordered based on favorite flavors and ingredients: *Le suprême de bar à la vapeur, citronnette à la
tomate et au basilic, en chaud et froid.* Steamed bass I like, lemon
and tomato with basil, these were good things. As a chef friend

of mine in New York says, "I can sell anything with basil on it. *Anything.*" He was ridiculing a world in which diners lunge for the familiar, without thinking about the totality of the dish, without taking the time to construct a meal. *Basil, I'll take it.* Sun-dried was another favorite. "I could sell sun-dried dog turds," he used to say.

Personally, I'm not sure what's wrong with this notion. It drove my friend crazy because he felt like he spent hours coming up with wonderfully delicate and complementary dishes only to realize that it was the obvious that was selling the items, not the subtle treasures within. But so what? Is it wrong for a chef to think more about his preparations than the diner? Is this whole restaurant business more about pleasing the diner or the chef?

Claire ordered *Les filets de sole, mousseline au riesling et aux crevettes grises*, which sounded terrible to me, soft and mushy and ill defined. But she said she loved sole and always ordered it. I started with *La salade composée au homard et truffes noires* because I love black truffles and used to hunt for them when I lived in Italy, and Claire went with *Les asperges de Malines à la flamande*. Why? She liked asparagus.

Easy choices.

Something about being inside Comme Chez Soi reminded me of the submarine in Jules Verne's *Twenty Thousand Leagues Under the Sea*. It must have been the funny glass and the wild curves, the light from the false skylights. And the conviction that this is what the future would be like, the self-conscious *modernism* of it all.

Claire was ranting about the Belgians. "The highlight of the week—this is important," she insisted, "is to cut Mass a little early to get in line at the pastry shop. This is the big thrill of the week in Brussels. That is Sunday. The rest of the week, there is nothing to do but carpet shop. They love the furniture store!"

The restaurant was not large—again, the submarine—and Claire's voice was not soft. I glanced around, wondering if others could hear her—and they could, of course. A table of middle-aged Brussels stalwarts, businessmen and their wives by the looks of it, exactly the sort of people Claire was ridiculing, were smiling with a nod of agreement. Yes, this is true. This is Brussels, you're right.

Then the salad came and I wasn't listening as closely. As soon as the kitchen door—which wasn't far away—opened and I caught sight of the salad, I was sure I could smell the truffles, like the best truffle pig on the block. I took a huge, embarrassing breath as it was laid before me; the waiter smiled, clearly a man who had smelled a truffle or two in his day. Lobster is a flavor—or lack of flavor—that's always bored me, but the texture worked well with the truffles. It was a gratifying combination, clean but musty.

The menu cover of Comme Chez Soi was a tribute to Art Nouveau, with a series of open doors leading to Magritte-like kisses floating in space. This did not go unnoticed by Claire. "They have one artist, you know—Magritte—and everything must have a Magritte reference. There may be a law about this . . ." She paused, a cluster of asparagus on her fork, and I had the sense that she was watching me to see if I believed her. Mostly I was focusing on the asparagus, which looked quite good hovering in the air. I wondered if she would particularly care if I just reached over and snatched the fork right out of her hand.

"And Simenon, he's their only writer. So everywhere we must celebrate Simenon!"

I was sad to see the asparagus disappear in her mouth.

"I *like* Simenon," I told her, and she nodded in agreement.

"Me too. But don't you think every country should have more than just *one* writer and *one* painter?"

"But at least they are good."

She stabbed the air with her fork. "Spoken like a true Belgian!"

"Do you know where I might be able to get a 1965 Mustang repaired?" I asked.

"You have a Mustang?" she asked, clearly astonished.

I nodded. "A very sick and troubled Mustang."

"Here?"

I nodded again.

"And it is broken?"

"Quite."

"We must go talk to my boyfriend about your Mustang," Claire announced brightly, and then she went back to her Belgian-bashing rant.

When we left Comme Chez Soi, I was desperate for sleep. The truth was, I couldn't really remember ever sleeping before. It might have happened long ago in another country, but I wasn't certain.

"My boyfriend will have suggestions on the Mustang thing," Claire said as she headed the tiny Renault into the blissfully uncrowded late-night streets of Brussels.

"Uh-huh," I agreed, trying hard to keep my eyes open. "Maybe tomorrow we could get together."

"We'll go now. It's better."

"No!" I shouted. She turned and gave me one of her penetrating looks. Please, I thought, don't start with this eye-contact stuff again.

"I'm tired," I explained. "Incredibly tired."

"It is okay," she assured me. "We live very close to the hotel."

"Don't you think we could do this in the morning?"

"We go away to my family's house in Normandy early tomorrow morning."

"We could meet for breakfast . . ." I pleaded. It was very important that I find a bed immediately. It was difficult to over-state the importance of this need.

"Oh, it will just take a minute!"

*I'm being kidnapped,* I thought, wondering if I might be able to grab the wheel and whip the little car onto the sidewalk and leap out. But I realized that I was too tired even to lift my arm.

"I think you are in a lot of trouble with the Mustang," she said in the same upbeat tone. "I really do. It is old, no?"

"Yes," I moaned.

"No one in Belgium has an old car. You have noticed this?"

I hadn't, but she was right, of course.

"Here, if you have a problem, you just call the Royal Automobile Club. That's it!"

"It works?"

"Yes. You should call them."

So I did.

# Chapter
# Six

I saw him from the breakfast room of the hotel.

He was walking around the Mustang with a clipboard, examining the car like a hard-eyed gambler looking over a prize Thoroughbred before the Big Race. Even from forty feet away, through leaded-glass windows, it was clear this was a very serious individual. A short, tough guy in hefty motorcycle boots, tight jeans, and a black shirt with some sort of crest: Royal Automobile Club, it said; I could see it when he turned toward the hotel and stared, as if demanding, "Well, isn't anyone going to come out here?"

His name was Marc. He reminded me of the Belgian paratroopers I'd known in Africa: hard guys, no nonsense, with an air about them that they could deal with just about anything and probably had. He inspired confidence but was not big on bedside manners.

"You're crazy," was the first thing he said to me, offering his elbow to shake in response to my outstretched hand, his own hands holding a piece of dirty rubber tubing.

I told him my name. He nodded. This was something he knew from the Royal Automobile Club and not something he particularly cared about.

"This is your car?" he asked.

I nodded.

"You're crazy," he repeated. "You brought this from America?"

Again I nodded. This was getting a bit predictable.

"Why?"

*Why had I brought the Mustang?* I thought very hard about this. It seemed most important to be able to come up with at least one solid reason. If I could just remember one reason, I was sure I would feel much better about life in general, with a special emphasis on the automotive.

"I thought it would be fun." I shrugged.

He laughed. Positively exploded in laughter. He whipped out a rag from his back pocket and wiped off his hands, then slapped me on the back. "That is very good," he said. "Excellent."

I smiled. I was open to any good news.

Then he frowned. "I must know," he said, "did you run over something big? A boulder, maybe?"

*Was this guy nuts? Boulders in Brussels?* For a brief moment I wondered if possibly there was a whole wild part of Brussels I hadn't seen, a boulder-strewn canyon just off the Avenue Winston Churchill? Some hidden Grand Canyon? Or maybe one of the tunnels had collapsed. This idea I liked, of course.

"How bad is it?" I finally asked him.

"In America, this is no problem. Here?" He shrugged, then suddenly grew very serious, drawing close, as if to share some great intimacy. "You must tell me. Please, I must know . . ."

"Okay." I looked around, feeling a tinge of embarrassment at sharing such a moment with a total stranger.

"Why is this car an automatic?"

Oh. That.

"Do you know ten cc?" he abruptly asked.

I thought hard about what this had to do with automatic transmissions.

"The band," he finally said, exasperated.

I still wondered what this had to do with automatic transmissions. I *hoped* it had something to do with automatic transmissions.

"They have a song about American tourists . . ."

Marc was driving not the large tow truck I would have imagined but a Renault only slightly bigger than Claire's. It was bright white and emblazoned with the imprimatur of the Royal Automobile Club, a ridiculously impressive crest for an organization that existed to fix broken cars. Marc open the hatchback of the Renault and exposed an intricate array of sparkling tools and parts. It looked more like a mobile operating room than a garage. He selected a long piece of black tubing and announced dramatically, "Now I go under." He said this as if he were about to dive to two thousand feet and rescue a crippled submarine. He had a certain flair, this guy Marc.

He slid under the car and asked me, "What do you think of Mobutu?"

"What?"

"Your opinion of Mobutu?"

It seemed all together too early in the morning to be discussing the relative merits of a minor African dictator. Particularly when my transmission and radiator were bleeding all over Brussels.

"Why?" I asked. Maybe something had happened that I missed, like Mobutu had just invaded France.

Marc slipped back out from under the car with a surprised look. "They were a colony of ours, you know. *Zaire*." He said this scornfully.

"What would you do with the Congo if you had it?" I asked.

"The *Congo*." He toyed with the abandoned name of the country. "Is finished. But we don't have a lot of colonies. We were never greedy."

"I see."

"There is a great debate about whether or not these former colonies are better off after being liberated than before."

"I see. Marc, what is the story with the car?" I tried hard not to shout.

He came out from under the car and looked at me with something of a hurt expression. "You think I can't fix?"

"Of course you can," I lied. I had no reason to believe, other than his resemblance to a paratrooper, that he could fix even a flat tire.

He was under the car for quite a while. Rat wandered out with a cup of coffee, took a long look at the spreading stains and Marc's feet jutting from under the Mustang, shook her head and went back inside.

Marc emerged to see her retreating. He looked at me, as if expecting an explanation. When none came, he broke down and asked, "Tell me, how many liters of transmission fluid does this hateful automatic take?"

The manual in the glove compartment—the original manual, which is a very big deal in the Mustang world, having the original manual, that is—said the automatic transmission took five quarts.

Marc did not believe this. He scrunched up his eyebrows and, in a very Gallic moment, muttered, "C'est impossible!"

I read aloud from the manual. There was no question. Five quarts.

"Here, give me that!" Marc insisted, grabbing the manual.

"Marc, I *can* read," I insisted petulantly.

He scrunched his eyebrows in a very de Gaulle-troubled-by-the-state-of-the-world kind of way. "When was this written?" he demanded suspiciously.

"It's the *original* manual," I said proudly.

"Then it is old!" he exclaimed accusingly.

"But Marc." I sighed. "This is the original engine and transmission. Nothing has changed."

He stepped back and looked at the car like one of those guys at the state fair that make a living guessing your weight and age. No, he decided finally, this car cannot hold five liters of transmission fluid.

There was a brief moment when we debated liters versus quarts, but he held firm. Liters *or* quarts, five of them were not going into this Mustang.

Marc, Marc, Marc, I begged, please. Let's just fill the thing up, and when it overflows, we stop. One liter, three quarts, who cares.

He shrugged, then asked, "Where is your transmission fluid?"

I stared hard at him. If, by chance, I'd had a quart of transmission fluid I would have gleefully poured it over his head. The image was clear and pleasing: a river of red, warmish fluid cascading over his dark hair and paratrooper's face.

"You are smiling," Marc noted.

"Yes."

"Then you have the fluid?"

"NO! OF COURSE I DON'T HAVE TRANSMISSION FLUID!"

"We search."


We spent most of the day driving around Brussels looking for automatic transmission fluid. It was actually a quite pleasant way to see the city. Marc behind the wheel was a formidable force. He *attacked* the city, swooping from lane to lane, rushing through caution lights, even honking his horn at pedestrians, unimaginable in quiet Brussels. It was a display of reckless anarchy that warmed my heart.

After we'd tried the third or fourth place without success, Marc announced, "I hate my ex-wife. But I really hate automatic transmissions."

Marc played in a rock and roll band. "We have the subtlety of Pink Floyd and the energy of Guns N' Roses."

I thought about this and couldn't quite imagine it. "What does that mean?" I asked.

"Soft rock," he said, looking chagrined. "But we are playing in a place that has the longest bar in the world—seventy-two meters. You must come and bring your friend. What is her name?"

"Rat."

"An American woman named Rat." He contemplated this thoughtfully.

"She's from Wyoming, actually."

"But that is in America!" he insisted, as if it were under question. "I know Wyoming!"

"You do?"

"I like the stories of the West."

"Zane Grey? *The Virginian?*"

He shook his head. "*Bonanza.*"

We finally found a stash of fluid in a little gas station with one pump run by a friend of Marc's. He had a bright silver hook for a right hand, and when Marc asked him if the cans of fluid were still good—they were rusted and dateless and looked to have been easily twenty years old—he plunged his hook into the lid of one, piercing it as easily as if it were aluminum foil. He took a long sniff, then passed it to Marc to smell. Like a couple of wine connoisseurs, they considered the aroma and nodded approvingly to each other. It must have been a good year.

Back at the hotel, Marc carefully lined up the five cans of fluid. Rat came back out, still carrying her coffee cup. "We have to go see the Magritte," Rat announced.

"You are Rat," Marc said.

"Yes."

"I am Marc."

They shook hands quite solemnly. "Personally," he declared, "I believe Magritte is vastly overrated and Belgians like him because he is all we have."

Rat launched into a defense of Magritte. Marc countered. I watched this sidewalk seminar, not quite believing it. Then I started emptying the transmission fluid cans into the car, one by one.

There was absolutely no doubt in my mind that the machine would take five quarts. It had to take five quarts. The manual—*the original manual*—stated emphatically that it would.

But it didn't, of course. Marc, to my not insignificant annoyance, was right. After two cans, it was full to overflowing. I stared at the fluid leaking out of the engine as if expecting it to burp itself and resume ingestion.

"You think it is still hungry?" Marc asked quietly, a terribly pleased look on his face.

I pouted, still staring at the confounding car.

"Why did you get so many cans?" Rat asked. "It only takes a couple of quarts."

"*How do you know?*" I shouted. "*The manual says it takes five!*"

There was a long pause. The charming couple who owned Les Tourelles stuck their heads out of the kitchen window.

"It's the original manual, too," Rat said, smiling broadly.

"This is very rare," Marc said.


We had dinner reservations at Bruneau at eight o'clock. There were three of us, of course, because Rat—just as I knew she would—insisted Marc should join us. He arrived at Les Tourelles on a large Suzuki motorcycle, wearing a buckskin jacket with trailing fringe. A bolo tie with a large turquoise medallion hung from his neck; he was squeezed into a pair of tight white jeans tucked into black motorcycle boots.

It was quite a look.

We took the Mustang, Marc looking most proud that it was functioning. "It is very loud!" Marc cried, delighted. "Belgians must hate it! Belgians hate noise! This is the quietest country on earth."

"It's holding!" Rat shouted over the throaty gurgle of the engine and the wind. "It" was the ruptured transmission line that Marc had fixed.

"What did you do to it?" Rat asked.

"I put adhesive tape on it."

"Adhesive tape?" Rat asked. "That's it? Just *adhesive tape?*"

"You think I'm a miracle worker or something?"

"How long will that hold?"

"Not very long, I wouldn't think," Marc said good-naturedly. "It's only tape."

"Oh."

Bruneau was across Brussels, near the Koekelberg Basilica, on an unassuming street of small shops. It had been renovated a year earlier with a very California look: sleek and spare with sliding glass doors and lots of marble, a large *B* the only sign that it was the famous Bruneau. There was even a small food boutique in the foyer, Boutique Traiteur, which resembled a chic Beverly Hills specialty food shop.

It was a space designed to impress rather than invite. Two town houses had been joined and gutted and filled with dramatic shapes: oversized columns, recessed pillars, and chrome. Everywhere there was gold—the walls, the light, even the flowers, which seemed to be on every surface.

It was presumably all the vision of Jean-Pierre Bruneau, probably Belgium's most famous chef. He would be forever known as having obtained three stars faster than any chef in Belgium's history: 1977 was the first star, then 1982, and finally the third in 1989. This is a great and daunting feat, and as with all serious achievements reached at an early age, the pressure to sustain such a level—from the Gods of Michelin, from his public—must be fierce.

Which, no doubt, influenced the million-dollar-plus renovations. Michelin does not shy away from proclaiming that a restaurant's physical presentation—everything from the attractiveness of the design to the cleanliness of the bathrooms—affects its star rankings.

This was the great edge that the food critics Henri Gault and Christian Millau used to launch their Gault-Millau guidebooks. Why judge the quality of the food by the bathroom, the flowers, the modernness of design? Anybody who picks a restaurant based on the hand towels doesn't deserve a fabulous meal! Gault-Millau would assign "toques " of greatness based on what goes in your mouth, not what's under your feet. And so the war was launched—Gault-Millau, screaming over the top, all youth and attitude and vibrating with reverse snobbism, versus the stodgy Michelin run by old men hanging out in the bathroom in white gloves looking for grime.

For a while in the late seventies to the mideighties, it looked like Gault-Millau would triumph and drive the ancient Michelin from the field. But like an aging rock star, Gault-Millau learned that a hip edge is difficult to maintain, and youth is even harder. What started out as a small labor of love became big business: books, magazines, television shows. All of this had to be fed by advertising, and with ads always come questions of favoritism. *They spend half a million a year with Gault-Millau, and they have fourteen toques. Have you eaten there lately? It's terrible! But they spend half a million a year with Gault-Millau.*

All the while Michelin slogged on: steady, dependable,

backed by millions of tires, and refusing, as always, to accept ads. They didn't try to out-hip the competition or suddenly reevaluate their criteria. They just kept on being Michelin, with the quiet confidence that in their heart of hearts, people really *did* care about bathrooms.

And Lord knows the chef-owners never quit caring about the glory and riches sprinkled by the Michelin stars. That third star always made you famous, and you had to be a fool with numbers for it not to make you a lot richer than those days, heady as they were, when the first star appeared next to your name in that boring red book.

For Bernard Loiseau, the chef and proprietor of La Côte d'Or in Saulieu, France, the supremacy of Michelin over Gault-Millau was forever confirmed when he looked out his window and saw the editor in chief of the Gault-Millau magazine standing in front of his restaurant reading the red Michelin guide. For a chef like Loiseau, long obsessed with moving from two stars to three, it was an oddly reassuring moment, confirming that his pursuit of Michelin glory was not in vain. If even the Gault-Millau editor relied on Michelin, what further proof was needed that Michelin still ruled the culinary world?

There was something about the whole Michelin process that must have driven chef-owners quite mad in the privacy of their own kitchens. It wasn't enough that they were great chefs, concentrating on their craft. They had to be showmen! They had to dazzle! And was it worth it to spend a few million francs on a fancy renovation? Of course, if it would help keep three stars for a few years! That was easy!

But what happened if you spent the money and still lost that star? Dropped to two stars, my God! What then? How do you claw your way back into the stratosphere? Renovate yet again? What do these people want? A flaming moat? Dancing bears?

So if you are Jean-Pierre Bruneau, it only makes sense to spend a small fortune converting your once small but charming town-house restaurant into a sleek showplace, combining two town houses, gutting them, and reconstructing the space into a futuristic fantasy. Which is all very intriguing to the eye but not very inviting. It makes you want to stare but not sit and relax.

Except for the garden, which shines at the end of one of the golden rooms like an allegorical painting. As soon as I saw it, I wanted to sit there in the worst sort of way. It was a soft summer evening when it seemed a crime to be inside, when twilight felt like it might never end and the world might have a chance to endure forever in some exalted state of golden light.

Which is why I assumed it would be impossible to get a table in the garden. Certainly in New York you would have to take hostages to get one of four tables in a garden when the house was full—and Bruneau was full every night. This is what having three stars in a wealthy city that likes to think it knows a lot about food will do for your business.

But there was no problem with seating in the garden. The staff seemed charmed by the suggestion. Astonishingly, none of the garden tables were taken, while every table inside was full. I began to wonder if perhaps there was something we didn't know, like there were snipers in the nearby basilica who loved to use diners for practice, or maybe every evening at 9:30 there was a sudden, very localized downpour or a hailstorm that only fell on the garden.

Whatever the reason, I was delighted. I could think of nothing more pleasant than our own little weird ménage having the garden to ourselves.

"This is the ugliest menu I've ever seen," Rat said pleasantly. It wasn't that she really cared, it just seemed important to record the fact for history.

She was right. It made me wonder if there was some sort of Brussels ordinance requiring menus to be surreal and unappealing, like really bad Magritte paintings. The powder-blue cover featured a drawing of the nearby Koekelberg Basilica floating in the heavens, with a white cloud serving as a tablecloth on which a drawing of the restaurant—the way the restaurant used to be, before the recent renovations—perched on a plate like an entrée, a cluster of flowers and one huge burning candle behind it, as if the restaurant were being served for dinner. This was probably intended to be very clever and allegorical, not just embarrassing.

Marc whistled at the prices. They were ridiculous, but then they always were, and I decided not to think about it in hopes we really could get Rat's lawyer boyfriend to pick up the tab. Living in New York, I had long ago developed a psychological defense to absurd restaurant prices based on specious rationalizations along the lines of "Well, it's cheaper than a car" or "Mormons pay this much every couple of months to feed the average family of fifteen." It helped, sort of.

Four *amuse-gueule* starters appeared right away. I was learning that this was very big in the three-star world, this freebie stuff they give you for just showing up, and really worthy of an entire separate critique. You could write a guidebook entitled *How to Eat Really Well for Free at Three-Star Restaurants*, complete with descriptions of the starters and the best excuses for leaving the table after the freebies were delivered but before you actually had to order any real—i.e., not-for-free—courses. Something like, "I'm sorry, my house is on fire and I really must get back to see what can be salvaged." Who could question that? Of course, it would be important to keep a running tally of the excuses used so that you didn't trot out the house-burning more than two or three times.

Bruneau did very well with the free starters—four different ones. A paté, a soufflé of lobster, something I can't remember, and my favorite—salmon wrapped in lobster mousse on a bed of alfalfa sprouts, which struck me as the most elegant sort of health-food dish imaginable. Rat liked it so much she asked for a repeat, which seemed to shock but not displease the wait staff. Probably it was the first time anyone had ever expressed excitement over the *amuse gueule*, since the etiquette seemed to be predicated around the idea that it was important to seem nonchalant about the basic service of a restaurant: the flowers, the charming maître d', the decor—these were things one was expected to quietly appreciate, not jump up and down and hail with great vigor. *Those are the prettiest flowers I've ever seen! What a nice waiter!* For some reason, you just didn't do this kind of thing any more than you were expected to be terrifically excited about the free starters. It was a matter of form.

There were a half dozen things I would have liked to order. For a starter—the real starter—I was torn between the *Salade de Homard aux Pommes Vertes* in an *émulsion au curry léger* or the *Coussinet De Raie Aux Pinces De Homard* in a *vinaigrette à la tomate*. And for the main course, the *Dos De Barbue Poelee Aux Epices* sounded wonderful, or *Filet de Bar De Ligne "Dos Bleu"* with *tartiné au caviar d'Iran*—I did not know that Iranian caviar was considered superior—and the *Ravioles De Celeri Aux Truffes aux essences aromatiques* was appealing, if only because I couldn't imagine what it would be like.

And then there was the *Galette De Pigeonneau de Vendée et ses cuisses caramélisées au soja* and the *Croustillant de Filet D'Agneau des Alpilles parfumé au basilic*.

"This is not easy," Marc said.

"Ordering is never easy," Rat agreed in a most serious tone. Marc laughed.

"I'm not joking!" Rat insisted, which naturally made Marc laugh harder.

"Do you do this often?" Marc asked.

"We've never been to Bruneau," I assured him.

"I think it is fun once in a while, but to eat like this every night . . ." He shook his head.

Rat and I looked at each other and didn't say a word.

I settled on the ray fish to start. It came in a tomato vinaigrette with red and green peppers arranged in diamonds. Pretty, but underwhelming, with a most strong resemblance to crab salad.

But next there was the *Fricassee De Homard Breton Au Jus De Viande aux chicons confits au gingembre et citron vert*. It was fabulous, contradictory but not conflicting, every taste a surprise. A warm wind was blowing through the garden. It was eleven P.M., but there was still an orange glow in the sky, as if darkness had been delayed until we could finish dinner.

Chef Bruneau wandered by as we were finishing dessert. He was a large, gentle-looking man with a quiet manner. When asked about the renovations, he seemed hesitant, as if wondering if we would think them too ostentatious. But when he learned Rat and I were from New York, he relaxed, assuming, I suppose, that we would understand the need for such showmanship, coming from the city.

"Do you know the Quilted Giraffe?" he asked, referring to the famous East Side restaurant. When Rat told him it had recently closed, he seemed shocked. "It is closed for renovation?" he asked hopefully.

"Finished!" Rat exclaimed. For some reason she appeared to be taking pleasure in delivering this bit of apparent bad news. "Shut! Over and out. Show closed!"

"But such a place? How is it possible?" he murmured, more to himself than us.

"Well, you know how it goes," I said comfortingly.

"Yep," Rat chimed in, "they were coasting for years. Big name, but that was it."

Chef Bruneau now looked absolutely miserable. Marc, ever the sympathetic soul, complimented him on the lamb he'd enjoyed, the *Cotes d'Agneau À La Mie De Pain*. Bruneau brightened and began to tell us how Belgian beer was the key to the lamb.

"They drink beer?" Rat asked skeptically. "The lambs?"

"Only the *best* Belgian beer," he confirmed.

"You can taste it, it's true," Marc agreed.

Rat looked at the two of them, then challenged, "You're making that up."

"We like to cook with beer in Belgium," Bruneau said. "It is part of our national heritage. Would you like to see the kitchen?"

While she was getting up, Rat was still murmuring, "Beer. I had a dog once who drank beer. Sheep?"

"You see," Marc said, "there are some who think Belgium is the most boring place on earth, but where else do you have sheep who drink beer?"

"I *like* Belgium, Marc. I just don't like the tunnels."

"Ahhh. And after midnight, they let sheep drink beer in the tunnels."

"Marc, shut up."

"It is a sight you must see. Tell me, can I drive the Mustang home?"

# Chapter
# Seven

The brake cylinders were waiting for us when we returned from Bruneau, delivered from the airport by some mysterious means. I held the package marked "Mid-American Mustang" in my hand, like a relic from another world. What were they eating for dinner in St. Louis, Mo.?

Marc had given me the names of several places where I might be able to get the Mustang brakes repaired. It took half an hour on the phone for me to realize that we were in big trouble. Everyone was very happy to work on the Mustang—in two weeks. We were heading into some mysterious Belgian holiday and the very suggestion of working even a half day caused people to laugh out loud. Quite literally. This did not improve my disposition. I called Marc.

"Remember what I said about Mobutu?" he asked.

I did only vaguely. It had not seemed very important at the time and did not seem more so now.

"We never had many colonies, and then we lost the ones we had. Now you begin to see why."

"What does this have to do with my brakes?"

Marc sighed. "It is about Belgium and Belgium is about your brakes. Understand?"

"No."

"Did you offer them extra money?"

"Yes."

"But no one cares. Once we worshiped the church and now we worship the holiday. It is a good thing Mobutu doesn't invade Belgium."

"Marc—"

"He could conquer us in a day. He is short but—"

"*Will you forget about Mobutu, for Christ's sake! What about my brakes?*"

"When do you leave?"

"We're eating at Romeyer tonight and then tomorrow we leave for Strasbourg."

"You're getting close to Germany. There is hope."

"I hate Germans, and how am I going to get there without brakes?"

"Carefully. It is not so bad. I drove it, you know."

"You drove it to dinner, not across France to Strasbourg."

"It *was* a great dinner. I think next time I will try the ray fish. Will you come tonight and hear my band?"

I was sitting in the hallway of Les Tourelles, where the hotel's one telephone was located. The hotel felt like an overgrown home more than a commercial establishment. Two cats, one black, one white, ran through the hall. Henry, who had taken an immediate liking to the place, sat placidly by the kitchen door, where he had learned he was likely to get treats from the young daughters of the owners. There was something about the place that was very comfortable, and I was beginning to think about taking up permanent residence. Why go anywhere? I could become the eccentric hermit of Avenue Winston Churchill, the aging bellboy of Les Tourelles. They could use a good bellboy; right now only the daughters carried the luggage. A beard would probably go well with this new life, or a goatee anyway.

"Stuart?" Marc finally said, breaking the silence. "You know what you should do?"

"You think we should drive to Strasbourg without brakes and find some German to fix the car."

"Yes. That is tomorrow. Today you should go to the comic-strip museum. You like comic books?"

It was a good idea.


Brussels is a place that likes to take itself seriously. It's a culture based on international trade and diplomacy, endeavors that make a virtue of blandness and neutrality. It's probably a preview of how all of Europe will end up if this crazed rush to European unity continues: big bland cities without cultural distinction. The Belgians pretend to love all of this and actually act as if it's important that they are the home of the E.U.—the European Union.

It probably makes sense that the Belgians have embraced with great fervor the concept of eradicating national distinctions, since they have never been very good at establishing a national distinction in the first place. A country for only a little over 150 years, they've tried to cobble together a national identity from bits of France and Holland, never with great success.

Having been twice conquered in their brief history tends to focus a nation on unoffensive tasks, like making money. The Swiss have done this deliberately and have at least managed to preserve some national dignity with the notion that they are in control of their own destiny, *intentionally* neutral, backed by a civilian army of great, if untested, repute.

It's clear the Belgians never should have tried to be important. When your own king—Leopold II—sums up the national character as "*Petit pays, petites gens*" ("Small country, small people"), this is hardly a call to national greatness. Perhaps out of boredom, Leopold tried to convince his country that they should play a role on the world stage, and certain delusions of

grandeur were inevitable. But a colony or two can not obliter-
ate a national culture, so when the Germans set up field kitchens in the Grand Palais in the central square of Brussels—as
they've done twice so far this century—the Belgians reverted to
form and did not take to their modest forests with pledges of
eternal struggle. Yes, there were heroes and, even more prominently, heroines, like Gabrielle Petit, but these were no *muja-
hideen*. They mostly decided to act as if they just didn't care and
called it passive resistance, an oxymoron if ever there was one.

This takes an inevitable toll on the human soul and pushes
one to a certain ironic detachment. Which probably has something to do with the Belgian love of the comic strip.

As soon as I heard that Brussels had a comic-strip museum,
I knew I had to go. It coincided completely with my belief that
you should always seek out the one museum which is unlikely
to be replicated elsewhere. Why drag around to see the bad
local imitation of the Louvre or the Met? In New York, I always
direct visitors to the Police Museum. Best photos of different ways
to die in New York. In Los Angeles, the Tar Pits. Dinosaurs! Real
dinosaur bones just a decaf latte away from Melrose Place! In
Seattle, go see Mark Toby. You'll never find him elsewhere!

The Centre Belge de la Bande Dessinée is in the heart of
Brussels, a city designed to look important. In many ways the
center of Brussels is a classic Potemkin village: massive, impressive buildings worthy of an empire in which not very much
happens. Take the comic-strip museum—it's in an exquisite Art
Nouveau former department-store building designed by the great
Victor Horta himself. Under the massive cantilevered glass roof
you'll find the most serious presentation of comic-strip art imaginable. There's something enjoyably inappropriate about it, as
if you'd walked into the Metropolitan Museum and found that
the Renaissance wing had been rededicated to the history of television sitcoms.

But who's to say Tintin doesn't deserve such lofty surroundings? Tintin, the most famous Belgian of them all, Tintin the hero. Since 1929, he has lived all the unfulfilled fantasies of the Belgian psyche. While Belgium was pulling back from colonization, Tintin was roaming the globe in comic-book volumes like *Tintin and the Picaros* and *Tintin au Pays des Soviets*. And when Belgium was facing an approaching invasion from Germany, their army might not have been ready to repulse the fascists, but Tintin was in *King Ottokar's Scepter*.

Tintin captured the imagination of Belgium because he was everything the Belgians in their hearts knew that they weren't: daring, bold, larger than life. As a repository of a national identity, Tintin and his author, George Remi, elevated the comic-strip format to an extraordinary level, so it only makes sense that this august building would be dedicated as a shrine.

And it only makes sense that the Belgians would be furious with George Remi for seeming to be too cozy with the Germans during the war. He continued to publish an innocuous version of Tintin for a German-controlled paper and was promptly arrested as soon as the Germans left town.

But when he resurrected the great hero in the bimonthly *Journal de Tintin* in 1946, the Belgians quickly fell back in love. The museum, dedicated in 1989, ten years after the creator's death, is really an excuse to honor Tintin, though it masquerades as an homage to the genius of the comic strip. Rat and I wandered through the impressive building, the scores of comic strips far better lit and presented than most of the masterpieces in Florence's Uffizi. I'd assumed the crowd would be hip-hopping teenagers scurrying around plugged into Walkman's, but of course it was serious Belgians, mostly forty and older, paying respect to the characters they had grown up with and that had inspired their dreams. A nation acting out its fantasy destiny in little strips of animation.

*  *  *

His name was Tony. I'd never particularly liked him, but I knew him and he lived in Brussels and since he was one of two people I knew in Brussels—the other was the diabolical driver Claire—I called him.

"De-lighted. Friggin' de-lighted!" he kept saying when I called. "Have to get together sometime," he chimed in a vague sort of way that implied the very distant future. It occurred to me that he probably didn't like me very much either and dreaded this kind of call. "Friggin' humans, strange lot, aren't they?" I could imagine him thinking. "Come to town and think they have to call, people you wouldn't see for good money at home. Stevens! Why's he calling me?"

"We're going to be in town until tomorrow," I lumbered on, God knows why, "and were wondering if you wanted to get together for dinner."

"Terribly sorry, not sure can do. Not sure at all."

"We have to go to Romeyer," I said.

"Oh, well, that's splendid!" He instantly switched gears. Maybe the old schedule can—"

"And Rat's with me."

"Super! What time!"

Tony knew Rat from our gym in New York. He was a reporter for the BBC who covered politics and fancied himself a ferocious squash player. He may have been, for all I know; I grew up in a state that didn't even have a squash court and I've never touched a racquet in my life.

I'd met Tony through politics, when he had wanted to cover a "real American campaign" and had talked me into letting him report on a race I was working on in South Dakota. My misguided effort to be helpful resulted in four long days of Tony at my side murmuring, "The vastness, oh, the vastness," every few minutes. He actually wore a Savile Row bespoke suit;

I'm not making this up, he really did. And brand-new cowboy boots fashioned from the skin of some unidentified endangered species. He also wore bow ties and was fond of quoting Kevin Costner from *Dances with Wolves*. We spent four days in South Dakota, and had we spent a fifth, I'm confident he would have been sent back to Brighton in a box, disemboweled by some disgruntled South Dakotan who couldn't take another word from this bow-tied, Savile-suit-wearing dandy in iridescent cowboy boots.

Now Tony was in Brussels covering the European Community for the BBC and working on his "true history of Waterloo." This was something he used to talk about a lot at the gym, and it's safe to say that there was not one person in all of New York City who was remotely interested, a minor detail that did not deter Tony in the slightest.

"You invited Tony?" Rat asked me in shock. "Tony? The Twit?"

"He's not so bad."

She laughed.

"And he's the only person we know in Brussels."

"So?"

Rat and I were in the Brussels Super Gym, just down the street from Les Tourelles on Avenue Winston Churchill. In a strange way, it seemed to be a perfectly logical extension of the comic-strip museum. The Super Gym, billed as Brussels's most modern, felt like a museum dedicated to the history of sport. The barbells were large round balls linked by a bent iron bar and looked exactly like the kind of thing you'd have seen the "World's Strongest Man" lifting at the county fair around 1900. Two old men in long Bermuda shorts and no shirts rolled a huge medicine ball back and forth.

Rat's black leotard was similar to what several of the middle-aged men were wearing. In shorts, a tee shirt, and running shoes,

I looked terribly out of place, as if I had wandered in off the street onto the stage of a period-piece drama.

"Tony remembers you," I told Rat in my best brother-teasing-sister voice, "he sure does."

Tony liked to hang around the weight room after playing squash—particularly when Rat was around. He always wore a clingy white tennis shirt and shorts so short and tight that they looked to have been stolen from a hooker.

"And I remember Tony," Rat countered, "and that's why I think you're nuts as a bunny to have called him."

And I knew she was right.


He picked us up at the hotel in a convertible Morgan.

"That yours?" He asked when he saw the Mustang parked out front. "Aren't you worried about it getting nicked?"

"You're a damn optimist," Rat said. She was wearing a short black cocktail dress and platform shoes, and if her goal was to discourage Tony from staring at her the way he used to at the gym, she had failed quite miserably. If that was her goal.

"Smashing!" Tony announced as soon as he saw her. "Just smashing!"

"Perhaps Tony would consider trading cars?" Rat asked, as if Tony were not present.

"Tony would not give a rat's ass for that junky American smoker but Tony thanks you very much."

We all squeezed into the Morgan, and though Tony was giving every sign of being just as great a jerk as we'd remembered, it was still difficult not to feel good about life, with the top down, heading to what was reputed to be a spectacular restaurant on a gentle evening that would grace us with hours of soft dusk like a very special present.

"It was a hundred and seventy-nine years ago almost to the day," Tony told us as we rolled through beautiful thick woods. Though we were only fifteen minutes from the center of Brussels, it seemed as if we were in the deepest of forests. "We're only five minutes from the battlefield," he said hopefully.

"Tony," I said, "the reservations."

"Yes, yes. Maybe after dinner."

"Tony?" Rat asked.

"Yes, love."

"What the hell are you babbling about?"

"Waterloo!"

"Tony is working on a BBC production on Waterloo," I told Rat.

"Actually, they haven't totally committed, but we're very close! It wasn't a beautiful day like this, no sir. Rained cats and dogs all the day and night before. Napoleon waited, you know, for the field to dry out. Didn't help at all, only delayed things and might have cost him the battle."

"Why?" Rat asked.

I gave her a sidewise glance. Didn't she remember how Tony could talk for hours—literally hours—about Waterloo? Had she never been around for one of these performances?

"Allowed the Prussians under Blücher to reinforce Wellington, didn't it?"

"Oh my God," Rat laughed.

It took a moment for Tony to realize that Rat was reacting not to him or Wellington but to the sight of Romeyer in the distance. The setting was fantastical: a large stone country manor surrounded by a lush park that felt like a manicured game preserve, complete with deer and a sparkling lake, where, I had no doubt, the fish had been trained to jump into your net.

We were met in the parking lot by a child waiter. There's

really no other way to describe him. He was, perhaps, twelve or thirteen and dressed formally, so he looked like an extra in some elaborate pageant.

He led us to the wide terrace that stretched the length of the building. The furniture was pink and reminded me of the tea-house look of the riverside gazebo at the Waterside.

"Just like the trailer I grew up in." Rat grinned, nodding at the AstroTurf that graced the floor of the terrace.

"A trailer?" Tony asked. Clearly he found this charming and exotic.

"You bet, honey. My stepdaddy used to chase me around and I had to fight him off with those little safety scissors they give you in grade school."

"My, my," Tony mumbled, both titillated and appalled. I didn't have the heart to tell him that Rat grew up in a four-thousand-square foot house with a father who was head of the Wyoming bar association.

The child waiter reappeared with a little plate of melon and prosciutto and another of sardines and eel on toast. Tony ordered a bottle of champagne. He drank champagne all the time, one of his more enjoyable affectations.

The sky was bright blue even at 8:00 in the evening.

"I think," Tony said, "that this might be really quite fantastic."

Fantastical, yes. But fantastic? No, not really. There was something just not right about the whole evening.

Rat felt it right away. We had moved inside to a table under one of the eight large windows that lined the dining room. "This is not a happy house," Rat declared. This was after we had ordered and were nibbling a second set of freebies, one some sort of mushroom confit and the other an odd chicken concoction. But it wasn't the food she was reacting to as much as the feel of the place.

"A museum," Rat said.

I laughed, still under the spell of the intoxicating evening and the lush surroundings and, yes, the Ruinart champagne. But I knew what she meant. The dining room, which probably sat fifty or sixty, was half empty, and there was no one under fifty, except us, in the room. With the exception of the child waiter, the staff was mostly older as well, and no one seemed to be enjoying what they were doing.

It all made for a repressed, formal feel that reminded me of restaurants in medium-sized American cities that take their role as the Important Place to Dine far too seriously. Invariably they were French, usually with a maître d' or captain or two who spoke English with a French accent and maybe were even French. It was memories of such places that for years had driven me from any establishment with a white tablecloth and into the bowels of Spanish Harlem and Chinatown in search of food that was, by God, fun to eat.

And what's the point of going to any restaurant if it isn't great fun?

The food at Romeyer certainly wasn't bad. My *Agneau à la fleur de thym, bouquetière de légumes* was terrific. Very satisfying. We drank a couple of bottles of a 1970 Saint-Estèphe, which was fantastic, and altogether, it was a meal you'd be lucky to have any time.

The mandatory predessert sweets were outstanding: a crème brûlée with melted drops of brown sugar and the usual plate of pastry-chef magic—a strawberry custard tart with coconut, chocolate macaroons, elephant-ear pastries, miniature cupcake-like concoctions. And, most oddly, a chocolate ice cream log. We ate them all, unthinkingly. This seemed to delight the waiter, who showed a smile for the first time that evening. Rat finished with crêpes suzettes, prepared at the table.

"Now," Tony said, "we have to make just a short detour. Won't take a minute," he insisted over our groans.

Which is how Rat and I ended up sitting on a hillside at the Waterloo sight, splitting a pirated bottle of the Saint-Estèphe, watching mad Tony roam around in the dark, hollering:

"Right here is where Wellington stood and shouted 'Up Guards and at 'em!' Charged the goddamn Imperial Guard with bayonets and drove 'em back!"

I fell asleep in the grass right about the time the Prussians were arriving to reinforce Wellington.

# Chapter
# Eight

We were just past Waterloo when the car began to smoke. Or steam, really. Big, billowing clouds of steam. Very impressive, in fact.

For a long moment—too long, no doubt—I ignored the steam, as if we were just driving over some giant manhole with escaping steam, like a late-night spin down Seventh Avenue in New York on a cold night.

But this pleasant fantasy—certainly one of the most pleasant, nonsexual fantasies evoked by Seventh Avenue, home to many a hooker—evaporated like the steam when Henry began to growl. This was no doubt an indication of my willful automotive ignorance, that even a dog was better at detecting impending disaster than I. Rat, to her credit, didn't say a word. She could be good that way, Rat could. Very un-nagging and prone not to state the annoying obvious.

She might also just have been concentrating on ways to kill Tony. That was a subject worth occupying the mind for quite a while.

We were in a deep forest, a tunnel of green that eventually would lead to the motorway to Strasbourg. The day was enjoyable and cool, and it seemed perfectly natural to pull over by the side of the road.

"Maybe it just needs to cool down," I said. For those of us who don't understand cars in the least, there is always a tendency to personify the machines, as if thinking of them as possessing human traits will somehow make them more comprehensible.

Rat looked at me. She was wearing sunglasses about the size of Frisbees and it was impossible to determine what she might be thinking. That was the point, I guess.

"Tell me again," she finally asked, "why it was important to drive around in a 1965 Mustang?"

"Why was it important to eat in all these damn three-star restaurants? Tell me that!"

"The food tastes good," she said, still in a perfectly level voice, unlike my own rising tone. "And Carl was going to pay. At least in theory."

"But I love this car! It's beautiful!"

"Fine. Let's take a photo of it and carry it with us every-where. This would be the perfect spot to take a picture. Then let's call a cab and go back to Brussels and rent a real car."

"And leave the Mustang! Just like that?"

"Yes. With any luck at all, some German will steal it and be driven mad with frustration."

She knew I disliked Germans. The idea did have some appeal.

A few cars, not many, had passed us without stopping. No doubt we looked like a happy couple out on a picnic excursion. Wrong on both counts.

"A German wouldn't know the brakes were bad. They might get in and drive away and plow right into a tree." This enjoyable scenario began to unfold in my head.

"Or maybe a big tanker truck. Lots of flames."

"But that would snuff the truck driver too," I cautioned.

"He would be German as well."

"Ahhh . . ." It was a delightful notion.

Holding onto this image, I got out of the car and raised the hood. The car burbled like a witch's cauldron.

A Peugeot headed in the opposite direction stopped alongside us and a balding man of late middle age leaned out and
asked in French if there was a problem. While I was constructing an answer in my head, he repeated the question in Dutch,
looking slightly embarrassed, as if he had committed a mild
faux pas.

I wondered whether if I remained silent he would keep
rolling out other languages. What would be next? German, probably. Then maybe some Scandinavian tongue. I could pass for
Scandinavian. German too, unfortunately.

"We have a problem," I eventually said in English.

"What sort of problem," he promptly responded in perfect
English.

A diplomat, I thought. He had to be a diplomat.

"The goddamn car is jinxed!" Rat shouted, smiling.

He blushed. Actually really and truly blushed.

"I see," he answered. "May I be of assistance?"

"Bet your ass," Rat told him, uncoiling from the car.

He turned so red I was afraid he might have a stroke.

We left the car by the side of the road and Lester the diplomat—yes, he was a diplomat with the E.C.—drove us to a village just a few kilometers away. "A little garage I know," he said.
"They will have a truck to tow."

He told us he had a sister in Iowa who'd married an American serviceman when they had been living in Frankfurt. His
father was a diplomat as well, second in command in the Belgian consulate in Frankfurt.

"Her son and daughter came to visit last year. You should
have seen them! Americans! Real Americans!"

He paused. Rat and I were not really listening, both still
inwardly fuming over the car. Henry was crowded into the
Peugeot's back seat with me. Lester had insisted, of course, that
Rat ride in the front seat with him.

"She was right, my sister," he continued. "To leave this country, become an American." His voice sounded suddenly quite sad. I watched his profile—a friendly, soft face.

"There is no future here." He laughed. "We try to construct imaginary futures, but there is no real future here. It is all about yesterday." He paused again. "Such a small country. An easy country to live in. Everyone taken care of. But is that a life?"

We drove in silence the rest of the way to the garage.

It was a true village, one long street lined with a few shops, one large grocery store, a small auto-parts store, and three bars, no restaurants. Though less than forty-five minutes from downtown Brussels, it existed in another world.

The garage owner was a Turkish-born, German-trained mechanic who had once, he said, been head mechanic at the largest BMW dealership in Paris. In his late forties with two young sons, he had left the city to find a simpler life.

"It was the housewives! They were the worst!" he asserted vehemently. "Always they need it by noon! A blown engine! By noon! As if they even needed the damn cars! A hundred-thousand-deutsche-mark vehicle to drive from one shop to another!"

He was named Franco because his parents thought he could do better in the world if he passed for Spanish, not Turkish. "Me, a Spaniard! Can you imagine such craziness!" He smiled broadly at the thought. "Still, better to be a Spaniard than a Turk in this new Europe." He shrugged.

He was a big fellow, with closely cropped black hair and a broad build. I could tell Rat thought he was handsome because of the way she didn't challenge his tirade against housewives. Not that Rat was quick to defend housewives. But still, they were females, even though French ones.

Franco's garage was on a side street, a simple one-bay affair, meticulously clean and well organized, with a small office adjacent to it that connected it to the house next door. Posters of Formula One racers and racing cars lined the walls. This was Franco's great passion, and he could not believe that we didn't know the great racers.

"You're joking!" he cried, quite serious in his claim, convinced that we were feigning ignorance as some sort of practical joke, like pretending not to know the earth wasn't really flat. "You don't know Juan-Manuel Fangio? Alberto Ascari?"

He was stunned by our blank stares and slapped his head, a wonderfully Gallic gesture of stupefaction. "That's incredible!"

Franco had two sons who looked exactly like him only smaller, as if he had fallen in the washing machine and been shrunk, then duplicated. They were ten and eleven and wore identical blue workmen's overalls with "BMW Service" stickers and "BMW Racing Team" shoulder patches. They both stood to the side of their father and anticipated his needs, passing over tools with crisp gestures and solemn expressions.

"Can you believe that?" Franco asked his sons. "They don't know who Juan-Manuel Fangio is?" The kids smiled at the preposterousness of the notion. Not big smiles, just little hints of a grin.

"They're adorable!" Rat said, nodding toward the children.

"Adorable? Hah!" Franco scoffed, but he was obviously pleased. "They will be great Formula One racers! Great ones!"

Though his hands had been working furiously under the hood, he'd seldom looked down to see what he was doing. There was something strange about it, as if his hands belonged to someone else who was paying attention.

"You must feel the machine!" he exclaimed, when he saw me staring at him. "That is what a great mechanic knows how to do. You can see very little. You must feel!"

Franco replaced the radiator hose, which had sprung a leak, and removed the thermostat. He held it out at arm's length, as if examining a diseased organ. "You will not need this until it is cold and your heater must work at maximum efficiency. Here." He handed it to Rat. "You must find a similar one that is not malfunctioning."

He had a way of throwing in quasi-technical language that sounded like it had been learned from a mechanic's phrase book: "maximum efficiency," "malfunctioning." I had an image of the young Franco, looking, no doubt, just like his sons, staying up late to memorize the proper automotive descriptions in French, German, and English so he could one day be a great mechanic and repair the fancy BMWs of Parisian housewives.

"We go for a drive to test now," he announced, sliding behind the wheel.

"Franco," I interjected, "there are a few problems . . . a few other problems."

"Yes?" He started the car and raced the engine, filling the small space with a tremendous amount of noise and not a small quantity of bluish smoke.

"Oil leak!" he announced. He turned to me—I was now in the passenger's seat—and asked in very serious terms, "You were knowledgeable about this problem of the oil leak?"

"Trust me, Franco, that is the least of our worries. There's a real problem with—"

He nodded absently and, scoffing loudly at the automatic transmission, threw the car into reverse and accelerated rapidly out of the driveway.

"Jesus!" he yelled as his foot hit the brakes without noticeable effect. The car hurtled backward across both lanes of the narrow street in front of his house, bounced over a low curb, and shot into a field, where it came to a slow halt after I reached over and turned off the engine. From across the way, Franco's sons stared wide-eyed. Rat was laughing. Henry ignored us.

"I was trying to tell you about the brakes," I said flatly.

Franco collapsed on the wheel, as if he had just run a very long race. His back was heaving and I was afraid that he was sobbing.

Then he leaned back and burst into laughter. "That was superb!"

We didn't make it to Strasbourg that night. We drove back to Brussels in Franco's chopped-up BMW and returned to our hotel.

"Back so soon?" the young woman behind the desk asked us.

"We couldn't stay away," I answered, smiling. It felt strangely good to be back, like coming home. That's what traveling did to you—stay in one place three nights and it's your new home.

"You can stay all summer!" she said, and at the moment, the invitation sounded very appealing. Henry came in and immediately plopped down in his favorite spot in the hall. It was all very cozy.

That night we escaped from the tyranny of three-star cuisine at a bistro not far from Les Tourelles. It was 10:30 by the time we headed out to eat, and a full moon was coming up in the light-blue sky. Café Roosevelt was on a corner, the door open, looking far more inviting than Romeyer.

It was L-shaped, with the bar extending down one long wall. The bar had a wood floor and the restaurant section was linoleum, with checkered tablecloths. The crowd was the sort of trans-generational mix that's hard to find anywhere in

America at eleven o'clock at night. Next to us were three handsome boys in their late teens, eating steak tartare and *pommes frites*
at an impressive rate. When Rat sat down, they looked at one
another and giggled. Two teenage daughters, maybe fourteen and
fifteen, sat across from them with their chic, attractive parents.
The daughters kept looking at the teenage boys; their parents
noticed and exchanged a quiet smile.

A working-class family of small men and large women with
thick legs came into the bar, and before they sat down beers were
waiting for them. We sat by the open door enjoying the warm
breezes. Everyone was smoking. Miles Davis began to play from
hidden speakers. It was improbably perfect. Women walked by
outside alone, with no hint of late-night fear.

It suddenly occurred to me that we hadn't eaten all day.
Looking at the menu, I wanted to order everything on it. This
was the best-looking menu I'd seen in days. Only La Tante Claire
could match it and the prices. Yes, well . . . take a look:

*Asperges à la flamande*—350
   *Mousseline*—350
   *Vinaigrettes*—300
*Magret de canard fumé*—390
*Assiette Nordique*—510
*Moules à l'Escargot*—320
*Jambon de Parme au melon*—435
*Saumon fumé d'Écosse*—540
*Foie gras*—560
*Capitaine mousseline*—585
MÉNU—880
*Potage du jour*

---

*Jambon de parme au melon*
      *ou*

*Foie Gras*

---

*Filet pur Béarnaise*
*ou*
*Raie au Beurre aux câpres*

---

*Mousse au chocolat*
*ou*
*Flan caramel*

LES SPECIALITIES
*Moules à l'Escargot—320*
*Omelette maison—320*
*Scampi fritti tartare—420*
*Scampi fritti provençale—420*
*Scampi meunière-fritti—450*
*Scampi curry riz—480*
*Osso buco pâtes ou riz—500*
*Calamari tartare—390*
*Fondue bourguignonne—670*
*Anguilles au vert frites—475*

Rat and I split a cheese-and-mushroom omelette that came burnt on the bottom and soft and gooey inside—just wonderful. Then we had the same meal the kids next to us had ordered, steak tartare and *pommes frites*, because it looked so good. With the white asparagus that were on every menu in Belgium, a simple vinaigrette on the side. We finished with a flan caramel, and I was a very happy man.

We had eaten mostly in silence, not wanting to disturb the balance of what felt like a perfect symmetry. But when the plates were cleared and Rat lit up one of the small cigars she'd taken to smoking after dinner, there was one subject we had to broach.

"So what do we tell Carl?" I asked.

"That's easy," Rat said. "I'll just lie to him."

"Oh. That."

She seemed quite pleased with her answer and tried to slip back into the pleasant postdinner calm we had both been enjoying.

"Rat," I had to ask her, "this whole thing about Carl paying for this trip, that's crazy, right?"

"Crazy?" She was as vague and noncommittal as an experienced criminal under questioning by a rookie prosecutor.

"Yes, crazy! He was never going to pay for this trip even if we did eat in every one of the restaurants on consecutive days. Why should he?"

"Why should he?" she repeated rhetorically, taking a long puff from her mini-cigar and blowing the smoke toward the open door. With her profile turned to the moonlit streets in the background, it was a painfully cinematic moment. Which Rat understood, no doubt. She was not one to be unaware of her surroundings. "Carl is the sort of fellow who would enjoy paying for something so that it would give him control of the situation." She paused, thinking. "Yes, that pretty much sums it up, I suppose."

Someone replaced the Miles Davis with Chet Baker.

"Don't look so shocked," Rat told me. "You do the same thing."

"No, I don't."

"Of course you do. Right now you're thinking that you don't like Carl"—she held up her hand when I started to interrupt—"or you think he sounds like a creep and you don't want him to pay for this trip even if he agrees to it. Right?"

I shrugged.

"Come on—"

"Okay, okay!"

"Isn't it annoying when I'm right?"

"Yes!"

"I know. But don't worry about Carl. I'll handle Carl."

"Fine. But—"

"You think you'll pay for everything yourself anyway, right?"

"Right!" I started to argue but there didn't seem any point to it. I was suddenly tired in a very pleasant way. The truth of the matter was that I really didn't care about Carl one way or the other. The notion of eating in all the three-stars on consecutive days—or almost consecutive days—was such a preposterous one that it had an irresistibly lunatic appeal. Why *not* do it?

Rat looked at me as if wondering what I was thinking. She had that pleasantly bemused expression on her face that reflected a certain New York ironic cool that could be either quite appealing or extraordinarily annoying, depending on one's state of mind. I was feeling not so bad about the world, so it didn't bother me.

"Wasn't that a great dinner?" I eventually said.

The bar had thinned out. The three boys who had been sitting next to us were now at the bar talking about World Cup soccer. The family of small men and large women were into their fifth or sixth beers and laughing uproariously.

"It was a *spectacular* dinner," Rat agreed. "Much better than Romeyer."

"God, yes."

# Chapter
# Nine

We were on the road to Strasbourg by noon the next day. Franco had worked a small miracle, installing the brakes with apparent ease, assisted, of course, by his sons. Today they had let drop their solemn demeanor a bit and several times re-enacted their father's great backward slide across the street into the field. This got better every time.

The revitalized Mustang was very fast and loud. We drove in something of a trance, lulled by the noise and the smothering heat of the day. Henry collapsed on the back seat, which was just large enough for his considerable bulk, and seem to sleep with his eyes open, his tongue hanging down almost to the floor.

Last night's meal was still with me the way a powerful book or film can haunt one for days. It had been simple and elegant and deeply satisfying. I could eat there again and again without a moment's hesitation, but the three-star palaces had been mostly a disappointment. Romeyer reminded me of the aging movie queen of *Sunset Boulevard*, gaudy pretense and show gone to seed. Comme Chez Soi was inoffensive, but the food was terribly predictable, a long-running Broadway show that desperately needed new life. And Bruneau, well, it was difficult not to feel that Bruneau was trying too hard to be hip, that its heart was not in the cool interiors and cute gourmet food boutique. It was like a face-lift that didn't quite work.

But what did I expect? Ask any foodie and they will swear that the really great food of Europe is far away from the three-stars. Personally, I've long considered myself a fellow traveler of Calvin Trillin and John Thorne, the author of the wonderful *Simple Cooking* and *Outlaw Cook*, hunting in back alleys for anything tasty to call dinner. I've actually enjoyed roasted ants at a roadblock in Africa, and I lived in New York for years before I ventured into any place whose existence was even acknowledged by the *New York Times*. And yet rarely did I walk away not pleased and never, ever hungry.

But I *wanted* to fall in love with the great food palaces of Europe! It was such a cliché that they were stuffy and predictable and full of Japanese tourists and German investment bankers, it was such an accepted truism that the really great stuff was down the street in that undiscovered place that just next year will be getting its first star and soon everyone from Paris will be flocking, that I wanted to be shocked and dazzled and stunned, delighted and amused by these great three-star battleships. For years I had been such an inverse snob that I was desperate to be proved wrong. I wanted to walk through a magical door and be elevated to a higher state of being.

La Tante Claire and the Waterside had tantalized me with possibility. I'd entered with precious few expectations—this was England, after all, even if they did have three stars—and left feeling far better about the world than when I'd entered, pleased that this was how I had spent a few hours of my life. But I was greedy! I longed for sustained, oversaturated, overindulgent gustatory bliss. That seemed straightforward enough, no?

There were twenty-nine three-star restaurants in the world and nineteen were in France. As we rode across the top of France in the impossibly loud Mustang in the fierce June sun, an image kept floating through my mind, like a cowboys-and-Indians heat mirage. I saw the Mustang as an arrow, probably a flaming arrow in the best American television tradition, headed straight into the heart of France.

Stuart Stevens

It made no sense, of course. Except maybe I did want to pierce France, cut into its heart and soul through overindulgence. France *was* food, and the three-stars were touted as the epitome if not of all French food, of a certain strain of the culture in its most rarefied and effete form. It would be like trying to understand America by spending a month traveling the rodeo circuit or touring truck stops. You would understand more about something that was quintessentially American.

And so it was with the three-star quest—my ridiculous flaming arrow headed into France.

You can walk anywhere in Strasbourg, and this I like. Best of all, the cathedral seems to draw everyone in town to the central square, so that only a few blocks away, the streets are empty. It's as if the one dramatic public space has been sacrificed to create the very private moments of hidden discoveries that lurk along the Ill river and the pleasant, quiet streets lined with chestnut trees. It has a simple, direct charm, and after the self-aggrandizing, Euro-loving *phoniness* of Brussels, I found this quite appealing.

Like the location of Restaurant au Crocodile. It wasn't a Palace-in-a-Park like Romeyer—and had it been, I probably would have run screaming from the door—but instead it was set in a little alleyway just down the street from a Marks and Spencer department store. I took this as a good sign. And there wasn't a little boutique in the foyer selling cookbooks or tee shirts but instead one huge crocodile suspended from the ceiling, reminding me for all the world of a few bars I'd seen in places like Bayou Lafourche in deepest, darkest Cajun Louisiana. I liked this too. I started wondering if maybe they would be serving huge stacks of crawfish that all the regulars would call mudbugs and instead of tablecloths there'd be butcher paper that old Cajun women who didn't speak a word of English rolled up after you'd eaten about half of your body weight in crustaceans.

But instead the foyer led into a square, quite symmetrical, bright room. It struck me after a moment that there were no real windows, just false skylights over wrought-iron wall sconces. It was a pleasant, unpretentious quirky space, and when I spotted one nice-looking family with kids in shorts, the absolute right thing to be wearing on a hot June day but surprising nonetheless for a three-star palace, I started to like the place.

Monique Jung, the wife of chef-proprietor Émile Jung, led us to our table. Crocodile had been created by her and her husband. She had an aging-showgirl sort of appeal, a glamour and attractiveness held together by sheer force of will. A less bright room would have been kinder to her heavily made-up face, but this was her turf and she moved through it with a forceful authority.

We sat next to the family I'd noticed with the children in shorts. The father, a big fellow, blond, who looked like he had been an athlete once, smiled with unusual friendliness, the kind of openness that seemed quintessentially American. They can't be French, I thought, maybe American, Californians on vacation; that would explain the shorts.

But he was German. They were all German. Which was very troubling when I quickly realized what a likable, genuinely friendly person he was. It always troubles me when I come across Germans I like. It makes maintaining my rabid anti-German fervor all the more difficult, which, naturally, I resent terribly.

I found out he was German when he was quick to engage us in conversation, starting with commenting on Rat's choice of wine. Rat always chose the wine. She knew her stuff far better than I, and besides, it seemed important to her. She had ordered a bottle of Château Siran, continuing her vow to only order Margauxs the entire trip. That was when the German overheard her choice and spoke up. Short of someone reaching across the room and grabbing a choice dessert just as a waiter presented it in front of you, it's difficult to imagine anything more annoying than someone from another table critiquing your wine selection, but somehow this fellow did it with charm. Honest.

"I think you may find it is an amputee," he suggested. Maybe it was his phrasing—"I think you *may* find it"—allowing for the possibility that we may not find it so, in fact we may just love it to death—or maybe it was the *amputee* that made us want to talk to him.

"An amputee?" Rat said. "An amputee?"

"I found it had no legs," he continued. "But perhaps I was having a difficult bottle."

"No legs?" Rat looked at me, a glint in her eye. "You mean like my brother Juan, who had both his legs chopped off in a car accident. Like that, you mean?"

The man blanched. A look of genuine horror flashed over his friendly face.

"I was thinking in his honor I would have the *Pied et Oreille de Porc truffés en Crépinette*."

He stared at her for a moment, then burst out laughing.

"Excellent choice. I had it last week. Accompanied by a truly sublime mixture of cabbage and apples."

"*Chou frisé et Pommes Darphin*," Rat read from the pastel-pink menu. Someone seemed to have sponsored an ugly menu contest, and each of the three-stars had entered with enthusiasm.

"My name is Hildegard," the man said, rising slightly. "And this is Véronique and our most charming children"—he said this in a teasing way that made the kids smile—"Henri and Hans."

The woman was blond and quite attractive, with the well-kept look of women you see on the Riviera—middle-aged, elegant, sleek. She was seated at the far end of their table and smiled, but it was too far for us to engage her without shouting.

"I don't really have a brother," Rat admitted.

"So I guessed," he said.

"Not anymore, anyway," she continued. "Not after he was killed in the war."

He found this very funny as well. His wife stared as if her husband were taking mad before her eyes. I wondered if he did this sort of thing a lot. It was something that could get rather tiresome, I imagined.

Our German friend—Hildegard did seem to be his real name; Hilde his friends called him—wanted to know what brought us to Strasbourg, and when Rat, who appeared quite taken with the man, began to explain our strange eating odyssey, he immediately wanted to know what we thought of Brussels. But before we could really answer, he threw in that he thought it was "the future of Europe."

"That bad, huh?" I asked.

He didn't quite seem to get this. "All this Euro-government nonsense," I elaborated. "It's ridiculous! The E.C., the International Court in The Hague. Please. The whole thing gives me a headache."

"But your own president, he spoke of a New World Order!"

"That was a good name for half a million soldiers and a bunch of laser-guided bombs beating the crap out of Saddam Hussein. That *is* the new world order, not impressive offices full of Eurotrash bureaucrats trying to feel important."

"Like me," he said, but with a smile. "I am with the Human Rights Court here in Strasbourg."

"The Human Rights Court," I repeated slowly. "Now *that* is impressive. Can you tell me, please, exactly what the Human Rights Court does?"

He paused for a moment. "That is somewhat difficult," he finally said.

"I'm ordering," Rat sighed.

The menu was excruciatingly pink, perhaps in solidarity with a quote on the inside cover from Paul Claudel of, it noted, l'Académie Française, which read, *Voir peu à peu, dans le brouillard, se découvrir et se dresser l'Ange de Strasbourg, en fleur, rose comme une fille d'Alsace* (To see, little by little, in the fog, to discover the angel of Strasbourg, in flower, rose like a girl from Alsace).

Inside the pinkness, I was reminded of Waverly Root's comment that Alsace did

> not possess any particularly dominant natural food re-
> sources to impose a definite shape on their cuisine, as
> the cream and apples of Normandy have formed the
> cooking of that province. . . . The cooking of Alsace
> would seem, indeed, to be to a considerable extent
> artificial—a borrowing, rather than a school imposed by
> the nature of the land. The cuisine of Germany has been
> moved bodily across the Rhine. There it has undergone
> naturalization for the better. The Alsatians have added
> a French subtlety to the often rather unimaginative
> heaviness of German food.

This is, for my tastes, a most modest compliment, rather like saying that the cuisine of Jackson, Mississippi—my home town—had been improved by the influx of Vietnamese refugees. This was true, but it still did not mean that you would go out of your way to find yourself in the Big J. for a meal.

But I liked the menu, if only because it was more quirky than the time-warped boredom of the hopelessly classical Brussels food museums. Here you had *Pied et Oreille de Porc truffés en Crépinette* and *Foie gras d'Oie au Naturel en Gelée de Gewurztraminer* and *Poulette et Crêtes de Coq au Riesling, Nouillettes à l'Alsacienne*.

There was an emphasis on German wines—which made sense, given the locale—and a focus on what Waverly Root calls "the economical meat-makers, the pig and the goose." The great Waverly was intrigued by how the food staples of a poor region could take hold in a not-so-poor area like Alsace-Lorraine. He chalked it up to "the eating habits of a people who came from poorer soils in Germany, where these were natural foods."

That was in 1956, when Root published the *Food of France*, and I was confident he would have found it even more interesting almost forty years later. The entire notion of food tastes based on regional availability was becoming as quaint as regional dress—the sort of thing to be trotted out once a year for special holidays.

But people seemed to like—even needed to believe—the idea that there was something irreplaceably special about their local cuisine. It didn't matter if it was Alsace-Lorraine or rural North Carolina, where I've witnessed fistfights over the question of wet versus dry barbecue, a difference in taste separated by a half dozen counties. There still lives a part of us that defines who we are by what we eat, and while food per se isn't worth fighting over, identity is always the stuff of great battles. The Crusades come to mind. So does the Junior League.

Yes, the Junior Leagues of America. Why is that every Junior League from Beaumont to Brookline feels the need to publish their own cookbooks? You know what I'm talking about—those spiral-bound wonders that usually have a picture of something old on the cover (and if not old, definitely cute) and are filled with some of the most frightening recipes the human mind can conjure. Stuff like pea casserole Hawaiian style or sweet and sour succotash fritters.

Yet I've always liked these cookbooks because there is something wonderfully proud and assertive about them, despite their oppressive cuteness. Right there *in print* these women are proclaiming to the world that their cottage cheese salad rings are *the best*! That no one can top their sponge cake deluxe! This is Muhammad Ali exulting in his greatness, Joe Namath proclaiming victory the night before the Big Game!

But it is about food. Food of the most banal and literally canned type imaginable. Still, it is *their* food! The cuisine of Cincinnati, the toast of Tyler! This is about bragging rights, this is about defining who they are and what they are about. You think you've tasted quick-frozen tomato salad? Forget it!

This irrepressible drive for regional culinary superiority is a great and glorious thing, but it's not without a dark side. In a world in which regional cuisine is mostly being driven by *tastes* and not the necessity of availability, when lobsters can be bought live at the Dallas supermarket and Thibodaux mudbugs—crawfish—can be had fresh in Los Angeles, there seems to be an inevitable human tendency to resent all this modern abundance as much as praise it. Chalk some of the feeling up to food nostalgia, I suppose, a conviction that "nothing is the way it used to be," and some to a cynical suspicion that we must be sacrificing a great deal—*something very important*—in exchange for this "abnormal" turn of events that makes strawberries available in January and Israeli oranges the preferred fruit in Newark, New Jersey. We have to believe, it seems, that this is just some Faustian bargain and we're losing more than we're gaining.

Which leads us to rumors about ducks. Yes, ducks.

I had ordered one for dinner.

"The duck, how is it?" our German friend asked.

"Not great," I admitted.

"Fatty?"

I shrugged. "And too salty. The juniper and ginger is a wonderful notion, but . . ."

"I have a theory," he whispered conspiratorially.

"Yes?" Rat and I leaned forward. We loved a good conspiracy.

"You know the Alsatians love of foie gras? It is an . . ." He searched for the word.

"Obsession?" Rat suggested.

*What are we doing?* I wanted to scream. Whispering madly about obsessions with foie gras like we were plotting a coup? Foie gras? Liver, for crying out loud.

"The goose," the German continued, "the goose which produces the best, most superb foie gras, it has thrived here."

This I had read in Waverly Root. I believed in Waverly Root.

"Well . . ." he whispered. At the end of the table his wife stared at us with a bemused confusion. "In recent years there have been many rumors—just rumors, to be fair—that"—he paused for emphasis—"that restaurants were serving the same ducks that had been fattened for foie gras. The whole ducks, not just the breasts *magret* or in a confit. But a *roasted duck* that had been prepared for the foie gras! Can you imagine?"

"No!" Rat finally exclaimed after an appropriate dramatic silence. "Do you really think?"

I glanced at her, trying to tell if she was truly shocked or just pretending.

The German shrugged.

"*C'est impossible!*" Rat exclaimed.

*C'est impossible?* I stared at her. Who was this woman from Wyoming trying to kid?

The captain approached, followed by a pair of back waiters bearing fierce-looking silver cutlery.

*Oh my God*, I thought in panic. They know we're talking about *their ducks*! I looked around for the exits.

The captain smiled and stepped aside as the waiters presented their knives. Rat and the German looked at each other wide-eyed. A fourth waiter appeared with a leg of the duck and the captain quickly carved it, presenting it to me with a flourish.

"If I was you," Hildegard whispered with a bright gleam, "I would eat every bite." He paused. "And tell them you *loved* it."

It seemed like good advice.

# Chapter
# Ten

L ife is an ironic business. Why else would it be that my faith in three-star greatness would be revitalized in Germany. *Germany?* I'm not making this up.

You see, there's a three-star that lurks just over the border from Strasbourg in the Black Forest. "The sport hotel and health clinic Traube-Tonbach nestles in the sunny municipality of Baiersbronn, situated in the valley of the Tonbach in the heart of the Black Forest, which is internationally renowned." That's how their charming propaganda read. It was the "internationally renowned" that I liked. Ahh yes, *internationally renowned*. But what? The hotel? The Black Forest? And more importantly, *renowned for what?*

This is Germany, after all.

And then there was the matter of the "sport hotel and health clinic" description. Ah yes, just your typical sport hotel and health clinic–three-star restaurant combination. This had to be, I was certain, some kind of joke fostered on the Germans by the French. *Hey, did you hear the one about the sport hotel that got three stars?* This was good.

Rat and I crossed the border talking, of course, about ducks. She was convinced that we had stumbled onto an international scandal and should call someone immediately and rip the curtain off this shameful practice.

"Like who?" I wanted to know. "The food police? There's a hot line we can call?"

"What about a newspaper?"

"DUCKS IN BONDAGE! Hell of a headline. I can see it now. *Das Stern* will love it. The Hitler diaries were nothing next to this. 'Just a rifle shot from the evil depths of the Black Forest, one of the great conspiracies of our time has been launched.'"

We stopped at a gas station, and still arguing about ducks, I filled the Mustang. We had gone about a kilometer down the road when cars behind us started honking their horns. This, naturally, I ignored. If there was something about my driving that was troubling to some BMW-driving German in a hurry to get to their bunker in the Black Forest, this was not a bad thing.

Rat and I went back to ducks and why it was no one seemed to barbecue ducks. Where I grew up in the Deep South, a chicken stood a better than average chance of ending life on the barbecue grill. Millions and millions of chickens sacrificed to the gods of barbecue, so why not ducks? This suddenly seemed like a very important question. In a paranoid frenzy, I wondered if there was a secret duck-eating barbecue cult from which I had been excluded. I had a friend from Mississippi who always barbecued his Thanksgiving turkey, and it was flat-out delicious. I was thinking about calling him as soon as we stopped to ask if he had ever slathered up a quacker with his favorite sauce.

But then I noticed the smoke. It was a fierce kind of smoke, black, acrid stuff that smelled like burning plastic. Glancing in the rearview mirror, I began to understand the angry and incessant honking of horns, which was growing louder by the second. The honking came from cars that were enveloped in the same black smoke, which was emanating from the Mustang.

Henry, who had turned out to be, I had to admit, a ridiculously placid traveler, sat up on the back seat and stuck his snout in the air, sniffing. Then he started to whine.

Seized by the impulse that perhaps we could outrun the smoke—as if someone were chasing us with a smoke gun rather than us being the *source* of the problem—I jammed my foot down on the accelerator. The reaction was not good. Instead of hearing that all-enveloping throaty rumble I had come to love even while it deafened me, the engine chattered like hail on a tin roof. That dependable thrust of anachronistic V-8 power was replaced with a sickly shudder. The car actually lost speed.

In my rearview mirror I caught a glimpse of a long line of cars trailing us, drivers waving wildly. Perhaps they thought the Mustang was on fire, or perhaps it simply disturbed their German sense of order to be trailing a 1965 Mustang belching black smoke. It certainly couldn't have been very pleasant.

"I think something is wrong," I said to Rat. She looked over at me and giggled at this inane observation.

"You do?"

The car began to lurch as if having a seizure.

"What kind of gas did you put in?" Rat asked.

"How the hell do I know? I just put some in."

"I have a theory," Rat said.

"Wonderful," I grumbled.

"My theory is that you might have put in unleaded fuel and 1965 V-8s probably need all the lead they can get."

She was right, of course. Rat had an annoying way of being right about things automotive. It was her Wyoming cowgirl roots.

"What do we do?"

"We could stop and siphon out the old gas and put in new."

"Siphon? Siphon with what?"

"A hose would probably be best, don't you think?"

I thought about killing her, maybe with a hose wrapped around her neck.

"Just a thought," she added, when she saw my look.

We were driving up a long incline, heading into steep hills.

Suddenly I started to laugh.

"Yeees?" Rat asked.

An insane image had crowded into my brain, that here we were plunging into Germany and were *actively going about the business of gassing Germans!* I giggled maniacally and tried to nurse the very sick Mustang over the foothills of the western Black Forest.

"Tell me!" Rat demanded, laughing. "Tell me!"


"Why?" I kept asking myself. "Why had this happened?"

It was, by any logical judgment, a most perplexing question. Why in the middle of the dreary Black Forest had someone gone to the pains to create a place where food was this good?

The "place" was the Sport Hotel and it would be hard to imagine a more oppressive environment. Perched on the side of a mountain, it looked like a 1930s Bavarian period piece, complete with heavy beams and dark wood and carpets, huge clocks everywhere—most with elaborate gold faces—and every available surface crammed with Bavarian kitsch, from cuckoo clocks to those awful porcelain figurines that look like they should be sold in Stuckey's restaurants across America. That some people actually pay lots of money for these things and consider them art is surely a testament to human folly and bad taste.

The total effect was like stepping inside some very special retreat for high-ranking German officers and their wives in the heady early days of the war, when the swastika was flying over the Louvre and London would be next. Stout, exceedingly pale German men, most smoking cigars, shuffled about the terraced grounds in sandals, draped in towels and trailed by either an even more stout woman, presumably a spouse, or a younger, thinner woman in a diminutive bikini, presumably a mistress.

While I will be the first to admit that I have paranoid fantasies of German evil, even a normal person would have felt some unease. I know this because Rat took to singing "Deutschland über Alles" under her breath as we wandered the grounds. (In the anti-German department, if not others, Rat passes the base test for normalcy, which is to say that she simply doesn't think about how much better off the world might be if Germany had been abolished after the last war.) I joined her, of course. We both seemed seized by an irresistible impulse, and I wondered if it were the result of some secret Nazi brainwashing ray emanating from the hilltop, the ultimate "Truth and Spirit" ray perfected after many years by one of the wrinkled old men so eager to flaunt their decaying bodies. It seemed very logical at the time.

Picture the dining room: a big, heavy room that felt like a beer hall that had been decorated for a wedding. The cheese tray was a half-barrel affair resembling the sort of devices from which failed beauty queens pluck winning lotto numbers on the ten o'clock news. The view down the valley was spacious and green, but how often does the concept of "great view" go with superb food?

So I sat down in this ponderous room, and the last thing I expected was a marvelous meal.

But, like a small miracle, it happened.

First, there were women working in the dining room. Captains and waiters, not just back waiters. I felt better about the world at once.

"Much improved," Rat said.

"I'll say. Women. Thank God."

She stared at me and shook her head, tilting it toward the dining room. A young, darkly handsome fellow was walking toward our table carrying a wine list. He wore a lapel pin insignia that I was learning indicated membership in the sommelier society.

Rat rolled her eyes and managed to look both quite pleased and about sixteen all at once.

He was French, very friendly, and surprisingly unchauvinistic about French wines. "No one wants to admit it," he laughed, "but the German wines are superb!"

Rat spent a long time, a very long time, discussing this with him in depth.

The food was shockingly good: chicken with shredded black truffles with asparagus and carrots in a champagne sauce. A salad of grilled sole with garlic and artichoke hearts in an herb dressing heavy with basil.

We were having a good time, a sort of time I could never have imagined having in Germany. Which is why, I'd like to think, the chef and owner quietly appeared at our table.

Harald Wohlfahrt was in his whites, of course, but he looked more like a shy apprentice than the master chef who had just so captivated us with his talents. Herr Finkbeiner, the owner, beamed at his side, like a proud father or older brother. There was something about the interaction between the two that was sweetly touching, without any of the Teutonic bombast that shouted from every corner of the Sport Hotel.

"We have been together sixteen years," Finkbeiner said, putting his arm around the chef, a gesture that struck me as acutely American. "Together we had this crazy fantasy that maybe one day we could get a Michelin star. In those days, it was impossible to get good food here." He gestured out at the valley, still lit by the midsummer sun.

"I would leave at three A.M. and drive to Strasbourg for market, two, three times a week," Harald Wohlfahrt said. He appeared embarrassed, as if confessing something a bit sordid.

"And the guests," Finkbeiner said, rolling his eyes. "Harald Wohlfahrt would make these extraordinary dishes and they would stare at them. Just stare!" He tapped his head. "You could see them thinking, 'Where's my sauerkraut! Where's my schnitzel!'"

"I cooked schnitzel," Wohlfahrt said softly. "I *still* cook schnitzel. I like schnitzel. You like schnitzel!"

Finkbeiner roared. He hugged his chef again, beaming with pride. *See what I have here, not just a cook but a wit! A funny man!*

"You've been here sixteen years?" Rat asked Wohlfahrt. Then, not waiting for an answer, she murmured, truly impressed, "That's incredible. You've spent your entire life here."

Harald Wohlfahrt was thirty-six years old.

Rat's comment seemed to please him, though I doubted she meant it as a compliment. It was just that the notion of working one's whole life at the same place was such a distinctly un-American concept that it was hard to grasp.

Finkbeiner asked us if we had enjoyed dinner. It felt like more than a perfunctory inquiry, as if he were genuinely concerned, like a good family doctor inquiring about your health.

Rat lavished the dinner with praise and went on about the disappointments of Belgium and the Crocodile.

"And in England?" Finkbeiner asked when we told him that we had liked both the Waterside and La Tante Claire, he nodded sympathetically.

"You see, for us, for any non-French-speaking country to receive three stars, it is terribly difficult. I believe we must far exceed the standards of France."

Harald Wohlfahrt demurred. There were wonderful restaurants in France and wonderful restaurants in Germany. It was a question of the food, not the rating. Had we ever eaten at Fredy Girardet's in Lausanne, Switzerland?

I had. During the years I lived in Switzerland we would make pilgrimages to Girardet from Lugano. That it took five hours or so on the train did not seem to matter.

And Girardet, Wohlfahrt pointed out, did not want Michelin to rate his restaurant at all. In the past he had been given three stars, but now he had decided that he did not want to participate in the whole rating system.

But here, Finkbeiner said, here we wanted to create great food. His family, he told us, had built a great hotel and when he took over, he asked himself how could he do more than just maintain standards. How could he do something that no one had ever done? So he found Harald when he was a teenager and together they chased this dream.

And now, Rat said, people come from New York to eat at the Sport Hotel. This is something.

The two men looked at each other, smiling. "He is the youngest three-star chef," Finkbeiner said. "Do you know that? We have been working together for sixteen years, and he is still the youngest chef."

"Tell me," Rat asked, leaning forward. "Have you ever heard anything strange about the ducks of Strasbourg?"

# Chapter
# Eleven

We were in Paris the next night for dinner.

People look forward to Paris for many reasons: romance, beauty, music, sex, and, yes, food. But me, I was thinking about laundry.

It was a serious problem, as I'm sure you can imagine. This running around, eating at a different three-star every night plays hell on a man's clean-to-dirty ratio. There were four three-stars in Paris, though, thank God, so it meant four days without having to crawl into the Mustang and thunder off to another destination.

Which meant I could get my laundry done. Or so I thought.

We were staying at the Hôtel Angleterre, not for any good reason except that it wasn't expensive, and Rat, once she heard Hemingway had stayed there some, she was a goner. We *had* to stay at the Angleterre. Which was fine by me. I had stayed there before and always liked it. Except there was this problem with the laundry.

"Of course we can do laundry," Émile, who mastered the front desk, said. Émile was charming, young, and, Rat thought, very handsome. She thought he was Lebanese; I thought Algerian.

He handed me an intricate laundry form to fill out. It included such items as "men's dinner jackets," "cummerbunds," and "tux shirts," and, my favorite, "shirts with collars." I ignored the column listing the extraordinary prices. This was something I was getting good at. I was learning that ignoring prices brought a certain mad freedom, like not looking down while climbing.

"How long will this take?" I asked Émile. He was definitely Algerian, I decided. They were the most hospitable people on earth, the Algerians, and he had that certain kindness around his eyes.

"How long do you stay?" he asked.

"Four nights."

He winced, pained by the information.

"Why?"

"We could forward to the clothes."

I paused, trying to figure out what he really meant.

"You know where you go next?" he asked.

"Yes," I answered. For a moment I started to explain about our mad eating quest, but I couldn't come up with words that didn't sound horribly embarrassing. This was usually not a good sign, when you couldn't describe something you were doing without feeling ridiculous.

"Then we could send the clothes." He smiled at this, pleased that he could offer a solution. He had to be Algerian. No other nationality would be this gracious.

"I think," said Rat, who had been hovering by the door, "that maybe it will take longer than four days to do the laundry."

Émile nodded, appreciative that someone else had stated this painful fact.

I shrugged and thanked him.

Which is why I was wandering around Paris with an armful of dirty clothes when I ran into Victor.

"You're homeless," is the first thing he said. "You are strolling the streets of Paris looking for a heating grate. Tell me what happened? How'd it all go so bad so fast?"

He said all this with the rakish smile that was what I remembered most about him. It had been three years since I'd seen him, the last time late at night in an uptown New Orleans club called Tipitina's. Then he had been dancing with what surely was the most beautiful woman in New Orleans and singing along with the Wild Tchoupatulis Indians. Victor knew all the words, having grown up on Bayou Lafourche, Louisiana, where most of the television and radio stations broadcast in Cajun French.

Victor was a cousin of mine in some complicated Southern sort of way I'd never really understood. His father had been a lawyer from New Orleans who dropped out and retreated to the bayou with a mad whim to raise crawfish. This had been met by predictable scorn mixed with pity in the stratified world of New Orleans society and general bewilderment within the family. The universal opinion, of course, was what a shame it was that Victor's father had doomed his entire family—Victor had three sisters—to a life of poverty to be played out in the unimaginable bleakness of subtropical New Orleans.

But a strange thing happened. It turned out that raising crawfish wasn't such a lunatic theory after all. In fact, raising crawfish turned out to be a wicked good business, and Victor's dad became the crawfish magnate of Louisiana, if not America. Perhaps the world, who knows? In fact, Victor's entire family flourished wildly on the bayou. They built a tennis court and launched the Bayou International tennis tournament, which received a moment of national attention when two of Victor's sisters, the one at Stanford, the other at Harvard, brought home their boyfriends from college to play in the tournament and the said boyfriends just happened to be top-ranked collegiate players and noted rivals.

But Victor had skipped the fancy schools his sisters attended and ended up at LSU, at least for a year or two, and had, the last I'd heard, moved to France to run the exporting arm of his father's business. The French loved crawfish and apparently were delighted to get them wherever they could, even from the banks of a bayou in Plaquemines Parish, Louisiana.

It had been years since I had seen Victor, but he did not seem to think it was odd in the least that we would run into each other on the streets of Paris, me with a handful of dirty clothes. I was standing alone on the corner of Rue de Buci and Rue Mazarine, staring at the window of Charcuterie Alsacienne, wondering why something like Alsacienne sausages could look irresistible on a Paris street corner and not a very big deal at all in Strasbourg, waiting for Rat to return from her search for water for Henry. She had decided he was dehydrated from the long ride in the convertible, and she was probably right. I knew *I* was dehydrated and I had been sipping on plastic bottles of water all the way across France. It was late afternoon, when the light was first beginning to soften, and after hours under the sun, I welcomed the encroaching dusk like sprinkles of cool rain.

Just as I was getting around to asking Victor where I might be able to have my clothes cleaned, Rat appeared, led by Henry. She was wearing black leggings, oversized Jackie O sunglasses, clear jelly sandals, and her favorite University of Wyoming tee shirt, the one with a bucking horse and a lariat emblazoned across the front. She had bought a thin leash for Henry that had fake rhinestones every few inches and looked like a prop from some bad prewar Berlin sex show, the sort of thing Sally Bowles would have found divine.

"Are you embarrassed," Victor asked after the introductions, "to be seen in Paris with a man clutching a bundle of dirty laundry like a life preserver?"

"Well, you know, Victor," she said without a beat, "most men are fairly embarrassing in one way or other and women just learn to ignore it." Then she smiled.

This left Victor, for the moment, speechless. I used the opening to press my case for a dry cleaner.

"No, no, no," Victor insisted. "Dry cleaners in Paris are impossible. Sophie will save you."

A few minutes later we were walking up the long, narrow flight of stairs leading to his apartment. The stairs wound around an open caged elevator. At the fifth floor, I asked about the elevator and, more important, why we were not inside it.

Victor shook his head remorsefully. "I think it is very dangerous," he said cryptically. "These elevators are very old. Have you ever thought about that?"

Rat and I looked at each other and kept climbing.

Sophie was waiting as soon as we opened the door. She was an attractive, midforties woman with shiny blond hair swept up on her head in an old-fashioned style. With her apron and her happy-to-be-cleaning way, she was like some sort of fifties housewife ideal come to life on the sixth floor of a Rue Visconti apartment.

As soon as she saw my sad bundle of clothes, she swept them from my arms and held them up to the light from the open window facing the avenue. She examined them critically, as if critiquing their design and construction. Then finally she nodded and said something to Victor in a language that sounded Eastern European, though I couldn't have placed it to save my life.

"That's it," Victor told me. "She'll have them ready tomorrow afternoon."

I thanked her profusely and she nodded, looking somewhat embarrassed. Victor steered me toward the door.

"Tonight you must meet my fiancée."

That he had a fiancée was news to me but I had hardly kept up with his life.

I explained that we were having dinner at Taillevent and he immediately said, "That's perfect. We have an early dinner party and we will meet you for dessert." He looked at Rat. "I'd like you to meet my fiancée," he said pointedly.

* * *

We rode to Taillevent in a subway car full of drunken French soccer fans singing drinking songs in remarkable harmony. They sounded so good I wondered if perhaps they were a soccer club-choir out celebrating a recent victory. Even a pair of the ancient but incredibly cute couples that seem to be a French speciality, him in the requisite blue beret and her dressed all in black, seemed pleased with the performance.

Rat was wearing some preposterous dress that looked, to me, like a little girl's ball gown, a bright blue thing that stuck out at a sharp angle, so that she resembled a flying saucer that was lowering its landing gear. She seemed very happy to be back in a city as obsessed with fashion as New York. Walking down Boulevard St.-Germain to the Metro stop, she had rattled off the designers' names of the clothing worn by the women, and a few men, strolling by as if on their way to a fashion opening. It was an impressive, offhand performance, like listening to a top strikeout artist reeling off the pitches an opposing team could never hit. "Slider inside. Armani. Heat high. Givenchy. Knuckleball. Dior."

Though it was nine clock, the sky was bright blue, and it felt like we were walking through a mist of soft light.

Taillevent is housed in a grand Napoleon III *hôtel particulier*, a stately place, dark and richly paneled with heavy oil paintings. This is the style so often adopted in America by any restaurant trying to take itself seriously, from Indianapolis to Seattle. The look is intended to impress, to convey a sense of importance and ceremony to all that occurs within. In such places you are supposed to bring important clients and celebrate anniversaries and birthdays.

Of course, in a strip mall just down from a 7-Eleven, the effect is merely pretentious and silly, somewhat pathetic in its overreaching for grandeur. But steps from the Champs-Elysées on a clear summer night, when the staff smiles and seems genuinely pleased that you have chosen to spend time in their presence, Taillevent felt warm and inviting, conveying less a sense of majesty and more sheer fun, like playing dress-up. The crowd looked happy but not smug, and the first floor, divided into separate areas of banquettes and small rooms, buzzed with the pleasant sound of humans engaged in pleasurable pursuit. *Look at us, aren't we lucky to be in this pretty space eating wonderful food?*

The menu came, a large and impressive document, presented with a flourish. It was the first handsome menu we'd seen, a solid piece of work with none of the kitsch cuteness that had made the menus of Brussels so appalling.

"A declaration!" Rat declared, taking the menu from the handsome, midforties waiter.

He seemed startled but then smiled broadly, nodding: "Oui, mademoiselle, a declaration of the rights of man!"

We were upstairs in a smallish room that felt like a drawing room. I wondered, without really caring, if this upstairs was a "Siberia," like the upstairs at "21" in New York, a place they put the tourists, most probably of the Japanese and American variety. The crowd was all French, though, and had the look of those that had been here many times. But of course that was part of the skill of a great restaurant, to make everyone feel welcome, like arriving at a party thrown in one's honor. A special party where great and glorious food was to be consumed, marvelous wines downed, and routine cares banished.

Which, I have to say, I was on my way to feeling at Taillevent. Before us appeared, quite magically, circles of artichoke and tomato. The dish looked pretty and boring and tasted wonderful, cool, refreshing. Finally I was beginning to understand the purpose of the mandatory complimentary starters. Yes, they were intended as a gracious gesture, a way to demonstrate that your presence is desired and expected and, indeed, appreciated. *Come into our home, we have been waiting! How nice to see you!*

But like a foyer to an impressive home, the starters that appeared so effortlessly were a transitional passage from one way of being to another. One moment you're on the Metro listening to drunken rugby songs, wondering if you're going to be late and whether or not one of the rugby players might throw up on you, and the next you're engulfed in a world constructed solely to give pleasure to every sense. It was all a bit disorienting and unsettling. The starters were needed to ease you into this new world. No questions asked, no decisions demanded. Just a little glimpse of the great things to come. *Here, relax. You'll enjoy this . . .*

And, of course, a chance for the chef to show off. Invariably the starters were designed to seem casual and offhand—*just a little bite of something we tossed off*—but the best were shockingly good. It was like a sports team, while warming up before the big game, doing something absolutely phenomenal with total nonchalance. *Oh, that? No big deal, we do it all the time.*

The room had an unusual organizational structure. There was no sommelier and there were no circulating captains. Each table had one waiter who handled everything, supported by what seemed like an endless cavalcade of back waiters. Since I liked our main waiter, I liked the arrangement. It lent a certain personalization to what was, in fact, a huge organization.

This feeling of intimacy was enhanced by the restaurant's design. Though the house itself was preposterously grand, the scale had been kept to a personal level by the use of a series of dining rooms. There was nothing overwhelming or intimidating about the space, even on the first floor, which held the most tables.

Taillevent has been a Great Restaurant for a very long time, always led by Jean-Claude Vrinat. Like any of the great Michelin gustatory palaces, it is, in theory, an easy place to criticize. *Too old, too predictable. Boring.* Patricia Wells in her wonderful *Food Lover's Guide to Paris* writes that "there will be no surprises in either service or cuisine" and then in the same breath calls it "perhaps France's most flawless restaurant."

No one has dealt with the Michelin paradox better than Jean-Claude Vrinat. *With three stars in hand, how do you stay on the top?* He's chosen to do it by focusing on service and food, thankfully leaving the great house to be what it is, a great Napoleon III period piece. "We wouldn't shed a tear," writes Gault-Millau, "should the drab blue velvet and the bibelot cabinets suddenly disappear." But this cattiness aside—and wasn't it Gault-Millau's mandate to focus on the *food, not decor?*—they are quick to praise "the menu's recent shift towards new, more subtle dishes," attributing it to the influence of a younger chef on the rise, Philippe Legendre, a protegé of Joel Robuchon's.

I started with *Fantaisie de Tourteaux, petits Légumes à la Barigoule*. Still fresh from the stifling Metro and the Paris in July streets, I was looking to be refreshed, revitalized. The crab arrived surrounded by sliced artichoke hearts with asparagus and carrots organized in a perfect circle. It was astoundingly good, with a light sauce that seemed to be a reduction of the vegetables with a touch of butter, just enough to flavor but not drown. Nothing complicated or pyrotechnical, it wasn't trying to be something that it wasn't—the greatest sin of overreaching chefs, particularly in America, particularly with New York hipster chefs. *Let's put mango and basil with the crab. Okay?* No, no, no. A light butter sauce is just right.

Rat had lobster sausage, *Boudin de Homard Breton à la Nage*. "I have to order it," she declared as soon as she spotted it on the menu, sandwiched between *Minestrone de Langoustines Bretonnes* and the *Foie de Canard à la Gelée de Coing*, both of which sounded spectacular to me. "Because of Chanterelle," she said. "Get it?" she asked with a look that said, "Are you dumb or what?"

But I did get it, actually. Chanterelle was one of our favorite New York restaurants, a small, white room that seemed to

exist on another plane of being, some Zone of Exaltedness that
not only consistently produced the best food in New York but
always presented it with a consistent graciousness and professionalism that is nearly impossible to find in New York (or America),
where there seems to be the waiter-actor world and the tired
French hacks, with little room in between. One of the Chanterelle signature dishes was an appetizer of lobster sausage.

A bite of Rat's *Boudin de Homard* brought me back: the
clean, spare room on the corner with the big windows and lots
of flowers and not too many tables and a couple of hours to spend
that was sure to make one feel better about being alive. The
Taillevent version had more butter and a strong tarragon flavor.
I wanted more. Rat would not hear of it. "You touch this plate
once more and I will bury my stiletto heel in your ankle." She
said this with the calm assurance of a woman who had buried a
few heels in her day, and I backed off, chastened. How many guys
were out there, I wondered, crippled for life by Rat's heels? Is this
what she meant when she said, "Do you know what it's like to
be single in New York and a girl from the West?"

Victor arrived just as we were finishing the entrées. He
walked in, cigar in hand, Phoebe in tow, looking every bit like
he owned the place. That was a talent of Victor's which I enjoyed—an ability to seem totally comfortable in any situation.

Phoebe, to my surprise, looked to be only a few years
younger than Victor. This was a radical departure from his former
girlfriends, who had all looked like they were plucked from the
ranks of New Orleans Saints cheerleading squads. But each of
them that I had met—five or so, I suppose—had had a certain
peculiarity that I'd found appealing.

One had been dressed completely in buckskin, not a com-
mon sight in New Orleans. When asked—and, of course, I had
to—she said it was because she had a thing for the "early Cher"
who often—she seemed to have made a study of this—wore

buckskin during the time Sonny was strutting around on *The Ed Sullivan Show* in a long car coat. "You're old enough to actually remember this," she had said, somewhat pointedly. She also said that she loves wearing animal skins because her ex-husband was an animal-rights activist. She seemed a bit young to have an ex-husband lying around, but she said they had fallen in love at a demonstration in front of a Vietnamese restaurant in New Orleans that was selling cold dog. Her family pet had disappeared and she was convinced he had been retailed out to an Asian lunch crowd. "It's pretty easy to fall in love under those circumstances," she explained and, naturally, I had to agree.

But Phoebe favored Chanel over buckskin. She had the classic good looks I associated with Parisian women of twenty-five years ago, an image driven home by European cinema: Catherine Deneuve in *Belle de Jour*, Dominique Sanda in *The Conformist*. She was straight and slim with high cheekbones and wide eyes. Victor seemed dazzled.

I assumed, of course, that she was, say, a P.R. director for Paris *Vogue*.

"I sell software," she said, taking a puff of Victor's cigar. He laughed.

"Phoebe *wrote* a lot of the software for the Minitel. She's the Bill Gates of France."

This time she laughed, shaking her head. "Bill and I," she said, holding up two fingers, "we are like this."

It seemed like they were joking, but I had no idea. It was difficult, but strangely appealing, to think of her writing software. Surely she would have been the most elegant software author in the world.

"So," Phoebe asked Rat, her eyes sparkling, "what was best?"

Rat laughed. She liked Phoebe. Slipping into her most exaggerated Cowgirl Accent, she launched into a positively pornographic description of the *Foie de Canard au Pain d'Épices et au Gingembre*. "Honey," Rat exclaimed, "that sucker was so rich I thought my mouth was going to lay down and die."

"Hallelujah," Phoebe cried. "Testify, sister."

"We just saw this documentary on gospel singers," Victor explained. "Phoebe has decided she is going to move to Alabama and become a black woman."

"A black woman singing in the"—she played with the words delightfully—"Ebenezer Methodist Church! Say Jesus!"

Around the room, heads turned toward this elegant woman doing a not-bad imitation of soul shouting. Victor, never a man uncomfortable in the spotlight, waved his cigar good-naturedly, like a proud impresario.

*Bill Gates? Gospel singing?* It began to dawn on me that Phoebe was a woman obsessed with American culture, the mirror opposite of so many Francophile Americans. I started wondering how she felt about Jerry Lewis. So I asked.

"He's an idiot!" she cried, blowing a perfect smoke ring. "A buffoon."

This clinched it. She did—or at least was trying to—think like an American. My theory had always been that the French embraced Jerry Lewis just to prove the superiority of their own culture. This notion that somehow he was an unappreciated comic genius languishing in America was nonsense. Deep down, reveling in Jerry Lewis's supposed greatness was a deeply condescending notion. *Oh, yes, he is amusing, the best America has, no doubt.*

"And you," Victor asked. "The dinner was good, no? You had . . ."

This was all a bit strange. Victor was sounding more and more French, while Phoebe was the American.

"The sea bass," I told him.

"Yummy?" Phoebe said.

"With rosemary and a sauce of olives and minced peppers and zucchini."

"And?" Victor asked.

"Good," I said. "Not life changing but very good."

"The French," Phoebe said, "they should do more with Asian. At least, these places should." She gestured around the room, as if conjuring up the Gods of Michelin—Taillevent as representative of Great Classical French Cuisine. Which wasn't too far off.

"So," I said, "do you really think so?" I leaned forward, just as Rat kicked me under the table.

"Did you hear I have a dog?" Rat said.

I couldn't really blame Rat for the kick and the change in subject. The last thing she wanted to hear was another rant from me about Asian cooking versus French. It was something she'd been hearing far too often, poor woman.

"His name is Henry and he is really the cutest dog in all of France."

# Chapter
# Twelve

The next day at the World Peace Gym, I was still thinking about Asian food, classical French, and the future of cuisine.

"Hubert," I said, "you have to admit that there is something ridiculously childish about French food."

"I do?" he answered, with the skeptical lift of the eyebrow that seemed such a stereotypical Gallic gesture I figured it had to be taught in the schools. "Tonight you tell me that Alain Senderens makes food for *children*? This is amusing, my friend."

But of course he didn't look amused. In truth, he looked like he was about to have a heart attack. It had been my idea to meet at the gym, and I was having serious doubts about the wisdom of my choice of venue.

Hubert was a friend from New York, a transplanted Frenchman from Brittany who had taught at a tony East Side prep school for two decades. In his late fifties now, he returned each summer to Paris, just long enough, he always said, to make him realize he was still in love with New York. I liked this, among other things, about Hubert. It was getting difficult to find people who still talked about being in love with New York.

In his youth, Hubert had been a Paris-based restaurant critic who had worked his way up to become one of the fabled Michelin inspectors. This made him, without exaggeration, one of the thirty or so most powerful men in the world of French cuisine, which, it's probably fair to say, made him one of the thousand or so most powerful men in France.

He had first come to America to explore the possibility of an American version of the *Guide Michelin*. The notion was to begin with a New York publication and work across the great cities of America. This was in the late '60s, when the great French restaurants of New York were in their splendor: Le Pavillion, Le Cirque, La Côte Basque, the Quilted Giraffe.

It seemed a splendid idea, and Hubert had, by all accounts, a spectacular run for a couple of years, roaming New York on a Michelin commission at a time when hedonism of all sorts, gastronomic and otherwise, was in full fever. But then it began to dawn on him that it was simply impossible. A *Guide Michelin* for America was a wonderful, hopeless idea.

"What is the essence of America?" Hubert asked me rhetorically when he first recounted his story. "Change." He sighed and took a long puff of his smuggled Cuban cigar. "Change, change, change."

"So?" I said. "That's why you need some smart French guys nosing around to keep everybody straight."

"But it is impossible in America! Here, restaurants come and go every few minutes. There is no consistency! How can Michelin put its name on a product that may be useless the day it is published?

"Other publications, they specialize in discovering new places. That is good. It is needed. Michelin does a little of that. But the *Guide Michelin* is most famous for charting the long history not just of a restaurant but of the chefs and the chefs' families. That is really what we write about. People, not buildings! It is like a novel. How can you write a novel if every chapter you have completely new characters?"

But Hubert loved America. He started going to Yankee Stadium, learned to drive for the first time and took long trips out West, discovered Studio 54, and confirmed repeatedly that, yes, American women really do like big, handsome French guys who can talk about baseball and wine.

Lately Hubert had started looking a lot like George C. Scott, an impressive figure inclined to disclaim enthusiastically on any number of subjects with absolute authority.

That he was doing so at the World Peace Gym seemed only slightly odd. He was wearing what had to be one of the last pairs of Bermuda shorts ever made, black dress socks with sandals, and a N.Y. Yankees tee shirt that had fit him about three hundred servings of foie gras earlier. But at the World Peace Gym, Hubert blended right in. Everyone seemed to be dressed similarly.

The gym was on a side street just off Boulevard Saint-Germain. It was a two-story affair that had the sort of stuff that YMCAs had in the midfifties: medicine balls, vibrating tummy belts, misshapen weights with bent bars. A badminton net was actually stretched across the floor and, to my astonishment, a furious game was under way. *Badminton? Who goes to the gym to play badminton?*

"Childish, Hubert," I reasserted. "That's the essence of classic French. No salads. No vegetables. Courses and courses of desserts. This is a Dennis the Menace cuisine!"

Hubert laughed so hard he dropped his medicine ball. "Ah, yes, your Dennis that is a menace, I can see him now slurping *langoustines et asperges* or *noisettes d'agneau rôti au celeri et truffes.* Oh, this is good."

"You can't tell me the French understand vegetables."

"You are mad!" he sputtered. "We love vegetables! We do amazing things with the onion! The *omelette à la lyonnaise* is a masterpiece!"

"Onions? Onions are a vegetable?"

"Of course they are, moron! And what about the artichoke?! I lived in Nice on artichokes one summer!"

"But a salad, a simple—"

"You mean lettuce!" he shouted accusingly. Everyone in the

World Peace Gym had stopped their medicine-ball throwing and electric-tummy-belt vibrating and ancient-iron lifting to watch Hubert shout at me. "Tell me you don't mean lettuce?"

I shrugged. "Okay, lettuce."

"Aha! See, I told you so! *Do you really think lettuce is a vegetable?*"

"Don't you?"

"Lettuce. Lettuce! *Lettuce!* I think lettuce is . . ." Hubert sputtered, trying to grab the right word. "I think lettuce is a *leaf!*"

Several people applauded.


Later, leaving the World Peace Gym, Hubert made a serious admission, at least for Hubert. "You know what is most wrong with French cuisine?"

"Not enough vegetables."

"Don't start with me! No, it is corn."

"Corn," I said flatly.

Hubert nodded vigorously. "I miss corn on the cob in France so bad it hurts. That was the first time I felt like a real American, when I was eating corn on the cob with my own two hands! Sweet corn! Not corn for cattle! Ahh, a treasure. A national treasure!

"You see," Hubert explained, "there is no glory in vegetables."

"Glory?"

"Of course. We feed corn to cattle. And this lettuce you love so much, what can you do to it besides wash it? Tonight we eat at Lucas Carton. You want to go there to see how well they wash lettuce? It is crazy."

"But if I like lettuce?"

"That is no excuse!"

"I see."

We were walking by the Jardin du Luxembourg. In the distance I could see Rat in gym shorts lying on the grass with Henry, two guys chatting her up. It was reassuring to think that the gardens had not changed much since Waverly Root's day in the early 1930s. One of Root's mentors when he was a young reporter on the Paris edition of the *Chicago Tribune*—fondly referred to by its writers and editors as *The Daily Miracle*—was the paper's sports editor, who "practiced one sport only: He was a sexual athlete. . . . He usually started his day by strolling over to the nearby Luxembourg Gardens, selecting one of the women sunning themselves there and leading her back to his newly abandoned bed."

What impressed Waverly Root the most, it seems, was his colleague's technique, "consisting of little more than a blunt invitation without time-wasting preliminaries."

"Don't you ever get your face slapped, Herol," Root asked him.

"Sometimes," he admitted as his slow grin began. "But I get an awful lot of sex."

"Alchemy," Hubert said, interrupting my silent tribute to Waverly Root.

"I'm sorry?"

"Cooking is alchemy. It is turning dross into gold through the application of heat. Without heat, there is no magic. And chefs, they want to be magicians more than anything else."

It was a clear, unusually cool day for July. The gardens were strangely calm, with none of the frantic exercising—the running, the biking, the rollerblading—that can make Central Park seem like some giant self-improvement zone.

I liked the alchemy conceit. Out of the earth comes base material and, yes, it was easy to call La Tante Claire's *consommé de homard aux épices et raviolis* gold. Spun gold.

"It doesn't have to be complicated," Hubert continued. "Take tomatoes. You can do more to a tomato than just wash it. I hope on my deathbed I can have a big bowl of tomatoes à la Provençal. Such a simple dish. Good olive oil, lots of garlic, a little parsley. But perfect, you know? You can prepare vegetables simply without having to steam them. Can you imagine? How much do New Yorkers spend in restaurants in which they order steamed vegetables. What possible reason would a chef want to steam a goddamn vegetable? To prove that he can really boil water? It is insulting!"

"But corn you like."

"Corn on the cob. To hold it in your hands. To feel the heat. A man cannot eat fresh sweet corn on the cob and not believe there is a benevolent God. It is impossible!"

That night we went to Lucas Carton and I didn't order steamed vegetables.

From the moment we stepped inside, it felt like a New York restaurant, and not in the best way. Maybe it was the lighting, flat and monotonous with no shadows, or the detached service. Not bad, just unenthusiastic. Nothing to signal that, yes, this evening will be memorable.

The space was stunning Belle Epoque but strangely uninviting. "This is," Hubert whispered with an evil chuckle as we followed the captain to our table, "the most expensive restaurant in France."

Behind us was a table of what had to be Swedish models dressed in black pants and white tee shirts, surrounded by aging French hipsters. Yes, it felt like New York.

"I used to come here to eat woodcock," Hubert said, as we settled down at the spacious table. It was one of the things I liked about the three-stars—the tables were always a generous size, and never crowded. "But then," he sighed, "they banned the eating of woodcock."

Rat looked puzzled.

"Not the eating," Hubert clarified, "but the killing. They were all getting slaughtered."

"How silly."

"But in Belgium, you know, you can still eat woodcock. You can eat any game in Belgium. It is almost worth a trip."

"Almost," I said.

Hubert looked around, taking in the restaurant. He seemed deeply happy, at peace, like he had returned home to someplace sacred.

"You should never underestimate what it takes to make a place like this run smoothly. The first chef will arrive around nine A.M. and do *la mise en place*. They prepare all the ingredients and reduce sauces. Most of the reduction is done in the morning. The meat sous-chefs, the fish sous-chefs, they do their preparation.

"Around eleven A.M. the Big Money Chef arrives. They eat for about thirty minutes, something prepared by one of the sous-chefs. Usually very conservative. They don't eat what they cook. The ingredients are too expensive. Around noon, they move to the next level."

Hubert opened the menu and peered at it with a delighted gleam in his eye. "It is like seeing an old friend," he said. "A very dear old friend."

The menu was handsome and understated thick white paper with deckle edges, a discretely embossed A.S. on the cover. The restaurant might be named Lucas Carton, but Alain Senderens wanted no mistake as to who was running the show.

"When the maître d' comes into the kitchen and barks orders—this menu, that menu—then he is like an orchestra leader. Everyone knows what to do and must do it with speed and grace.

"It is called *coup de feu*, the 'shot.' It lasts for two to three hours. The discipline is to allow each person to eat as long as they like but not to keep anyone waiting. If you can't do that, if you can't follow the conductor, you should do something else."

"Then the grand turmoil of the day started, the dinner hour," George Orwell wrote in *Down and Out in Paris and London*. From his perspective of a lowly *plongeur*, "no better than a slave," he describes the madness of dinner at one of Paris's best hotels. "The essence of the situation was that a hundred or two hundred people were demanding individually different meals of five or six courses, and that fifty or sixty people had to cook and serve them and clean up the mess afterwards. . . . The chargings to and fro in the narrow passages, the collisions, the yells, the struggling with crates and trays and blocks of ice, the heat, the darkness, the furious festering quarrels which there was no time to fight out. . . . Anyone coming into the basement for the first time would have thought himself in a den of maniacs."

Our first courses arrived. *Raviolis de pétoncles aux courgettes*. Ravioli with tiny scallops with a cap of zucchini. The sauce was a reduction of the scallops with butter, impossibly rich. Hubert reached across and unselfconsciously took up a spoonful of the sauce. "Butter is sacred," he announced.

Rat dived—as only Rat could—into *Langoustines et asperges aux fritons de poulet*. Lobster with green asparagus and bits of chicken that seemed to have been fried, with shiitake mushrooms. It seemed an odd combination that somehow did not come together. I've always felt that lobster was best left alone, that almost any kind of sauce treatment only drowned the delicate taste. This was a reduction with tons of butter, and the lobster seemed lost. The chicken was an odd touch that seemed overcooked and hard.

Hubert had a blissful look on his face. In front of him was *Assiette de poissons façon bourride au gingembre*. "You must," he said, pushing the bowl my way. It was extraordinarily rich, like a bowl of heavy cream flavored with fish sauce and garlic. I could not imagine eating the whole thing on a bet. Hubert devoured it.

"So look it, Hubert," Rat suddenly demanded. "Just what is it with everybody in this country that they want to pretend that nouvelle cuisine never happened or what?"

Hubert paused, twirling a glass of Château Gloria. It was, he had exclaimed with no little passion, his favorite wine. "One of the few good things to come from a politician," he'd said with a smile, explaining that the vineyard was owned by the mayor of Saint-Julien, Henri Martin.

"That," he said now, aiming his wine glass in Rat's direction, "is what I first fell in love with in America."

I looked at Rat, who seemed a little confused. "I thought it was corn on the cob."

"The way American girls talk."

"Yeah, yeah, yeah." Rat waved dismissively. "I'm tellin' you, you mention nouvelle and a hush falls over the room, like this guy over here"—she pointed to me—"asking old Germans if they were Nazis. You know?"

"You do that?" Hubert asked me.

"Of course I do! Why doesn't everybody, that's what I want to know?"

"Maybe they don't care."

"Don't care?!"

"Please," Rat said, "I will stand on this table and dance naked before I let you go off on some rant about Nazis and Germans."

"Well," Hubert said, clearly savoring the image.

"About nouvelle, Hubert."

"Yes," he sighed, his mind visibly shifting. "No one— no one with three stars by their name—wants to *follow*." He pronounced the word with great disdain, an evil obscenity. "Escoffier, yes, they will all say, of course, they follow in the tradition of Escoffier. That's okay. He's dead and can't compete. But for an Alain Senderens to say, 'Yes, I am nouvelle,' that would be humiliating. It would make them smaller.

"But it's there, you know." He gestured to the kitchen. "Nouvelle changed everything. To me, the greatest nouvelle gift was to make it okay to eat with the seasons. Sixty years ago, the three-stars would have five hundred items on the menu. If you want a leg of giraffe, okay, we have one rotting in the fridge. It was the range that marked a great restaurant. The idea of haute cuisine was doing what you couldn't do at home. No one believes this, but nouvelle helped break down the barriers between the haute and the bourgeois."

My hero Waverly Root would have liked Hubert's thesis. He loved to rail against the boring cuisine that had become, by the late 1950s when he wrote his epic *The Food of France*, synonymous with "fancy" French food.

"The Touraine and the Île-de-France both based their cuisines on the same foundation, the cuisine bourgeois, the hearty fare of the good trencherman. The Touraine chose to rest satisfied with that. Professionalism, in the Île-de-France, built on this foundation the haute cuisine, which, having conquered smart hotels and chic restaurants all over the world, is now what foreigners think of as French cooking."

"Now," Hubert continued, "it is okay to try and do fewer things well and with the seasons. And seasoning from all over, not just France. Like your pigeon . . ."

Our next courses were arriving in a scattershot way. First mine, then Rat's, and finally Hubert's. It was, well, sloppy. And it disturbed me that it disturbed me. I was truly developing horrendously high standards of service.

This three-star eating binge was going to ruin me and in ways I'd never anticipated. What had worried me most about the prospect of twenty-nine days of unending gastronomic overkill was the logical assumption that such gross indulgence of superb eating would ruin my enjoyment of the food. It seemed inevitable that I would come to dread each evening as a duty and my body would rebel at being inundated with daily doses of foie gras and butter. But the scary reality was that I found it perfectly normal to spend three or four hours an evening eating. With horrifying rapidity I had become adjusted to the idea that the biggest decision of the day was what to order for dinner. In my heart, I knew if I ended the three-star streak tomorrow, I would go into a long, painful withdrawal of deprived sensory overload. My options were clear: I had to keep on eating my way through France or face terrifying prospects. My fate had been sealed: I had become a three-star junkie.

I had ordered *Pigeon grillé au colombo et vermicelle chinois*. "The 'colombo,'" Hubert asked, "what do they mean? Some kind of African spices they say"—we had asked—"but what does that mean? It could mean anything or everything or nothing. He puts on it what he wants. But the very idea that it would have a name that was non-French, in a three-star, that would never have happened before La Point graced our world."

"'The influence of Fernand Point today is immeasurable,'" writes Rudolph Chelminski in *The French at Table*, "'as great as was the fabulous reputation of La Pyramide, the paradise he began creating in 1924 in Vienne. . . . La Pyramide's kitchen was graced with an astonishingly great number of internationally recognized names of French gastronomy today.'" Indeed the list is impressive: Paul Bocuse, Pierre Troisgros, Alain Chapel.

"Point taught them," Hubert said, "that it was okay to experiment if first they learned the classics. A whole generation fell under his influence and went on to create what became nouvelle cuisine."

The pigeon was superb, shockingly red at the bone. "You can thank nouvelle for that," Hubert said with a grin. "They never would have served something so uncooked before."

"You look happy," Rat said to Hubert gently.

He smiled and sat back in the banquette, surveying the room. "This, for me," he said with a sigh, "is the closest I come to going to church."

For a moment, I thought I saw his eyes cloud with tears. Then he leaned forward and whispered, "I think we must order two desserts apiece. What do you say?"

# Chapter
# Thirteen

E ach day brings only two opportunities for field work,"
A. J. Liebling wrote in *Between Meals* on the challenges
of writing about food, "and they are not to be wasted minimiz-
ing the intake of cholesterol. They are indispensable, like the
prizefighter's hours on the road."

I took comfort in the great Liebling's advice as I found
myself wandering the streets of Paris perpetually hungry. Given
the fact that I was spending three hours at least a night gleefully
stuffing my face, it did not seem physiologically possible that I'd
ever wake up hungry. But somehow every morning I seemed to
hit the streets with extraordinary eagerness to eat anything that
wouldn't eat me.

Liebling honored those who could consume vast quanti-
ties of food. "In the heroic age before the First World War, there
were men and women who ate," he wrote nostalgically, "in addition to a whacking lunch and a glorious dinner, a voluminous
supper after the theater or the other amusements of the evening."

Like the defeat of Napoleon at Waterloo and the fall of Paris
in 1942, Liebling counted as one of the tragic moments in
French history the discovery of the human liver and its vulner-
abilities. "From that time on, French life has been built to an
increasing extent around that organ, and a niggling caution has
replaced the old recklessness; the liver was the seat of the Maginot
mentality."

A large man who spent considerable effort becoming larger, Liebling took as one of his personal heroes the writer and restaurateur Yves Mirande. He was a man who would think nothing of sitting down to a "lunch of raw Bayonne ham and fresh figs, a hot sausage in crust, spindles of filleted pike in a rich rose sauce Nantua, a leg of lamb larded with anchovies, artichokes on a pedestal of foie gras, and four or five kinds of cheese, with a good bottle of Bordeaux and one of champagne," while looking forward to a dinner of "larks and ortolans . . . with a few *langoustes* and a turbot—and, of course, a fine *civet* made from the *marcassin* or young wild boar. . . . 'And while I think of it,' I once heard him say, 'we haven't had any woodcock for days, or truffles baked in the ashes, and the cellar is becoming a disgrace—no more '34s and hardly any '37s.'"

The thought of such a man was reassuring. Something had happened to me, as if the on-off switch of normal hunger functions had shorted out in the permanently on mode. The more I ate, the more I wanted to eat. And it wasn't just a simple matter of quantity. I wandered the streets of Paris thinking of little but food, hypersensitized to every smell and sight.

This is very dangerous.

In my feeding frenzy, Paris loomed as one giant meal waiting to be devoured. While Rat and Victor were at the Louvre, I wandered from bakery to bakery, using Patricia Wells's wonderful *Food Lover's Guide to Paris* the way soldiers had once used the famed *Guide Rose* to pick brothels. At the Boulangerie Beauvallet et Julien on the Rue de Poissy, I devoured half of a *pain rustique*, marveling at its rich dark color and strong flavor, then walked to Michel Brusa, 16 Rue Mouffetard on the Place de la Contrescarpe, to try his heralded sourdough baguettes. I stood out in front, the other half loaf of the *pain rustique* jammed into a coat pocket, and pulled the baguette apart, burying my nose in the strong sourdough smell and delighting at the texture of the bread.

With pockets stuffed with hunks of bread, I embarked on a mad search for cheese. The thought of finding the perfect Camembert, a tart Swiss, a creamy chèvre actually sent my pulse rate racing. It was like I was stalking some elusive animal, the trail growing fresher, and an encounter likely just over this next rise.

Without a moment's hesitation, I moved through the crowd streaming into the Louvre in search of Chez Tachon on the Rue de Richelieu. The thick crowd annoyed me and I wanted to shout, *What are you doing? You could be eating, not standing in line for some quick peek at a Cézanne. Where are your priorities? Art over cheese? Are you mad?*

I'd argued the same point earlier in the day with Rat and Victor, who inexplicably had chosen a day of museums over bakeries, cheese shops, and markets.

"Look," Victor had said, "I don't want to put too fine a point on it, but we are talking about the *Mona Lisa*, Brueghel, Rubens, Caravaggio—"

"So what?" I'd shouted, turning heads in Bistrot du Clos, where we were sipping huge pots of café au lait. "You can see wonderful photos and reproductions every day of the week anywhere in the world. But what good is it looking at a photo of one of Michel Brusa's great baguettes? Have you thought about that?! Can you taste the texture? Smell that incredible fresh smell that makes you glad to be alive? Huh? Can you?"

Victor and Rat looked at each other for a long moment. "Look," Rat finally said, "we're going to do you a favor. We're just going to forget that we ever had this conversation."

"That's probably best," Victor agreed, far too gravely for my taste.

"What? You guys think I'm ashamed that I intend to spend the entire day running around from bakeries to *fromageries* to markets to pastry shops?"

"Then eat a three-star meal at L'Ambroisie tonight," Rat reminded me.

"Okay? So?"

"There just might be a role for some moderation here, that's all," Victor suggested.

"Moderation? MODERATION? WE'RE EATING AT A DIFFERENT THREE-STAR EVERY NIGHT, VICTOR, I'D SAY WE'VE ALREADY KIND OF FLUBBED THIS MODERATION THING!"

They stared at me. I took a long drink of coffee. "Okay, Victor, fine, fine. But let me ask you one very important question."

"Yes."

"In your opinion—your personal opinion—where do you think in all of Paris you can get the best *boudin*?"


That evening we walked from the Angleterre to L'Ambroisie. It was a clear, surprisingly cool evening and the light was soft and gentle, a sort of glow that lingered so long it was easy to forget that it wouldn't last forever.

Victor and Phoebe met us at Les Deux Magots, where Rat had promised to rendezvous with one of the guys she'd met at the Luxembourg Gardens.

"The Deux Magots?" Victor asked, disbelieving. "That's where my *mother* wants to go when she comes to town."

"I'm sure she's a charming woman with impeccable taste," Rat said.

"Coffee is twenty francs a cup at that place," Victor insisted. "It's only five francs if we stand at the Café Napoléon bar. We can close our eyes and pretend we're at the Ducks May Go."

"What?" Rat balked.

"Rat has been reading de Beauvoir," I said.

"Oh." Victor nodded. He looked at Rat, started to say more, but Phoebe jumped in.

"I love Deux Magots," she said with true convictions.

"You like it because it's full of Americans," Victor teased.

"You should be glad I like Americans, silly boy. Maybe my taste will change?"

Victor shut up after that.

I knew why Rat wanted to go to the café. She had read me an excerpt from *The Second Sex* on the ferry from England. "I sat in the Deux Magots and gazed at the blank sheet of paper. . . . I wanted to write about myself. . . . I realized the first question to come up was: What has it meant to me to be a woman?" I, of course, had been teasing her about this ever since she had read me the passage.

Rat's friend arrived on a motor scooter, impossibly cool in white linen pants, shoes that looked like bedroom slippers, and a blue-jean jacket. His name was Michel and he was an architecture student whose family lived in Algeria. We talked about which route was better driving through the desert, the straight shot down through Tamanrasset or the longer route through the Sahara and Mali near Timbuktu. He preferred the latter, because he was fond of Timbuktu's architecture.

I described a meal I'd cooked once by the River Niger. The centerpiece was an oversized gar I'd caught, the only fish longer than six inches I'd ever caught in Africa. It was a bony prehistoric-looking thing about as appetizing as a display in a natural history museum. I filleted it, which was the only thing I could imagine doing, wrapped the fillet in tin foil with bits of onions and some old garlic cloves I'd bought in the Timbuktu market, and buried it in the coals of a driftwood fire. It was shockingly good, moist and sweet. I ate it with half a can of peaches and a mix of fried yams and onions, which was about all the shelves of Timbuktu's largest grocery had to offer.

"He's been thinking about food a lot," Rat said when I'd finished my lurid description. She said it in the same half-embarrassed tone you might use to describe the eccentricities of a doddering uncle.

Michel, with the natural graciousness that is quintessentially Algerian, added quickly, "I think about food all the time."

"Oh, God, we're all going to be nice to each other," Rat sighed, making it clear that she saw this as a terribly dreary prospect.

I started asking Michel a lot of questions about what it was like now in Algeria since the Islamic fundamentalists had rebelled against the government. Had his family stayed in the country? Did they feel safe? Did he have friends who had been killed?

His responses were very matter-of-fact, as if he were talking about a country that was not really his own, even though he had grown up there. But he saw himself as French and Algeria as a place where his family worked, a place he liked a great deal, but it was possible for terrible things to happen there, as they were, and he saw it as a problem to be solved, not a failure of a culture or a society for which he was responsible or to which he was deeply attached.

Yes, he had friends, both females, who had been murdered by the Islamic resistance. One was a teacher whose father had been a hero in the French-Algerian war. Her crime was to be smart and Western influenced—her classes watched CNN—and, most important, she was a very, very good teacher. She affected waves of students the way only a powerful teacher can. They had killed her just outside of her school, in view of her students; a knife was used, a large Islamic dagger plunged into her back, ripping up through her lungs and almost severing her spinal cord, so that she was left flopping around and spewing rich clouds of oxygenated blood.

When Michel talked about this, he did so quietly, as if reading from a medical report. "Rich, oxygenated blood" was his phrase.

The other was a journalist, the mother of a friend. Her family had pleaded with her to quit writing and leave the country, but she had refused. Her head was stuck on a fleur de lis wrought-iron fence in front of her church. She had also been a Christian.

But no, his family felt safe, more or less. His father owned a small factory and kept a low profile; they lived outside of Algiers with good security. "There are bombings in Paris, you know." He shrugged. "Anything can happen."

Around us, people were laughing and making plans for the evening. Across Saint-Germain-des-Prés, a group of Japanese tourists was earnestly heading for Picasso's bronze bust *Homage to Apollinaire*, which was sitting in a tiny garden adjoining a church, among bits and pieces of the original twelfth-century church. It was an odd, disconcerting arrangement that gave the impression of Great Meaning—the impressive head of a poet and friend of Picasso's, Apollinaire, the ruins of an ancient church. But like a bad poem drawing on failed metaphors, there simply was no larger meaning. There was, however, an unavoidable appeal to such a casual display of a Picasso bust.

An elderly couple in identical berets came out of La Hune bookstore next door, with a handful of books and a copy of *Paris Match*, featuring a cover story on Princess Diana's revelations that she'd had sex with other humans beside Prince Charles. It seemed to be important to her that Everyone Know This. Soon, no doubt, she would be appearing on daytime American television sharing the pain of bulimia with millions.

"You have to come to dinner with us," Phoebe insisted to Michel, breaking the long silence we'd fallen into after hearing his Algerian tales.

Yes, definitely, we all agreed. He demurred, of course. "I'm not dressed—"

Rat cut him off. "It doesn't matter. You'll be my date, and no place is going to turn me down, now are they?"

We all laughed. It was an appalling Restaurant Truth. It wasn't Rat's fault, it was just the way the world worked. No restaurant was likely to turn away any male accompanying a beautiful woman elegantly dressed.

We walked over to the Seine, passing the Charcuterie Alsacienne, where Rat had to hold me down to stop me from going in for a quick bite of their Westphalian ham.

"Look," I pleaded, "this is a long walk. We could get lost."

"I have a compass," Michel said, quite sensibly.

"A compass, a little food, all we need are some matches and we'll be properly equipped," I insisted.

*"We're only walking across Paris!"* Rat yelled, *"Not the goddamn Sahara."*

"I didn't say a word about water. We can always get water." She pulled me away.

We took the Rue Saint-André-des-Arts to the Place St. Michel, then looped by Saint-Séverin church just to smell the Greek restaurants. We crossed the Seine on the Petit Point and continued along the river. Victor, who was most proud of his knowledge of Paris, kept a running narrative of landmarks: *This is the mounted statue of Étienne Marcel, who presided over the first city council of Paris. Around the corner over there is the memorial to Parisian Jews who died in the Holocaust and, look, just over there, an extraordinary carving of a lion's head over the doorway to the Hôtel Châlons-Luxembourg, built in the seventeenth century . . .*

Victor talked all the way to the Place des Vosges. No one was really listening, but no one seemed to mind. Phoebe was talking quietly to Michel, and Rat walked alone a few steps ahead. She liked to do that a lot, walk alone, either ahead or behind, it didn't matter, just far enough to be by herself but close enough to remain connected. It seemed a not bad reflection of her worldview.

I was still thinking about Algeria. Coming out of the Sahara, I'd turned up at a desolate Algerian border post so sick I literally could not drive. By reputation the post was one of the nastiest in North Africa, with a supposed lust for long searches and seizures of hard cash that somehow violated Algeria's complicated currency laws.

But when they quickly learned I wasn't French and saw how ill I was, they took me in like a lost relative. For days I was taken care of in a crude military field hospital. It was like that wherever I went in Algeria—once they knew that I wasn't French, the hospitality was extraordinary, the people graced with an irresistible gentleness. For weeks I had camped out, never worrying for a second about danger.

And now if I returned, there would be people trying to kill me because I was a foreigner. It was difficult to imagine and somehow profoundly sad.

As I was mourning for a country I'd loved and seemed to have lost and wondering when I would be able to return to Algeria we suddenly passed under the archway of the central courtyard into the Place des Vosges.

The transformation was abrupt and affected all my senses. The temperature seemed to drop a half dozen degrees, the courtyard shaded from the drooping sun by the high walls. There was a fresh smell of greenery from the squares of grass and the center garden ring. It was quiet, the square deserted. An irresistible sense of calm settled over me.

L'Ambroisie felt like a small, extraordinarily elegant residence. There were two adjoining rooms, each with fewer than ten tables. A huge seventeenth-century Flemish tapestry dominated the first room, along with an oversized vase of massive sunflowers, chrysanthemums, and goldenrod. They were lit from above like a religious shrine, evoking the sense that kneeling in supplication was expected. A single candle sat on each table.

It was cool and quiet, like a very old church. Footsteps faintly echoed on the white tile floors. After the flat lighting of

Lucas Carton, the shadows cast by the candles and the recessed lighting were soothing and inviting.

We sat in the front room. Across from us, under the Flemish tapestry, a young Japanese couple dined in silence. They each had a bottle of wine—one red, one white—sitting in front of them, and I wondered if they were totally silent because they were angry, had nothing to say, or were simply drunk. They ate at a deliberate pace with no visible enjoyment.

The rest of the room, except one empty table for two, was full of Americans. There seemed to be not one Frenchman in the entire restaurant.

It was the scale of L'Ambroisie that I liked best. After Taillevent and Lucas Carton—true palaces and proud of it—the two rooms of L'Ambroisie felt intimate, personal. Madame Pacaud, the wife of chef Bernard Pacaud, met us at the door, a petite woman with smart eyes and a bemused smile that seemed to be saying, *Come in, this will be fun. It's all a bit silly, but let's have an extraordinary evening together.* The menu design was perfect: an understated textured brown, simple, elegant. And inside, it was a mere two pages with the fewest items of any three-star menu I'd seen: seven first courses, six fish courses, six meats, and six desserts. This compared to the forty-five various dishes at Taillevent.

Rat and Phoebe were given menus without prices, but wine lists were distributed to everyone, which I liked. The sommelier was short and charming, with sparkling eyes that looked absolutely mad. We decided a bottle of 1985 Château Kirwan would be the right stuff.

I started with *Pastilla de thon aux abricots secs, vinaigrette composée;* tuna in a phyllo-like crust with olive oil and capers and bits of lime. Crushed pistachios decorated the top. *Crushed pistachios?* They look lonely and silly.

It was a whopping big piece of tuna cooked far too long for

my taste. Dried apricots were inside. The list of ingredients reads like a gag dish: tuna, olive oil, capers, lime, pistachio, apricots? But somehow it was wonderful, the best dish I'd had since I'd come to France—but would have been even better if cooked less.

Madame Pacaud passed by and we had a quick exchange about the nature of tuna. To cook it less, she said with a smile, would mean that it had to be served red in the middle. This we simply don't do. Do you like it red? she asked. Almost raw, I answered, and she seemed intrigued. We could do that, she said. You can come again? She explained that they had just changed the menu the day before because the tuna and tomatoes had become available. They changed the menu four or five times a year, sometimes more.

The tomatoes just available? I asked. Is that possible?

*Good* tomatoes, she answers. The kind of tomatoes we want to serve.

While I was talking with Madame Pacaud, my *Croustillant de bar braisé, étuvée de fenouils aux olives vertes* arrived. The aroma was extraordinary: rich olive and saffron mixed with the earthy tomato and hints of fennel. I laughed. Madame looked at me and then chuckled.

"Good, no?" she asked.

"Very, very good," I said.

And, of course, it was. It was light, which was what I wanted, given the heat of the day and the amount I'd already eaten on my cross-Paris binge, but complicated. Fennel, olive, saffron, the light, flaky bass that was most definitely not over-cooked; each flavor you could taste individually. But any chef can construct a dish with distinctive flavors, just as any composer can write a piece in which you hear the separate instruments. The genius comes in the arrangement.

An older man in an electric-blue sport coat and a brilliantly blond woman dressed in bright pink arrived to take the one empty table. In the room full of earnest Americans and the even more earnest Japanese couple, the pair stood out like peacocks. The woman wore a lot of jewelry, mostly gold, including a wedding ring.

Phoebe nodded toward them and whispered. "French. You see, it is a myth that the French have stylish taste."

"That's ridiculous," Victor said.

"He looks like a gangster and she's a hooker," Phoebe whispered, more loudly and with an edge. "Look at the Americans here."

I took a look around. They seemed a pretty boring lot to me. Across from us a middle-aged woman with screaming red fingernails was working hard on pleasing her husband. She had been smiling and winking at him all night over her wine glass, like some gross parody of a first-date romance. Her husband was older and bored.

"I like our table," Michel said.

Rat laughed. "I like you."

He blushed.

"And look at the waiters," Phoebe added. "Their ties!"

The front waiters wore black double-breasted coats, white shirts, and paisley bow ties.

"It could be worse," I said. "They look comfortable."

"Comfortable?"

"Don't you hate it," I asked, "when waiters look like they are wearing ridiculous costumes? It's embarrassing and humiliating for them. A paisley bow tie? Not so bad. And the back waiters, they're in white. Classic."

Phoebe shook her head. It was clear I just didn't understand.

Across from us, the American with the wife who was trying hard to please took out a huge cigar and began to work it roughly in his mouth. She smiled harder.

I started to think about dessert.

# Chapter Fourteen

Hubert made us promise to go to Tour d'Argent with him. "I understand perfectly," he'd said. "You are not excited about going but curious. Like you would be about a train wreck. You want to see it, but you don't think it will be fun."

He wasn't far off.

"But you are wrong, of course," Hubert said. "Tour d'Argent is a treasure, you just have to understand it."

We were at his apartment in Paris, just behind the Musée d'Orsay on the Rue de l'Université. It was a deeply pleasant space on the fourth floor, facing a garden of chestnut trees. Hubert called it a tree house, and in Paris, that's not the easiest thing to come by.

"Mark me down for terribly skeptical," I said. "Skeptical, as in, I think you're probably crazy."

"You *know* I'm crazy." He smiled. "But I'm right about Tour d'Argent. Read this, it might help. I found it at the Strand. From 1929."

He handed me a faded book with a tattered cloth binding. Under the title—*Where Paris Eats*, by Julian Street—there was a drawing of a champagne glass that evoked an era of flappers and bathroom gin. It was silly and gay, the sort of book everyone would have been reading at the Stork Club before getting on the boat to Paris.

"Another famous restaurant on the Left Bank of the Seine is the Tour d'Argent, which lays claim to being the oldest eating-place in Paris, an inn of this name having been opened on the present site in 1582, less than four score years after the death of Christopher Columbus."

Even then Tour d'Argent was an institution, a place that drew crowds as much for its history and spectacle as food. "It is said," Street wrote, "that Henri III once stopped there for supper on his way home from hunting; that the fork, most useful of table tools, was first introduced to Paris as an improvement over fingers . . . and that the hostelry was indicated by Dumas as the scene of certain adventures of his three musketeers."

Since the reign of Napoleon III, the restaurant has been famous for its pressed duck, "well known to countless American and English travellers who went to the Tour d'Argent not only to eat the famous pressed duck, but also to watch the ritual of preparation. Frederic himself used always to perform the rites, and people at the tables put down knives and forks and stared, fascinated as, with waiters grouped round him in devout attitudes, he deftly carved the bird, placed the carcass in the silver press, mixed the savory brown sauce, and with it anointed the tender slices."

"Frederic" was Frederic Delair, the chef-proprietor who ushered the restaurant into the twentieth century and then passed it on to the Terrail family, who still owns it today.

"I come here like I go to the Old Vic," Hubert said with a certain reverence, as we stepped off the elevator into the main dining room. "To see how much things have *not* changed."

It was a sizable room with huge windows looking out over Notre Dame. Outside a light rain was falling against a sun that was still bright at 7:30 in the evening. A large, silver press for the famed ducks was prominently displayed, along with glass-dome serving platters awaiting the ducks. American accents filled the room.

The menus were presented, large, impressive things of brushed silver embossed with the Tour d'Argent crest of a medieval tower with "1582" hovering above its castellated walls. Hubert held it for a moment before opening. "For what I want, I don't need this, but it's like seeing pictures of an old friend. It brings back many good memories."

"Duck?" Rat asked. "If you have duck, I'll have duck."

The duck dishes were all for two persons.

Hubert gently shook his head. "Not tonight. I want to visit an old friend."

Rat and I looked at each other, shrugged, and opened the menus. They opened outward, like heavy swinging doors leading to a world of hidden delights. Which was, I suppose, the point.

The organization of the menu was intriguing. In the middle of the center panel there was a section labeled "*Canetons,*" listing six different ducks. On the left there was:

> *Caneton au fil des temps*
> *Le caneton Tour d'Argent*
> *Caneton Claude Foussier*

And on the right:

> *Caneton grillé aux pommes de reinette*
> *Le caneton Marco Polo aux quatre poivres*
> *Caneton Elie de Rothschild*

Underneath them—what Rat called "the duck section. A whole section of these damn ducks"—was a reproduction of an etching of sixteenth-century Paris with the inscription, "Eastern Aspect of the Notre Dame Church, Bridge of the Hostel Dieu and Notre Dame Island with views of St. Bernard."

It was all very logical and direct. Right in the center of the menu were the two compelling reasons diners came to Tour d'Argent: it served famous duck dishes and it had been around forever. (And the stunning view, referenced in the etching, wasn't bad at all.)

There was an honesty about Tour d'Argent that was appealing. It was, most important, an elegant tourist attraction and did not pretend otherwise. "There is no use pretending that the tourist Venice is not the real Venice, which is possible in other cities," Mary McCarthy wrote in *Venice Observed*, and so it was for Tour d'Argent. "Venice is a folding picture-post-card of itself," she wrote, and there on the menu of Tour d'Argent is an etching that is really a Tour d'Argent postcard.

Outside on the Seine, boats full of tourists passed the restaurant, turning spotlights upward. *Here is the famous restaurant Tour d'Argent, the oldest . . .*

"I am about to order a dish I had thirty years ago," Hubert announced, as if we'd been dying to know. "And it is my sincere hope that it has not changed one bit." He then preceded to order from the darkly handsome young waiter *Filet de sole cuit au champagne et petites écrevisses à la Cardinal.*

Rat and I had the Caneton Tour d'Argent. It was good. And Hubert had a blissful look on his face when he took his first bite of the sole. It had not changed, or so he remembered.

We had a bottle of Château Gloria and watched the lights come up on Notre Dame.

"Are you really going to Michel Guérard's tomorrow?" Hubert asked.

Michel Guérard's three-star outpost was in Eugénie-les-Bains, a day's drive south of Paris, almost on the Spanish border.

I told Hubert that we were leaving Paris early the next morning.

He nodded, and I thought for an awkward moment that

he was going to ask to come with us. A frightening image of Hubert crowded into the back seat with Rat's dog flooded my mind. Or, worse yet, *me* in the back seat with the dread dog.

"What's wrong?" Rat asked.

I shook my head.

"I envy you," Hubert finally said. "Guérard has made a little paradise down there, he really has. And he's probably the best chef in all of France."

When the Mustang shuttered to a stop, the silence was overwhelming. As my ears slowly returned to normal after hours of the thundering V-8, I could hear birds, lots of birds, voices laughing, and somewhere children playing. Henry sat on the back seat, panting in stunned silence from the heat. Rat was reading *The Sun Also Rises*.

I spotted him right away. He looked like an elf dressed in white. A charming elf who probably had magical powers. Trailed by a pair of female assistants, he was walking across the lawn, like a doctor hurrying between patients, an image reinforced by the sense that we had arrived at a very elegant sanatorium or maybe a very chic nuthouse.

The air was fifteen degrees warmer than in Paris, the light soft and gentle. A long walk led to the hotel, which looked like the estate of a Spanish nobleman or an elegant Bel Air mansion, surrounded by a cornucopia of near-tropical flora: palm trees mixed with banana and orange, huge stands of bamboo laced with roses. Across the immaculate lawns were statues of nymphs that seemed whimsical and silly.

We were in Eugénie-les-Bains, in the foothills of the Pyrenees, not far from the Spanish border. Once the area had been a bath spa erected as a resting point between Spain and Paris for the Empress Josephine. Now it was a small village of red-tiled roofs and wrought-iron balconies, a few cafés, a farm-implement store, a shop selling tins of the local patés.

Twenty years ago, Michel Guérard had come here from Paris to recover, by all accounts, from a near nervous breakdown brought on by too much success, too much food, too much work. The son of a butcher, Guérard apprenticed as a pastry chef but soon had his own restaurant in Paris, Pot-au-Feu. From its beginnings as a bankrupt bistro purchased for twenty thousand francs in the suburb of Asnières, Pot-au-Feu quickly became a sensational showplace for Guérard's talents, earning two stars more rapidly than any restaurant in Michelin history.

Then, when the restaurant was forced to close because of the government's insistence on building a road through his tiny dining room, Guérard found himself adrift, eating and drinking too much. He met and fell in love with a woman whose family owned a dozen or so health spas, and together they left Paris and retreated to this far corner of southwest France. He invented a new "diet" cuisine, *cuisine minceur*, lost twenty-five pounds, and set about constructing, with his wife's money, something the world had never seen: a three-star restaurant that was also a reducing spa. The notion was laughable: come to the three-star and lose weight.

But Michel Guérard and his wife had a concept that was more than just food: they wanted to construct a true retreat, a little piece of paradise stuck off from the rest of the world. A fantasy.

I wandered around the grounds, leaving Rat with her book and Henry, who seemed to have been paralyzed by the Mustang's noise and the southern sun. It was a sprawling compound. The main building housed hotel rooms and Guérard's three-star kitchens and dining rooms. There was a separate structure off to the side that looked like an elegant apartment building. I walked in and seemed to be alone. It was airy, with hardwood floors and a gentle breeze blowing the curtains.

Outside, I stopped a young man dressed in a sous-chef's whites who was walking toward the side of the main building.

"Who lives here?" I asked and he seemed puzzled.

"Lives?" he answered in a Scottish accent. "We all live here, don't we?"

He smiled and seemed to be thinking, *What an incredibly stupid question, but I'll be nice about it.*

"No, I mean in this building. Is it just for hotel guests?"

"Spa guests," he answered. "Here for the treatment, they are."

I nodded, wondering what all the treatment involved. "But doesn't it drive them crazy," I asked, "to come to a place to lose weight that is fifty feet from a three-star restaurant?"

"You haven't had the cuisine, now have you?" he said with a smile. "The best three hundred and fifty calories in the world, it is. And served right there in the dining room." He gestured toward the main building.

"Let me get this straight," I said. "People actually come and pay lots of money to eat three-hundred-and-fifty-calorie dinners while somebody at the next table is having a three-star feast?"

"It's three hundred and fifty calories of Michel Guérard's *cuisine minceur.* It's unbelievably good."

He was laughing, and so was I. There was something cinematically nutty about the two of us standing, me in shorts and a tee shirt, he in his doctor's whites, on the perfectly manicured lawns dotted with statues of nymphs passionately arguing about the relative qualities of 350 calories. If there was a second French Revolution, we doubtless would have been quickly led to the guillotine.

*He was eating in a different three-star restaurant every night? Can you imagine? Off with his head!*

*And he spent his days perfecting ways to lose weight with food that tastes like a three-star! What waste!*

"Tell me, that your Mustang over there, is it?" he asked, nodding toward the front of the hotel.

I nodded. Rat had fallen asleep in the passenger's seat and Henry seemed to be dozing as well, his head resting on Rat's shoulder. The bright red car shimmered in the late afternoon southern heat.

"It's a 'sixty-five and a half, isn't it?" he asked.

"You're a Pony head?" I asked, though the answer was obvious. Anyone who could recognize a '65 and a half from a '66 was a man who knew his way around Mustangs.

"When I have my own restaurant," he said with more certainty than wistfulness, "I'll get a 'sixty-seven Cobra with the original Pony interior, four-speed. I'll park it out front every night."

I laughed. "Do you think it will help attract customers?"

"I think it will help attract women, don't I?" he said with a smile. "Like that fellow in New York I read about, David Bouley. He drives a big Honda bike and he sleeps with a different model every night, right?"

"It's a big *Harley*," I corrected. "And maybe not every night."

"Every other then, fine. I'll settle for that. Particularly after a couple of years down here. Don't have a lot of single women wandering around Eugénie-les-Bains, now do we?" he said. Then, looking over at Rat, he asked, "Is that your wife in the car with the dog?"


The dining room was airy and white, with ceiling fans turning slowly and louvered shutters. Each table had a candelabra of five candles, a green linen tablecloth, and matching china. A sheaf of wheat tied with straw leaned against the candelabra. The silverware was Art Nouveau with a leaf-and-trumpet-flower design, formal, of course, but still slightly playful.

The contemporary French sense of interior design is famously unfortunate. It's not uncommon to see some of the most handsome and elegantly dressed people in the world sitting in restaurants or hotels that looked to have been designed by trailer trash from the outskirts of Dallas. The tendency is to go for loud and bright, with lots of geometric patterns. Textured wallpaper that seems to glow is a particular specialty. And in the country that has produced some of the greatest art in history, there is a decided fondness for lithographs and fountain-statuettes of little boys urinating.

But in Eugénie-les-Bains this was all different. Here, clearly, there was a sensibility at work with very serious good taste. And most impressively, it produced an understated elegance that seemed to blend naturally with the environment. There was no effort at a contrived formality. This part of the world was rural and southern, and with the white wicker chairs, the orchids in huge pots, the verandas with rocking chairs, this was perfect, relaxed but pleasing.

It started with cumin-flavored wafers served with a tomato pesto sauce, slightly heated. The waiter was a young woman. Rat liked this, and they talked about what it was like working with so many men.

With Monsieur Guérard, she explained, it was much better than most restaurants. He is a partner with his wife. She's the one who designs everything, so he respects women. Other chefs . . . she shook her head.

Rat wanted to know who was the worst she'd worked with. She laughed. You think I would tell?

The menu was intriguing, with things we hadn't seen . . . a salmon "Sweet and Sour" et les Beignets Croustillants de Grenouilles.

The Oreiller Moelleux de Mousserons et de Morilles aux Asperges Vertes was one of the few pasta dishes I'd seen since the spree had

begun, back at the Waterside in England. It was the kind of dish
you saw a lot of in New York or Los Angeles: a basic pasta tricked
out with interesting combinations and some asparagus thrown
in to make it appear more healthy. It appealed to various current American food fetishes: high carbohydrates are healthy (not
really true, but . . .), mushrooms are chic (look at the chanter-
elles for sale in Safeways across America), and the need to always
have something green, i.e., healthy, in the mix. There was
a whole subculture of inexpensive but good pasta houses
in New York that had blossomed offering exactly these kind of
combinations.

But Guérard served it with a cream sauce, about as hard to
find in New York or L.A. as footstools for ladies' purses. It arrived
rich with the earthy aroma of the morels floating above it like
an aura. For a long time I just let it sit in front of me, content to
gulp down the flavors in the air, enjoying watching a very com-
petent but not fussy dining operation go about its business.

The back waiters presented each dish with flair: large covered silver dishes were laid down before each diner simulta-
neously; a pause ensued that cried out for a drum roll, and then,
with a nod from the watchful captain, the assistants lift the
covers. The first time I ever saw this presentation was years ago
at Le Cirque, a celebratory dinner after winning my first political race. At the next table, an older, strikingly good-looking
woman with a Texas accent had told her much younger male
companion, "Watch this, sugar. They gonna attack all at once."
And they had.

Ever since then, I've enjoyed that moment of theatrical
presentation. I love the expectation, the slight edginess in the
air, the look of the serving dishes. And then there's the unveil-
ing, which, at its best, should be intoxicating both visually and
aromatically. It's a candle-lit, seductive moment, uncannily like
the moment between two lovers when they first undress.

As soon as I finished the dish, I wanted to eat another plate of exactly the same. All day I'd eaten nothing except half a baguette from one of those wonderful French gas stations that sell everything from cheese to baguettes to wrenches to pornography. The pasta was richly satisfying, complex and interesting but solid. It was like a bowl of hot oatmeal with butter and maple syrup just before heading out to ski. You had that sense you were eating exactly what you wanted.

But just as I was truly considering another round of the *Oreilles*, the *Griblette de Bar aux Rondelles d'Oignon Meunière* appeared. It was gorgeous: a fillet of sea bass topped with onion rings and little white *champignons de Paris* in a light butter sauce with shallots and white wine. It was really like nothing I'd ever had in my life. The onions—which I took a big bite out of first, naturally—were gratifying in that way only fried onion rings can be, and the bass was delicate, the flesh flaky and so richly flavorful I wanted to draw every bite for hours.

"You look happy," Rat said.

She'd ordered *Le Saumon Frais "Sweet and Sour" et les Beignets Croustillants de Grenouilles*. It was an amazing concoction: a filet of salmon in lime, sugar, and ginger sauce (I quickly scooped it up, fighting off Rat's defensive fork stabs), surrounded with beignets of frog legs, pink peppercorns, and seaweed bread.

"You take one more bite of this and you die," Rat said, and I didn't blame her a bit.

Michel Guérard appeared in the dining room for the second time that evening, beaming like a mad leprechaun. It was good to see the chef-proprietor working his audience. At none of the three-stars in Paris had the chef appeared, though at the wonderful L'Ambroisie Madame Pacaud's presence had filled the room.

Why did it matter that Guérard was making the rounds? Any well-trained staff could produce the same food night after night. But it was part of what was so unique about the concept of three-star restaurants. Yes, these were the great eating palaces of the world; yes, their chefs were stars, but they remained craftsmen and artisans who focused on what had made them great in the first place: running a restaurant that produced some of the most stunning food in the world. That was the idea, at any rate. Some did it better than others. There were the tales of chefs who were too busy opening places in Japan or consulting for chains to tend to their own restaurants.

But Michel Guérard was as famous and successful as any chef in the world, and he was right here in his own dining room, in the middle of nowhere, pursuing his craft. And he looked preposterously happy in the pursuit.

I found Rat eating a can of paté in the herb garden in front of the convent. She was wearing a bright white sun hat that she'd bought in Paris, black jeans, and a black tee shirt with a small, very discrete Harley-Davidson logo. Henry was perched at her feet and she was eating with her fingers the local paté straight from the tin. Around her was the large, intricately laid out herb garden that provided many of the seasonings used by the kitchen. And behind her was the stone convent converted to guests rooms.

The entire scene resembled some Dali takeoff on a classic Renaissance portrait: *Lady Rat in Black and White with Paté at the Convent.*

I had just finished a long run through the rolling hills around Eugénie-les-Bains and was soaking wet. Not quite sure how to begin, I plunged straight ahead.

"How would you feel," I said, watching in amazement as she fed some of the paté to Henry, "if we cheated."

Rat gave me a funny look.

"Cheated," I explained. "As in didn't leave today to go to another three-star."

The nearest three-star was Alain Ducasse's Louis XV in Monte Carlo, a long drive away across the belly of France.

"That would be cheating," Rat confirmed. "We've already cheated once in Brussels."

"Did you ever think that you might be poisoning that dog with paté?"

"Henry loves paté."

This, it seems, was true.

"Rat, talk to me. Does your ridiculous boyfriend still think we are going to eat at a different three-star every day?"

"He believes what I tell him." She put the paté can down on the stone floor for Henry to lick. "Unless he doesn't want to."

"Have I told you that it sounds like you guys have such a great relationship?"

"We have a Modern New York Relationship."

"Nightmare."

"Yes."

"So if we stayed here another day before going to Monte Carlo, that would be okay with you?"

"If I never have to get in that car again, it's okay with me."


At ten o'clock I turned up at the kitchen door to meet Alan Darr, the fellow I'd encountered the day before in front of the spa. He was dressed in his neat kitchen whites and sweating slightly, with a sharp-looking paring knife in his right hand. "Hey, you want to see the guts of this place, do you?"

I followed him across a neat gravel driveway to a large shed. Inside, stacked in perfect order, like everything else at Eugénie-les-Bains, was a treasure trove of food: crates of South African oranges, crates of leeks, sacks of garlic.

"They do it right here, huh?" he said. "Only the best stuff. That's the problem in England, isn't it? Hard to get the best stuff, still is. When I open my place, I want it to be like this."

He motioned for me to follow him back inside the kitchen. It was a madhouse. I counted twenty-seven people, each of whom seemed focused and intensely busy. With the rush of white-clad bodies, the neatness, and the flash of steel instruments, it reminded me of an operating room on a busy day. An operating room where the aroma of wood grills and spices replaced formaldehyde and alcohol.

As I watched, organizational patterns began to emerge. Four people were working in the *garde-manger*, which was next to the dry storage, which was a smaller version of the shed I'd just left. A walk in the cold room had revealed the pastry section, where five people were turning out the delicate petit fours, an entire plate of which Rat had devoured after dinner last night.

Alan took me on a quick tour, pointing out the different stations for meat, vegetables, and fish. A stove fifteen feet by ten feet dominated the wall with its combination of gas burners and wood-burning grill.

"What's that?" I asked Alan, pointing to a white device that looked to be a cross between a dishwasher and a trash compactor. "A Cryovac mate," he explained. "You take your leftover paté, or maybe a nice piece of salmon you want to save, put it in here, and let it go to work. It'll blast freeze, suck out all the air, and seal it up tight. Hell of a thing, right?"

It was a long way from the rule laid down by Fernand Point that everything must be cleared from the kitchen each day to begin anew with fresh ingredients each morning. "Point's ironclad rule was that La Pyramide had to begin every new day completely naked, with nothing in the fridges (there was no freezer) and nothing on the stoves," writes Rudolph Chelminski in *The French at Table:*

Point took cruel pleasure in playing hide-and-seek with
the smart alecs who thought they'd put something aside
for the next morning. He was tall enough to see onto
most shelves, and what he couldn't see he felt with his
hands which he poked into every cranny of the kitchen
every night before closing down shop. A lobster came
back untouched, or someone had reduced too large a
quantity of perfect pellucid *glace de viande*, shimmering
amber and delicious, just the thing for the kind of sauces
that most people dream about? *Tant pis*—into the garbage with it!

Alan described a typical day: in the kitchen by 8:30, a mad
rush to get everything ready by 11:30, an even madder scramble
during the lunch service, a break at 3:30 for two hours, and then
back in by 5:30, finishing usually around 11:30, but later in the
summer, when diners tended to linger later.

He was from Edinburgh and had trained at Glenn Eagles,
the famous golfing resort. His goal was to open his own restaurant
in Edinburgh. "Truth is, there just aren't good restaurants in Edinburgh. Terrible trick, but it's true." He was determined to learn
from the best and had pursued a position with Guérard for two
years before being accepted. "You can't open a great place if you've
never worked in one, it's as basic as that." When finally accepted,
he packed up his case of knives, his most cherished possession, and
came to the South of France to learn from a master.

He started out at just 5,600 francs a month but moved up
to 7,000 francs a month when he was promoted to *chef de partie*.
He had one of those chiseled Scottish faces filled with determi-
nation, with large eyes and short cropped hair. It was easy to
picture him going into battle as a member of the Highlander
Guards.

"You want to taste something amazing?" he asked.

With a practiced hand, he dipped a spoon into a medium-sized saucepan filled with a milky liquid. He held it up for me like a parent feeding a child. I inhaled it eagerly.

The taste was sweet and laced with an herb I couldn't identify.

"Ice cream," Alan said with the sort of grin his ancestors probably had when they discovered you could build houses out of peat. "We make it all ourselves from the herb garden. *Tilleul* ice cream."


That night we broke our three-star rule and ate at Guérard's new restaurant, La Ferme aux Grives. It was a few hundred yards from the main complex of spa, hotel, and three-star, set in an old farm that Guérard's wife had renovated.

It was a magical place: a big two-story, stone farmhouse with a fireplace large enough to park a car in. Country hams swung from an iron chandelier over the rough plank tables set with oversized brown china; each place setting included a folding clasp knife, the sort carried by French peasants for generations. As in the three-star, a sheaf of wheat lay on each table, bound with a ribbon.

We sat upstairs in the barn's loft, with a view of the fireplace below. It really was an amazing structure, so large that two cooks were working with three different kinds of grills. There was a vertical grill that held meat in front of the flame; searing it on one side, another grill that positioned the meat directly over the flame; and yet another that was really an open, wood-fired oven.

The waiter saw that I was intrigued and nodded toward one of the cooks, a beefy young guy with blond hair in a ponytail. "He's English," the waiter said. "They like to grill, you know."

He said it with a touch of teasing irony, like *You know how those English are.* "But he's good. He has eleven stars already."

Eleven stars?

"He's worked at restaurants with eleven stars between them. Not so bad, huh?"

It was a phrase I liked. *He has eleven stars.*

The menu was a single page, a relief after the elaborate documents we'd grown accustomed to confronting each dinner.

The waiter brought hors d'oeuvres of *La rostie de pain au fromage blanc et ognoasses*—grilled bread with little onions. The bread was smoky and crunchy, the onions tart. I had to stop myself from eating the entire plate.

Which I didn't want to do, because I had ordered a brochette of grilled vegetables as a first course. I had been salivating over it quite literally since walking into the restaurant. We ordered a bottle of Château de Perchade, which came from a village just a few miles away. It exploded in my mouth, a powerful, young wine a world apart from the Margauxs we'd been drinking.

A young, handsome man sat behind us with a woman who looked to be in her early forties. She had dark black hair, cheekbones that swept to the sky, and a pleasing smile. Michel Guérard came in, and when she stood up to shake his hand, I saw she was wearing a short black dress. Rat watched her with an appreciative smile. She loved anyone who could carry themselves with a certain uncontrived elegance.

"She used to be a model," Rat whispered, pointing out at her.

"You know her?" I asked.

She shook her head. "A runway model. She's got the moves."

She complimented Guérard on the suckling pig she was eating. There was something remarkable about a woman like this sitting down to a big meal of pig. Clearly she was a regular and seemed comfortable chatting with Guérard about how difficult it must be running two restaurants plus the hotel and spa.

Throughout it all, her companion sat quietly, with a vague smile on his face. She did not introduce him.

*La brochette de légumes grillés sur une soupe de poule à "l'aioli" d'herbes* arrived. It was sort of a ratatouille salad, with bits of cheese on the eggplant, all seared on the grill and served with a basil and garlic vinaigrette. Rat and I shared it with *La vinaigrette de poireaux grillés au jambon de campagne*, grilled leeks served with prosciutto.

Off to the side, out of the corner of my eye, I could see the woman kissing her date and stroking his face. She smiled at Rat across the table, as if to say *Look what I have. Isn't this nice?* Rat giggled. "I like this woman," she whispered.

"You're jealous," I said.

"Of course I am, don't be ridiculous."

"Do you think he feels stupid, being fondled over by her?" We were both whispering conspiratorially.

Rat laughed. "He looks happy to me. He looks like the happiest guy in France to me."

I glanced over, trying to seem casual. She saw me and knew exactly what I was doing. She winked and I whipped around.

"You're blushing," Rat laughed.

"No I'm not."

"*You're* jealous," Rat said.

"That's ridiculous." But I was, if only a little. He did seem to be having fun.

That night we walked through the village. It was the kind of night that drew you outside, warm and clear and lush with smells that made you feel like you were in the tropics, not France. Above shuttered shops, sounds filtered down to the street: a radio tuned to bad French pop, a couple arguing, a television game show, a young woman talking on the phone.

We stopped in the one café-bar that was open. It had a few tables, a long bar, and a television with the Tour de France on the screen. Two teenagers were banging on a pair of beat-up pinball machines in the rear.

Michel Guérard sat at a table, talking to a weather-beaten man who appeared to be in his early sixties. When he saw us, he nodded in a friendly way and motioned us over.

We shook hands and introduced ourselves, but he acted like he already knew who we were; it was a gracious gesture since, in a way, we were his guests and it would seem rude not to know one's own guests. He introduced his companion—I didn't get the name—and gestured for us to sit down. We hesitated, even more so when the man sitting with him rose to leave. We muttered the usual niceties about interrupting him, but he insisted.

"How old do you think he is?" Guérard asked, nodding to his departing friend.

"Sixty, sixty-five," Rat answered.

"I think closer to ninety," Guérard said, shrugging. "He doesn't really know."

We both uttered exclamations of amazement. He asked what we thought of the Farm.

"I like it," he said, after we told him how much we enjoyed it, "because now I can cook three different kinds of meals: the three-star, the *cuisine minceur*, and the Farm. It is my baby now, and I feel like when I first started Pot-au-Feu many years ago. It keeps me young," he said with a smile, "this trying to do different things with food. It's like music, you know? Trying to hit all the different notes."

I asked him about something that had long intrigued me. Why was it that there had been such an explosion of creativity twenty or twenty-five years ago with himself, Bocuse, the Troisgros brothers—that whole generation who came to prominence challenging the establishment with nouvelle cuisine and now had become the establishment?

"You have to realize what it was like in the kitchen in those days. Everyone followed Escoffier to the letter. It was like the spirit of cooking was being strangled. What we all wanted was a freer way to express ourselves.

"It wasn't a revolt. We didn't throw down our saucepans and declare that Escoffier was wrong. We built on our classical training the way a painter does. Monet said, 'I want to paint as the birds sing.' We were classically trained but we wanted to be able to do more.

"That's what I liked about the challenge of *cuisine minceur*. Could you make wonderful food and do it with less calories? And still maintain the form of what you are eating?"

"The form?" Rat asked. We had been sitting quietly, letting him talk.

"The form is critical. It is part of the total experience that must appeal to all the senses. My wife understands this better than I. I understand plates, she knows about how everything should look.

"You know, it was dangerous what we did. For so many years, if you wanted to succeed at cooking in France, you did things a certain way. It was mandatory. Now that we succeeded, it seems easy, but then we had no strength except our belief that we had to explore."

I asked him what he thought of current American restaurants. With his typical smile, he shrugged and said that he really had no way to keep up with the latest restaurants. "They change so fast," he said. "But I tell you, the chefs in America, they are very talented. It's the waiters."

"I was a waiter!" Rat cried, laughing.

"And how many years did you study?"

"Almost one whole day. But then they put me to work that night."

"And I have an idea, I believe, why you were selected," he said, looking at Rat with that twinkle he had that was hopelessly cute.

"I can juggle."

He frowned in confusion, and Rat picked up three salt shakers and proceeded to juggle them.

"*Formidable!*" Guérard exclaimed. "Here, it takes two years in school to be a waiter. An apprentice waiter."

"And to be a wine steward?" I asked.

"It takes a lifetime to know wine," he answered, shaking his head. "I'm only getting started."

It was such a self-consciously solemn proclamation that I thought for a moment that he might pause for a beat and then erupt into one of his trademark broad smiles. But this was clearly serious stuff for Guérard. The calm of the café and the late evening settled over us. In the background, the television was talking about the Tour de France and the kids beat on the pinball machines without great enthusiasm.

"It's been a very interesting life," Guérard said. "A different life than I would have thought. Eugénie-les-Bains? But every day in the kitchen I try to do something I've never done before and sometimes, it even works."

# Chapter
# Fifteen

I never wanted to go to Monte Carlo.

"You're crazy," Rat said. "It'll be beautiful, wonderful. Spectacular."

"You sound like an adjective-mad tour operator," I told her.

"Ducasse, idiot," she said, smiling. "Alain Ducasse. You remember what Guérard told us."

Yes, I did. He'd raved about Ducasse's talent, praising him as one of the best of the new generation that had come up since himself, Bocuse, Troisgros.

"Yea, but Monte Carlo . . ." I shrugged.

"You just don't want to leave."

"That's ridiculous. We've already left."

But of course she was right. I didn't want to leave Eugénie-les-Bains. Truth was I could easily have spent at least five or ten years staying right there in the converted convent, alternating between Guérard's three restaurants and running every day in the hills. It was the kind of life I'd aspired to for years.

We were sitting in a little town called Nogaro, not far from Eugénie-les-Bains. The Blue Guide to France mentions it in a fragment of a sentence, noting that it contains "a curiously debased eleventh-century church." This was vaguely interesting—exactly what kind of debasement rated a Blue Guide designation as "curious"—but it was not why we had stopped, drinking café au lait at the Café Rugby.

Bastille Day had stopped us. Or more specifically, a dozen or so people on stilts wearing white caps with red tassels, red kerchiefs, and blue smocks. Turning down a narrow street trying to find a road marked N124, I'd come very close to plowing through the crowd on stilts. As I screeched to a halt, sending Rat and Henry lurching forward toward the instant-death dashboard, that jutting piece of vinyl and steel that seemed to have been designed by the Mustang creators with the guillotine in mind, I had an instant image of the impending carnage: broken stilts, oddly painted in stripes of yellow and red, strewn like kindling, and tasseled caps flying into the town band that followed, interrupting their intense concentration in the best *Music Man* tradition.

The little parade was headed from the Place Jeanne d'Arc to the city hall, trailed by the town's cycling club. The markets were full of olives, and foie gras was everywhere—people were either selling it, buying it, or eating it. A woman in tiger-striped spandex hot pants stopped and stared at the Mustang, as if we'd stolen some prop she needed to complete her ensemble.

"With supreme artistry," Rat read from her worn Gault-Millau, "'Ducasse combines the sensual, keen flavors of Provence and the Italian provinces of Liguria and Tuscany to produce the most delicate and authentic dishes ever offered . . .'"

"Okay," I admitted, "that does sound eatable."

"It also says the interior is a shrine to the showy and extravagant, is ostentatious, frequented by a clientele whose gastronomic knowledge stretches all the way from caviar to lobster."

"Sounds perfect."

"I'll even drive," Rat assured me.

We traveled through the heart of Gascony toward Toulouse. While Rat drove, I read *A White House in Gascony: Escape to the Old French South*, by the English writer Rex Grizell. "'The land is beautiful, and benevolent and spacious . . . farming country—

fruit, vegetables, cereals, wine and livestock. It has been so from time immemorial, and so it still is.'" He describes a people fiercely independent and "traditionally great fighters. The Three Musketeers were Gascons. The famous d'Artagnan was from a poor farm—it still exists—in the heart of Gascony. . . . The courage of the Gascons was again in evidence in World War II when the region was a stronghold in the Resistance."

His portrait is a bittersweet, familiar one, of a people increasingly threatened by an unfriendly modern world, the economic base of their agricultural lifestyle jeopardized by "inflation, increased mechanization and the establishments of EU quotas." These are the farmers you see on television dumping unsold produce in the street, protesting the disruption of the E.U. Still, despite their sense of encroaching dangers, they maintain a "lifestyle where a village may have three bakers, each baking their own "real" bread, and where farmers still have their own vineyard and make their own wine, and where there are markets in every town which have been taking place on the same days every week for a thousand years, and are still crammed with the produce of the local fields and woods and orchards."

I was reading this aloud to Rat just as we passed a series of signs hammered to telephone poles that advertised 3615 SEX—TÉLÉPHONE SEX, and a billboard that read 3626—LUV, and then another. "Three bakers and lots of sex-phone lines—our own little Gascon paradise," Rat said. The phone-sex ads were interspersed with fields of sunflowers and freshly cut hayfields dotted with impossibly neat rolls of hay.

The bright morning heat was broken by rows of trees lining the narrow asphalt road. As we shot into the dark tunnel of trees, the temperature plunged and we were momentarily blinded by the sudden shade. Driving fast in the Mustang through this long corridor of trees had a mesmerizing effect, each individual tree merging into one long blur.

We crested a hill and rolled into the outskirts of Auch, past a simple roadside shrine with a crucifix and Virgin Mary. It was a beautiful little town enhanced by a sense of discovery after the long, empty stretches of rolling hills and fields. Near the town's central rotary intersection, a store advertised local mushrooms on a chalkboard likeness of a chef, complete with white toque:

*Chanterelle—Girolle*
*Bolet Stan*
*Entolome Livide*
*Amanite Mortelle*
*Russule Charbonnière*
*Salliote Champêtre*

Five different kinds of *amanite mortelles* were listed, with a skull and crossbones drawn next to each.

Leaving Auch, we found, across from the modern royal blue Peugeot dealership, a small stand that sold roasted chickens for forty-five francs. They were blistering hot, slathered with rosemary. At another stand down the road, we bought sweet melons. It was a fabulous combination, the hot rosemary chicken and the cool, sweet melon.

We stuffed ourselves from Gascony through the Haute Garonne, bypassing Toulouse and shooting southeast on the motorway toward the Mediterranean, to the Autoroute de Sol. We passed under old aqueducts, dipping down through chalky hills with the sea glinting in the distance, sunflowers pointing toward the sun.

I'd fallen in love with French gas stations along the autoroute. Stumbling into them, dazed from the sun, deafened by the Mustang's V-8, I was intoxicated by their irresistible sensual appeal. If not careful, I could waste unbelievable amounts of time wandering from one aisle to the next, luxuriating in the rare air-conditioning, staring at the elaborate display of tools, wondering what I'd need next to keep the Mustang on the road, or hovering in front of the refrigerated section that offered a half dozen different kinds of paté—paté at a gas station!—and a dozen or more cheeses.

Then there were the magazines, everything from the *Herald Tribune* to the lurid porno comic books the French adore. Next to a rack of the latest synthetic oils there'd be a basket of surprisingly good baguettes and a collection of the beautifully colored Michelin maps that I could spend hours pondering.

At a typical stop just off the Autoroute de Sol, I was standing in front of the magazine rack holding two cans of oil, some automatic transmission fluid (I had been collecting it, quite needlessly, ever since Belgium; the trunk was jammed with the stuff), two baguettes, and a hunk of Muenster cheese, when the older woman–younger man couple we had seen the night before at Guérard's Farm walked into the station. They were laughing and looking delighted with each other when our eyes met. The young man looked slightly embarrassed, as if he'd been caught doing something naughty.

The woman smiled and, nodding toward my armful, said, "A little better last night, I think."

"I've been eating this great rosemary chicken all day," I told her, and she seemed slightly startled.

"You had Michel's chicken last night, how did it compare?"

"You noticed?" I said, impressed.

"It looked very good." She laughed. "I wanted to steal a piece."

She was charming and very direct in a way that was instantly appealing.

Rat came in looking for me. She was always having to drag me out of these gas palaces. Recognizing the couple from the night before, she stuck out her hand and said in her best Wyoming twang, "Rat Kelly."

The woman took her hand. "Rat?"

"Like the big furry things you shoot at the town dump," Rat told her, which probably didn't do too much to clarify the situation.

"My name is Anne-Marie Vognas, and this is Lucien."

We shook hands all around. Rat spotted my can of automatic transmission fluid and rolled her eyes. "The man," she said, meaning me, "has become obsessed with collecting these little cans of automatic transmission fluid wherever we go. It's all because in Belgium we had us a little problem." She paused and caught their uncomprehending stares. "You had to be there. But now he's like one of those concentration camp survivors who are always buying food even when they've got an icebox full. You know?"

They nodded and I stared at Rat. *Icebox?* For some inexplicable reason, she was doing a world-class imitation of a Dallas Cowboys cheerleader. She pulled at my sleeve, dragging me toward the door.

"We're already late for sure. Y'all ever been to that place Louis XV in Monte Carlo?"

"You go there tonight?" the woman named Anne-Marie Vongas asked.

Rat and I nodded. "It's this thing we're doing," Rat said, starting to explain but then letting it drop.

"I can take you to a better restaurant tonight," she said.

"Yes?"

We both stopped, intrigued.

"Not a three-star, not even one. A no-star," she said, laughing. "But it is spectacular. I promise." She looked at us both with her direct, open gaze that was terrifically appealing. "You should come," she insisted, seeing us hesitating. "And it is much closer than Monte Carlo. That's too far for one day!"

"Why the hell not?" Rat said. "We're already lying to Carl."

"Who's Carl?" Anne-Marie asked.

"Her boyfriend," I said. Then after a pause added, "It's complicated."

"You can explain at dinner. I introduced Lucien, no?"


Le Verger was just over the hill from Ramatuelle, maybe thirty kilometers from Saint-Tropez—an old farmhouse surrounded by vineyards. Huge double doors opened to a terrace filled with flowers and about a dozen tables.

The proprietor was a woman somewhere in her forties or fifties; she had the stylishness of the French that masked her age well. She seemed to know Anne-Marie, but Anne-Marie was the sort who seemed to know everyone. It was a manner that reminded me of certain Southerners, without the sugary, over-the-top, incessantly cheerful quality that could make Southerners so annoying. The proprietor—I never caught her name—was harried and a bit rushed. At a three-star it might have seemed unprofessional, but here it didn't matter in the least. After all, she had a lot to do. It was more like being invited into someone's home; if they were busy seeing to other guests, so be it.

We sat at a table on the edge of the terrace, overlooking the vineyards. "My husband and I discovered here ten years ago," Anne-Marie said.

"Not Lucien," she said, laughing at our looks. "Lucien is the nephew of close friends. I have known him since he was just a little boy."

I nodded nonchalantly, or so I thought. I waited for her to elaborate, but she only smiled and picked up the menu. Lucien shrugged and looked ill at ease. I plunged ahead.

"What do you do, Lucien?" I asked. Under the table, Rat kicked me, as if I'd asked him how long he had been sleeping with his mom's best friend.

"I'm a student," he answered. "A student of political science."

Rat jumped in to tell him that I directed television commercials for politicians. He lit up and immediately began to ask me long, insightful questions about politics. What I really wanted to talk about, of course, was his relationship with Anne-Marie, but I stumbled on, as if we were having a little political seminar perched on the back hills of Grimaud.

The restaurant had a serving staff of just three, a relief after the fleet of waiters and back waiters of the three-star world. The senior fellow was perhaps forty, helped by someone who had to be his teenage son and a woman in her early twenties. The teenage son poured a bottle of Coteaux d'Aix-en-Provence and stood formally by the side, presenting the bottle as if at Tour d'Argent. Even if the wine had turned to vinegar, I wouldn't have had the heart to say a word.

I had a simple grilled fish, a *loup*, served with a sauce of olive oil, vinegar, and onions that was almost a warm salad-dressing concoction. The older waiter brought the *loup* to the table whole, then quickly filleted it, using the stone wall of the terrace as a sideboard.

Rat and Anne-Marie were talking about what people were wearing in Paris. The sun was setting behind the vineyards. Behind me, I could see into the kitchen. It was a crowded, hot space, no walk-in cold rooms or fancy stations bustling with *chefs de partie*. Inside, the chef was working with one assistant. I knew, without being told, that this was his restaurant and the woman out front scurrying to deal with her guests was his wife. He looked at me with a quizzical smile, wiping his hands on his apron, his chef's toque tilted at a jaunty angle.

I raised a glass in salute and, smiling, he plunked a glass from a crowded counter and joined me.

It was the Mustang's finest hour. We were driving to Monte Carlo along the Mediterranean, around Mount Boron jutting

into the sea, with Saint-Jean-Cap-Ferrat in the distance, through
the little villages of Villefranche and Beaulieu, past Eze, slipping
into Monaco at twilight. In the reflected light of the setting sun,
it was like driving through clouds of warm, shimmering gold.

The restaurant was in the Hôtel de Paris, facing the main
square of Monte Carlo. It was wonderfully overdone in Louis XV
style. Beige marble columns with gilded capitals reached past the
crystal chandeliers to the high ceiling. Cartouches with portraits
highlighted by lintels surrounded the room. Rococo paintings
of landscapes decorated with rose swags hung over the dozen or
so ornate tables; next to each chair was a little footstool for a
lady's handbag. A painting of Venus by Hyppolyte Lucas gazed
teasingly down on the room. Three massive doors opened up to
a terrace overlooking the main square, beige damask curtains
blowing in the breeze.

The total effect was fantastical and intoxicating. I found it
hard not to laugh at the grand silliness of it all. Fortunately, the
female maître d' seemed to understand. She had a smile and a
teasing look that said, *Yes, isn't this wonderful and ridiculous, but
let's playact for a night and have a spectacular time*.

Rat loved it from the moment we pulled up, the hotel and
casino lights just beginning to brighten against the darkening sky.
"It's just like the prom," she said happily, rising up to sit on the
edge of the seat and then jumping out of the Mustang without
opening the door, a feat that moved the valet parking squad to
break into applause.

"You went to the prom?" I asked. It was an image I could
not conjure.

"Honey, I went to a half dozen proms. I was the designated
prom date for most of Wyoming."

The waiters and captains all seemed refreshingly friendly—
never a bad thing, but here it was critical. The place was so over-
the-top grandiose that a chilly staff would have made it seem like
an insufferable museum. But the captains, waiters, and back

waiters seemed to appreciate that there was something magnifi-
cently absurd about this rococo extravaganza which was, after all,
*in Monte Carlo, in a casino, for crying out loud*! This was showbiz,
seen and be seen, Grace Kelly, paparazzi, *money, money, money*!
What in God's name did this have to do with food? Who came
to Monte Carlo *to eat*?

And who was more out of place in Monte Carlo than Alain
Ducasse, the man who'd brought fame and three stars to Louis
XV? This is a man who asserts to Bryan Miller of the *New York
Times* that the real gastronomic genius is Mother Nature and that
"more than half of my cuisine is the quality of the products."
*Mother Nature?* In Monte Carlo? Alain Ducasse, who is renowned
for his seriousness of purpose, was enhanced to a legendary status after he was the only survivor of a plane crash in 1984 that
killed four colleagues. "That changes your attitude about everything," he's said.

So, fresh from a near-death experience he comes *to Monte
Carlo* to find the meaning of life? But this is a man with ambition, confident that he could be taken seriously for his cuisine
wherever he worked, a chef who predicted that he would win
three stars for the Louis XV in four years and did it in under
three.

What did it feel like walking into the Louis XV? A celebra-
tion, actually. It was one of those unexpectedly delightful spec-
tacles that transformed an evening into something joyous, but
with none of the self-importance of a Big Night Out, which
haunts the restaurants of the world that beat their chests with
the Deadly Seriousness of the Special Occasion. Maybe it was
the beautiful drive along the sea, maybe it was the warm wind
blowing the curtains through the wall of double doors, or maybe
it was just that there was someone at work executing a vision who
realized a Spectacular Evening doesn't have to be spectacularly
stiff and boring.

"Olive oil is my butter," Ducasse has said, and the menu was laced with Mediterranean influences: *Un mélange de salades de Printemps, homard bleu et supions de Méditerranée assaisonnés de tapenade a l'huile d'olive Ardoino; Légumes et herbes des paysans de Provence en friture, tomate confite à l'huile d'olive et gros sel, mesclun d'ici; Daurade royale en pavé à la meunière, au goût mediterranéen, pommes de terre moelleuses et croustillantes.* There was a simple directness about the menu that was vastly appealing. Nowhere else had we seen a dish listed as *Les poissons de la pêche locale du jour cuits entiers comme on aime sur la Riviera, jus tranché à peine amer* ("A fish from the local fishery of the day cooked entirely as one likes it on the Riviera.")

The *amuse-gueule* course was simple and satisfying: basically just prosciutto wrapped around breadsticks. This was followed with tiny crawfish on sautéed eggplant served with sun-dried tomatoes, accompanied with lightly fried basil leaves and mozzarella. I followed with *Gros ravioli à la roquette et artichauts violets, du caillé de brebis "cassé" assaisonné de poivre de Java et gros sel*—arugula ravioli with crisp slices of deep-fried artichoke, all in a beef consommé. It had that difficult combination of tasting interesting and complex but not too cute.

Rat had *Légumes et herbes des paysans de Provence en friture, tomate confite à l'huile d'olive et gros sel, mesclun d'ici*, which was basically a lightly fried salad. Quite amazing. Fennel, zucchini flowers, basil leaves, a small eggplant, scallions, and mesclun. Underneath everything was a tomato coulis and on top was a delicate handkerchief of fried parmesan. Crisp, not a touch greasy, and tons of fun to eat. It reminded me of a drive-in movie in Jackson, Mississippi, where I grew up, that inexplicably served fried pickles. While trying to steal as much of Rat's dish as possible, I swore I would learn to cook it and have it every night back home, which, of course, I haven't. But I'm still hoping.

We followed with *Agneau de lait des Pyrénées cuit à la broche*, *jus à la sariette, gnocchi fondants et légumes sautés à cru, gratinés au suc de viande* and *Risotto à l'encre de seiche et supions de Mediterranée*. The lamb was my idea, and I regretted it right away. Not that it wasn't good—it's no surprise it was, but it was too easy, not interesting enough. I'd ordered under the chef's head. I started to explain this to Rat and she stared at me like I was crazy.

"You really are losing touch with all reality. Here you are sitting in this wonderful goddamn place complaining because your damn *Agneau de lait des Pyrénées* is *good?*"

"Yeah, but the risotto is better. This is probably the best risotto I've ever tasted. This is risotto to change your life!"

"Sick. No doubt about it. *Just think, what is happening to you?*"

"Okay, okay, I'm happy. I'm preposterously happy, okay? And appreciative. We're lucky. But I still wish I'd ordered another entrée. Hey, I'm a big boy. I can take life's crushing disappointments, don't get me wrong."

The risotto was rich and musky, and tasted like the ocean.

Rat dropped a napkin and, instantly, a smiling back waiter had replaced it with a fresh one. She beamed. "I could toss these all night," she said.

While the plates were being removed between courses, the single candle on the table was replaced with a fresh one and lit with a flourish. The waiter smiled and gave a hint of a shrug. *I know this is silly and you know it's silly but what the hell.*

As we left, the Mustang sat proudly in front of the hotel, surrounded by the hotel's valets. On the back seat was a bag with a half-eaten baguette left over from lunch. The senior valet, a wise-looking fellow in his late fifties, nodded and asked, "A good meal?"

"The baguette?" Rat said. "The baguette was terrific."

"To have a good meal here, that's to be expected," the valet said, "but to find a good baguette, that's not so easy."

I agreed and nibbled on the bread all the way back to Nice.

# Chapter
# Sixteen

Carl was waiting for us when we got to Florence.

Or rather, he was waiting for Rat, I suppose.

I'd met him before, but my memory was vague—a biggish guy, black hair swept back, telling jokes at a party in New York. I think he wore suspenders, but this was a few years ago when everyone wore suspenders, or at least everyone who traveled in Carl's circles.

But once I was sitting across from him at the L'Enoteca Pinchiorri in Florence, he was a vivid figure: six foot two, with a face that looked to be part Italian and part American Indian. It was a dramatic face, set off by black eyes and eyebrows and a slightly crushed nose. He was still wearing his hair straight back. I couldn't imagine waking up every morning and slicking back my hair in that style.

Maybe because Rat talked about him in such gray terms —a New York lawyer, you know—I was surprised at what a striking figure he cut. He was wearing jeans and a black double-breasted blazer over a black polo shirt. But it all made sense, seeing them together. It was hard to imagine Rat falling for a gray lawyer.

And she had fallen for him, at least a little. That was obvious by the way she acted when she first saw him.

He was sitting at a café just off Piazza della Repubblica. Rat was heading out to the English bookstore on the Via Tornabuoni

and I was going running in the Cascine park. I had been reading Eric Newby's *Love and War in the Apennines*, the wonderful
story of his capture and escape from an Italian prisoner of war
camp and the beginnings of his lifelong love affair both with Italy
and his wife, Wanda, whose family hid him from the Germans
while he was an escapee.

Newby, who was surely one of the few British commandos
with a background in the women's fashion business, describes
the difficulties of evading detection in Italy if you were lucky
enough to escape. "The Italians are fascinated by minutiae of dress
and the behavior of their fellow men, perhaps to a greater de-
gree than any other race in Europe, and the ingenious subter-
fuges and disguises which escaping prisoners of war habitually
resorted to and which were often enough to take in the Germans
. . . the suits made from dyed blankets; the desert boots cut down
to look like shoes and the carefully bleached army shirts were
hardly ever sufficiently genuine looking to fool even the most
myopic Italian ticket collector and get the owner past the bar-
rier, let alone survive the scrutiny of the occupants of a compartment on an Italian train."

I was thinking about this watching the Italians watch each
other and the throngs of tourists wandering across Piazza della
Repubblica. It had rained the night before and the air had a fresh-
ness that felt like September, not July. Then Rat screamed—the
first time I'd ever heard her do this—and everyone stopped and
stared, mostly at me, as if it were obvious that I had just stabbed
Rat. Or something.

Carl stood up and waved while Rat ran across the square
and jumped into his arms. It all had the look of some kind of
commercial, probably a shampoo commercial, what with Rat's
hair bouncing around and Carl's super-slicked look. A few
people standing around applauded. Rat seems to have this knack
of getting people to applaud her.

"How you doing, big guy," he said to me, offering his hand and a crooked smile. He was the kind of fellow who called everybody "big guy" and made it seem perfectly natural. He'd been doing it all his life, I suppose.

"Hey, you know what I think we ought to do?" he said. "I think we ought to go get something to eat."


I left them alone and found the Cascine park for a run. On this cool Sunday morning, the park felt like fifty years ago. It was crowded with people *strolling*—not rollerblading or running or any aerobic madness. Just *strolling* and they were dressed up! Suits, fancy dresses, the clothes they wore to church. A few wore old-fashioned Adidas running suits of the sort Russian athletes are fond of, but there was precious little spandex and hardly a microfiber to be found.

Vespas darted about, with girls riding sidesaddle, clinging to their boyfriends. Long lines wound in front of the gelato stands. A club team of bicycle riders leaned against their Campignola Bianchi bikes watching the pretty young girls in tight dresses parade through the greenery. Everyone tried to stay in the shade and everyone smoked.

The park was decidedly *untidy*, very un-French. It felt wild and decrepit, as if almost abandoned. There were no neat rows of potted flowers, no intricate flowerbeds or well-kept fountains. Newspapers blew across the cracked asphalt walkways.

An outer loop ringed the park, exposed to the bright sunshine. I ran it in complete isolation, passing only an occasional cyclist. When I turned back into the heart of the park to the green tunnels, dazed by the sun, it was like stumbling onto a hidden world teeming with life. Everyone stared at me as I ran past, dripping wet.

\* \* \*

It wasn't right from the beginning. The wine steward hovered over me with the first truly condescending look I'd seen since the three-star odyssey began. "We don't serve beer," he said rather proudly, which was silly, of course. You can get beer at L'Ambroisie, why not at L'Enoteca Pinchiorri? The earlier coolness of the day was fading into rising humidity. I'd run eight miles and hurried across Florence to L'Enoteca, and all I wanted was a nice Italian beer.

But I wouldn't really have minded if the wine steward had let it drop with "We don't serve beer." But then he followed with "Or Coca-Cola, either. *Vino* or *aqua* only."

Rat rolled her eyes. Then this unfortunate Canadian woman who apparently served as some sort of assistant hostess stepped in and began to lecture us—there was really no other word for it—about how Italians drink only wine with dinner. I knew she was Canadian because when I said something innocuous, or so I thought, about her being an American, I was sternly corrected. She was an attractive woman in her twenties who *looked* Italian, a fact about which I suspected she was inordinately proud.

All of this was unfortunate, particularly given that there was a truly charming proprietress-chef in residence. L'Enoteca Pinchiorri was the only three-star restaurant with a female chef, Annie Feolde, a large ebullient Frenchwoman married to an Italian. We'd met briefly when, wandering around looking for a bathroom, I'd literally bumped into her. She was a smiling woman with a shock of gray in her red hair and a pink face who reminded me of Bill Clinton's mother: funny, no-nonsense, and a terror if crossed.

Walking through the restaurant, Annie Feolde dominated the space, leaving a wake of intimidated staff wherever she moved. Some sixth instinct of successful restaurateurship must have drawn her to our table just as we were about to fillet the Canadian woman. She urged us to try the Tuscan menu or the

pigeon. To Carl she said, "You would enjoy the pigeon. I promise," and then she moved her considerable force over to the next
table, a young English couple on a first date. He was nervous and
had not stopped smoking since sitting down. She was long and
lithe in a sheath dress.

Rat frowned. "You *do* like pigeon. How'd she know?"

"Gutsy woman," Carl said. "I like her."

The wine steward was annoying, the Canadian woman a
problem, but the menu was a dream. Its combination of French
and Italian was irresistible. There were maybe one or two dishes
I didn't want to eat that very minute.

I scribbled down my favorites, and reading over them, a
hunger washes over me that is like a lovesick longing: thinly
sliced rack of lamb filled with pepperoni, lobster and barley salad,
sea bass topped with a salt-crumb, little potato tarts, red mullet
fillets with red wine sauce, big shrimp and chicory on the grill
served with rosemary-breaded marrow, whole wheat tagliatelle
with frogs legs and rucola, porcini mushroom consommé, pigeon
and lobster tortellini . . .

That was just from the à la carte menu. There was also the
Tuscan menu, eight courses:

> *Coccoli col pesto toscano* (deep-fried pasta with basil, pine
> nuts, and anchovies)
>
> *Triglie in bianco e frittura d'erbe* (red mullet fillets flavored
> with lemon and garlic)
>
> *Gamberoni allo spiedo e passato di gran farro* (big shrimps
> wrapped into pancetta slices and served with bean and
> pearl-barley cream)
>
> *Bavette al ragno* (homemade fettuccine, with sea bass, to-
> mato, and hot pepper)
>
> *Tortelli di Altopascio* (ricotta and spinach tortelli, with
> pecorino and cinnamon)

*Faraona in tegame* (guinea fowl, vegetable, and potato stew)
*Tortino di riso allo zafferano, salsa Morellino* (rice and saffron tart, tuscan sweet wine sauce)
*Biscotti di Prato e piccola pasticceria*

The Tuscan menu seemed like far too much, too many courses, too many tastes. So, naturally, I ordered it. I had to.

The shrimp wrapped in pancetta was one of the best things I'd ever put into my mouth, smoky and delicate. And the red mullet fillets with lemon and garlic were stupendous. But Lord, think about it: you started with deep-fried pasta, moved on to fettuccine, then ricotta and spinach tortelli . . . this is serious stuff. As someone who has always been able to muster a passionate appetite, I never thought I'd falter, but by the time the guinea fowl rolled around, I was in deep, deep trouble.

The Tuscan stew of guinea fowl tasted salty, but I wondered if it was me. Was I losing it? I reached over for some of Rat's John Dory, which was served with a parsley sauce between the Italian soda crackers they call *sfoglio*. It was light and smooth and made me feel there was hope. Maybe it wasn't just me but the concept of serving eight courses of regional Tuscan cooking. God knows the Tuscans were not inclined to sit down to eight courses of their regional greatest hits.

"Florentine cooking begins with careful attention to the selection of raw materials of the highest quality," wrote Waverly Root in *The Food of Italy*, "and continues by cooking them with a minimum of sauces and seasonings. It is spare home cooking, hearty and healthy, subtle in its deliberate eschewing of sophistication, which is perhaps the highest sophistication of all."

Later, when the restaurant was clearing out, Annie Feolde wandered by and sat at our table. Sitting in the open courtyard on a clear night, we were in no hurry to leave. She immediately began to tease us about not drinking enough wine. Her husband,

Giorgio Pinchiorri, ran the wine cellar, and he took it very personally.

"We started as a wine bar, you know," she said. "Back in 1973. I wanted the food to be more Italian, he wanted French," she laughed. "We could never get the right ingredients then to cook true French. Now it's easier, but why have just a French restaurant in the middle of Tuscany? It makes no sense."

Her husband joined us, thin and handsome in an elegant suit, full of nervous energy. She looked like a woman who worked twelve hours a day; he resembled a creature of nightclubs, the kind of guy you saw closing down Au Bar in New York or sitting at Le Dôme in Paris with a handful of models at 4:00 A.M.

"Everything comes from Florence," he said with understated pride, gesturing out at the table. "The silverware, the tablecloth. And in the cellar, we have a hundred and fifty thousand bottles." A deep sadness came over his face as he talked about a fire they'd had in the wine cellar, costing them thousands of bottles. "The little window in the cellar, they tossed a bottle with gas."

Who was "they"? I asked.

He shrugged and looked at his wife. She was pained, as if discussing the death of a loved one. "Maybe someone who worked here once." He paused. "Maybe not."

He brightened when he talked about the restaurant they had just opened in Tokyo. "It's the same as here," he said, "everything there comes from Florence. It is like you are stepping inside Tuscany. We shipped over thirty thousand bottles of wine."

"The Japanese love this cooking," Annie Feolde said. "More than the Tuscans," she laughed. "Tuscans, they don't want to come to a fancy restaurant and pay lots of money and eat Tuscan food. They want French food. Tuscan food is what Grandmother makes."

"But they can drink great wine here. Tuscan wine. French wine. Whatever they want."

"You still want us to have just a wine bar," she teased.

"A great wine bar. The best wine bar in Italy."

They were an impossible pair not to like. And I loved the *idea* of what they were trying to do, combining her classical French skills with Tuscan ingredients. But I couldn't shake the feeling that the L'Enoteca was trying too hard. The waiters in tuxes stiffly serving Tuscan stew? The menu "digestuin" serving fettuccini? No beer? Or Coca-Cola?

But of course it was really my fault. To depend on the French Michelin establishment to choose the great restaurants of Italy was as ridiculous as turning to Italians to select French greatness. The Michelin Gods would like that there was a French chef and they would like the stunning Renaissance house, the formal service, the commitment to an eight-course menu, the extraordinary cellar.

But was it a Great Italian Restaurant? I thought about this the next morning when we were having an early lunch at Dino's. Ignored by Michelin, of course, Dino's is hailed by *Le Guide de l'Espresso*, the Italian equivalent to Gault-Millau guides, as "a glorious old Florentine restaurant," and I remembered it from my first trip to Florence as a teenager, when I'd been dazzled equally by the beautiful waitress, to whom I was ready to propose, and the food, which was easily the best meal I'd had in my eighteen years.

Each time I'd returned over the years, it had never disappointed. There was a comforting consistency of ritual to walking into the hushed room with its vaulted ceiling and seeing the crisp white tablecloths and the Renza family, Dino and his wife and their son, Massimo. There was never an effort to impress, only to please.

The classic Tuscan dishes appeared: *crostini misti*, made with porcini, liver, or tomato, served on fat slices of *pane toscano*, the saltless loaves baked in wood-fired ovens with a characteristic thick crust and a beige heart laced with irregular holes.

Then the *risotto del Renza,* selected from Dino's "Ancient Tuscan" menu. I had been reading Burton Anderson's *Treasures of the Italian Table,* in which he writes about the complexities of Italian rice. "Among 120,000 known varieties of rice, Italy grows about fifty. They are grouped in four categories according to size, ranging from the small *commune* or *orginario* to *semifino, fino,* and *superfino.* Among the superfino, which is generally best suited to risotto, Arborio is popular, but specialists often prefer Carnaroli from paddies around Vercelli in Piedmont."

When researching the book, Anderson was astonished to learn that rice has vintage years like wine and "that certain growing areas produce superior quality and could be considered *crus.*" This had a particular resonance for Anderson, as the author of the definitive books on Italian wines, *The Wine Atlas of Italy* and *Vino: The Wines and Winemakers of Italy.* Years earlier, when renting a house in Italy, I'd discovered that Anderson lived just up the valley. He was a big, handsome guy with the most unlikely story.

He'd moved to Paris from the Midwest and, as I later heard from a mutual journalist friend, had done a stint at the *International Herald Tribune,* which was mainly an excuse to learn everything he could about wine. Somehow Burton had hit upon what was truly a nutty idea: he would move to Italy and make great wine *by importing Concord grapes to Italy.*

It was the kind of brainstorm you have late at night over a bottle of Côtes du Rhône, and when the sun comes up the next day, you quickly realize it was sheer madness. But Burton Anderson had been seized by a vision, struck blind on the road to Tuscany, and there was no turning back. By the late 1970s, he'd actually moved his family to a little vineyard outside Cortona, Italy, and succeeded, as he put it to me the first time we met, "in making some of the worst wine you ever tasted in your life. Total failure," he said with his nonchalant, very American grin.

Total failure except that in learning exactly why the Italian wine industry had not been hopelessly thwarted through an absence of Concord grapes, Anderson learned an immense amount about Italian wines, probably more than any American. His articles and first book, *Vino*, had a tremendous influence in dispelling the image of Italian wines as cheap stuff with a screw top. He appreciated Italian wines with an infectious love that has spread to all things gustatory and Italian.

In *Treasures of the Italian Table*, his latest book, Anderson tracked down the creators of the quintessential elements of Italian food, the best bread, pasta, olive oil, pizza napoletana, the white truffles of Alba. And the beef slaughtered to make the classic *bistecca alla fiorentina*, the "statuesque white cattle whose ancestry has been traced back to pre-Roman times when the Etruscans raised them in the Chianti Valley of eastern Tuscany."

I was at Dino's, looking forward to eating one of those Etruscan-raised cows. Or at least a close relative. "Florentine butchers," Anderson writes, "whose cutting methods differ from others, slice and chop the steaks from a triangular rack extending along the loin, or *lombo*, and rib cage, or *costa*. One end renders a *lombata*, a type of T-bone with the fillet, the other a *costa*, or rib steak. Either cut may be called *bistecca*."

Dino presented it *molto al sangue*, almost raw in the center, with rosemary and sage along the edges. It was simple and wildly satisfying, cooked quickly over coals to sear the exterior in a crust and doused with salt, black pepper, and a touch of olive oil.

Rat had ordered grilled porcini and they arrived thicker than the *bistecca*, emblazoned with heavy grill stripes. Her eyes gleamed. Carl, who I was beginning to like, had taken the sensible precaution of ordering *both* the *bistecca* and the porcini. This left Rat and me to fight over each other's plates. But for once we reached a quick, amiable solution; a fifty-fifty split was only sensible. Both dishes were so good, it was inconceivable not to indulge in each.

It was a simple, almost primal meal, not laden with artifice. It was not about showing how great the chef was but how good the food could be. While every French chef was quick to highlight the importance of the ingredients, here there was no question. The *bistecca* was nothing more than a piece of superb meat thrown on a grill, and the same for the porcini. Had the steak been tough, the meat unflavorful, the porcini dry and tasteless, the meal would have been a disaster. There was no complicated sauce to redeem it, no visual distraction of a stunning presentation. It was a gutsy performance from a chef who believed in his food.

I'd spent the morning at Florence's main markets, engulfed in the ingredients on which Dino has based his life. The Mercato Centrale was the hub of every kitchen in Florence, restaurant or private. An extraordinary, huge structure, it resembled one of the great train stations of Europe, a vast open space under a translucent roof of frosted glass supported by an elaborate superstructure of girders. Pigeons cruised through the upper levels. At first glance it gave the impression of an utterly chaotic jumble of vendors selling every imaginable element of Italian gustatory life, but there was an underlying order, like any American supermarket.

Fruits and vegetables of all kinds were upstairs, while the ground floor had sections dedicated to fish, meat, and cheeses. Prices everywhere seemed similar, with the competition driven by selection and quality and the varying charms of the individual vendors.

Upstairs the Banco Gianni sign advertised *erbe aromatiche—radici—lattughini—radicchio*. For lettuce, Banco offered *ricciolina, foglia di Quercia, rucola, o ruchetta* and a mixture called simply *le insalatine di Gianni*. There were *favolui*, *Fiorentino*, *San Marzana*, and *nostrali* varieties of tomatoes. He had beautiful *carciofina minutina*, the little artichokes that Rome went crazy over every spring, serving them *carciofi alla giudia*, fried whole and incredibly delicious. His herbs included *erba cipollina*, *finocchio*, *salvia*, *timo*, *origano*, *basilico*, and *erbe aromatiche costano*.

A few feet away, huge Plexiglas tubes held different varieties of porcini. *Porcini casalingi* sold for 10,000 lire per 100 grams, *porcini seccati al sole* for 17,000, simple porcini at 22,000, and the extra-large porcini for 25,000 lire.

Next to a butcher offering massive cows heads that looked fresh that morning, still dripping blood, a poster of a topless girl was on the wall with "*Impariamo ad amare la carne*" ("Learn to love meat") under it in bold block letters. The fish stands were massive, with everything from tiny fresh sardines to wicked ugly dogfish with gaping mouths of little sharp teeth.

I thought about what Waverly Root and Richard de Rochemont had written in their 1976 book *Eating in America*. "Unfortunately, ideally fresh or nutritious food is not readily available, even at a price, in most small American communities. Only banal prepared and semi-prepared food is generally at hand." Personally, I don't mind coming down on the side that the last twenty years have seen an improvement in the available food, contrary to most predicted trends. Chalk it up to the yuppie gentrification of the world, but the simple truth is that it's not uncommon these days to find all kinds of things in a chain grocery store in, say, Jackson, Mississippi, that would have been impossible to find a dozen years ago: cilantro, plantains, arugula, basmati rice, tandoori paste, fresh basil. All those little talismans of yuppie life are now haunting the shelves of America.

But there's no escaping that there's something decidedly intimidating and even frightening to Americans at large about the concept of *undomesticated food, food in the raw*. It's the same old "I won't eat it unless it's wrapped in plastic phenomenon" that A. J. Liebling observed:

> The reason that people who detest fish often tolerate sole is that sole doesn't taste very much like fish, and even this degree of resemblance disappears when it is submerged in the kind of sauce that patrons of Piedmontese restaurants in London and New York think characteristically French. People with the same apathy toward decided flavor relish "South African Lobster" tails—frozen as long as the Siberian Mammoth—because they don't taste lobstery. . . . They prefer processed cheese because it isn't cheesy, and synthetic vanilla extract because it isn't vanillary. They have made a triumph of the Delicious apple because it doesn't taste like an apple, and of the Golden Delicious because it doesn't taste like anything.

I had Liebling on my mind as I was drinking a double espresso and staring at a fresh load of tripe being artfully displayed in the meat case of Oreste Carroccis's handsome stall when Carl appeared out of nowhere, a beer in hand.

"Cheap," he said, nodding toward the tripe as the elderly man in a white smock and white peaked cap put out a notice reading *Trippa nostrale 7,000 kg.* "Only seven thousand lire a kilo. That's a hell of a deal."

"We could get a bunch for Henry," I suggested.

"Too good for that dog." Carl was still getting adjusted to the reality of Henry's constant presence and the affection showered on him by Rat. "Used to eat a lot of that stuff in Vietnam, you know," he said. "Developed a real taste for it."

"They served tripe to troops in Nam?" I asked. This was unimaginable.

Carl laughed. "That was all burgers and dogs or that field crap. I was SOG—Special Operations Group. We were the black-arts guys. In country, no uniforms, Laos, Cambodia. Worked with Nungs myself. Toughest little guys you ever saw. Loved pig tripe. Big feast for 'em."

"How long were you over there?" It seemed to be an odd turn of conversation, to be discussing Vietnam at 9:00 A.M. in the Mercato Centrale in Florence.

"Eight months, then got sick as a dog and sent home. Wanted to re-up but it didn't work out."

I nodded, unsure of quite what to say.

"Got to tell you, man, I loved it. Nasty, nasty but I loved it."

"What did you do?" It was a stupid question.

"Jumped out of helicopters and shot a lot of people. Great time."

"Sure," I said.

"Look," he said, turning serious and taking a big gulp of his Moretti beer. "I've got to talk to you about Rat."

"Rat," I said calmly, thinking, *Oh, this is great. First this guy tells me how much he liked jumping out of helicopters and killing people and now he wants to talk about his girlfriend, who I just happen to have been traveling with for the last month.*

Carl put his hand on my shoulder and looked me hard in the eyes. He was a big, impressive guy. "What's your honest-to-God take on Rat?"

"Rat?" I repeated bravely. I thought for a fleeting moment about denying knowing Rat, but that did seem a bit preposterous. I wasn't sure how smart Carl was, but I knew he wasn't *that* dumb.

"Do you think she hates me?" he asked.

He had a sudden look of vulnerability that made him resemble a scolded puppy.

"No," I answered. "That's ridiculous." Which was true.

"But she thinks I'm stupid."

This was a tougher call. "Not stupid," I answered. "I wouldn't say that."

"But close. I know. You know why she thinks I'm stupid? Because I make a lot of money. She still has this whole hippy-dippy Wyoming thing about guys in New York who make a lot of money."

"That sounds right to me," I said.

Carl slapped himself on the forehead and wheeled around, a startling gesture from a man this large. "See!" he shouted. "I told you!"

"But that doesn't mean she doesn't love you," I said.

He nursed his beer and thought about this. "She thinks I drink too much," he said.

"Do you?" I asked. It seemed a reasonable question.

"How much is too much?"

I nodded toward the beer he was drinking.

"Aw," he said sheepishly, "I'm on vacation." Then he brightened up. "Where are we going to eat next?"


"'The short trip from Milan to the little town of Cassinetta di Lugagnano is enchanting,'" Rat read aloud over the roar of the Mustang and the tearing wind. "'You'll travel along the Naviglio Grande (Great Canal) both in town (where it runs through the neighborhoods where it has preserved its ancient characteristics) and outside, going through toward the beautiful green Milanese countryside with its melancholy winter mists.'"

"Bullshit," Carl said matter-of-factly. "You're making that up."

"Melancholy winter mists? I could make up a line like that?" Rat asked, turning to face Carl, who was scrunched into the back seat with Henry. Neither one was looking very happy.

Rat was reading from *Le Guide de l'Espresso*, which I thought was a terrific book. But the "enchanting" Cassinetta we were seeing looked more like Eastern Europe on a bad day. The sky was gray and trying to spit rain. Tall apartment blocks in the Nuovo Romanian tradition dotted the road, interspersed with depressed and depressing hotel-bar-restaurants like Le Chat Noir.

"I don't think I'd have to think very hard to come up with a better name for a hotel than the Black Cat," Carl said.

I was beginning to like Carl.

"Dead Trucker's Nightmare, that's an improvement. Or how about the Dead Drop Inn?"

We passed a sudden stretch of cornfields, looking as forlorn as everything surrounding it that was man-made, then the ill-named Fiesta del Sol garden center and a combination camping and statuary store. Buy a tent and statue of Venus for the lawn.

"Hey, you know what this looks like?" Carl asked.

"Romania," I said.

"Queens. Like the part of Queens where I go to get my Harley repaired."

We were in front of the restaurant without realizing it: a simple house with a red tiled roof, next to a bridge. It looked like the kind of place that neighbors would stroll into for a special night out, a Friday, end-of-week pleasure. A local place, not a Food Palace.

"Thank God," I mumbled as we crawled out of the Mustang.

"What?" Rat asked, leaning over to give Henry a very wet kiss.

"Jesus, Rat," Carl said. "There's bound to be a law against having sex with animals in public."

"Look at this place," I said.

We all took a step back and stared up at the yellow stucco walls of the two-story house.

"Yeees?" Rat asked.

"It's small. It's simple. It actually looks Italian."

Carl looked around. "Lots of things look Italian around here, bro. Funny about that."

"I am willing to bet dinner that there will be no footstools for purses—"

"I'm leaving," Carl said.

"And if you drop your napkin, you might actually have to pick it up yourself."

"I'm out of here," Rat said.

We started to walk up the stone steps.

"What about the dog?" Carl asked. "We just leave him?"

"Sure," Rat said. "He's a dog. He'll be fine."

"What if—"

"Somebody kidnaps him?"

"I don't know . . ." Carl looked genuinely pained. Rat slid up next to him and gave him a kiss.

"You really are very cute," she said.

Seeing Rat like this was very odd, like meeting an entirely different person. She actually seemed to be in love, a state that I had never associated with Rat in the least. All in all, it was very charming.


Carl grabbed him. We had just finished what was truly a perfect meal and Ezio Santin, the Antica Osteria chef-proprietor, was standing near the entrance to the kitchen reading sheets of typewritten pages. It might have been brilliant recipes to try; it could have been an order of next week's supplies. He was an unimposing man with none of the flamboyance of a celebrity chef. He had a kind, approachable face that would have looked at home behind the counter of any small grocery in Italy.

Concentrating on his papers, the chef literally jumped when Carl pounded him on the back.

"That was fabulous. Unbelievable."

He brightened when he realized this very large American was not going to pummel him but actually was trying to express gratitude. He was a shy man who seemed truly modest.

"You enjoyed, yes?" He asked. "And what did—"

"All-porcini dinner."

The chef laughed. "Yes? This wasn't too much?"

"Too much? Are you crazy? I started with the *Scamponi con patate e porcini,* then the *Filetto di sogliola* with porcini, and then we split"—he nodded toward Rat—"the *Costa di vitello in salsa* with porcini."

I was impressed. Carl had rattled off the names without notes.

"You've got to understand," Carl continued, looking right at the chef with eyes that seemed just a touch mad with intensity, "I eat out every night of my life in New York."

"Out? What—"

"In restaurants. Every night. Six out of seven. It's business, but I'm addicted too, okay? But this was something."

The chef's wife, who ran the front of the house, came by and stood, protectively, I thought, by her husband. Carl's presence was a bit overwhelming.

"Hey, can we talk?" Carl asked. "Just for a few minutes. You got to tell us more."

And so we ended up sitting in the Antica Osteria's lobby-anteroom, which felt like a comfortable living room, talking about Ezio Santin's view of the world.

Somehow, immediately, we were talking about olive oil. He was adamant about using only one local producer. "It is *everything,*" he insisted. "The quality must be there or we are . . ." He struggled for a gesture.

"Dead," Rat said.

The chef laughed and almost blushed at the same time. He

buys three grades of oil from his producer, he explained, graded by the elevation where the olives are grown. The high trees produce the most flavorful, best oil, which he uses for salads and dishes where he wants the olive taste. The oil from the lower elevations he used for *frittura*, the deep-fried dishes.

Though his training was classically French—he had worked for Madame Point at Lyons's La Pyramide, which for years had served the same purpose for French cooking that West Point does for the American military, both training ground and accreditation—he was immediately drawn to nouvelle cuisine. "It was more like Italian," he told us.

This seemed odd. *Nouvelle?* Olive oil?

Of course, he told us. In Italy we were never afraid of the taste of food. We liked simpler food that brought out the flavors, he explained, and that is so much what the nouvelle movement started. Look at the menu; it was all simple food, he insisted, which made us laugh. No, it is true, he said and asked his wife to bring a menu from the evening's dinner.

It was two plain pages with no more than two dozen items. Like a kindly professor, Ezio Santin read off a few dishes:

*Gamberoni marinati al caviale e verdure alla greca*
*Tortino di funghi porcini alle noci*
*Scamponi con patate e porcini*
*Scaloppa di branzino arrostita con pomodorini al forno*
*Filetto di sogliola alle erbe e funghi porcini*
*Scaloppa di tonno fresco, cipollotto novello e erba ruta*
*Rognoncino di vitello cotto intero in salsa alla diavola*

He paused and looked up. Have we been to Venice? He smiled broadly, with a certain wistful look to his eyes. It's his favorite Italian cuisine, he said, the only one that really has a tradition of using spices as well as herbs. It all goes back to the

days of the doges, the great trading days of Venice, when Eastern spices were introduced to the cuisine.

*Foie gras fresco di oca al pepe di Setchuan*

He stopped again and told us that he was fascinated by
Asian cooking. Not the spices or the tastes so much but the
approach to food, the love of vegetables, the quick cooking
methods, the lack of sauces, the presentations.

Rat asked him when he was going to open a restaurant in
Japan.

His wife laughed and shook her head. It appeared to be
something they've discussed before. He's taught seminars there,
he explained, but a restaurant . . . ? He'll leave that to Bocuse.

Was he jealous of Bocuse? I asked, in a half-teasing way.

He laughed. "There is room for only one Bocuse," he declared. "And one is quite enough, don't you think?"

# Chapter
# Seventeen

I woke up the next morning feeling blessed. There had been something wonderfully calming and satisfying about the entire evening at the Antica Osteria del Porte, more like dinner in someone's home than a commercial transaction.

Without thinking about it a lot, I'd assumed that Rat would leave with Carl and that the Big Eat, as I had come to think of this whole adventure in excess, would come to an end. Now that Carl had appeared, there was no reason to continue this crazy pretense, which I'd never really believed, that he was going to pay for everything if we just ate on consecutive days. With a wistful kind of regret, I made a list of the restaurants that we would miss: Pic, Pierre Gagnaire, Paul Bocuse, Georges Blanc, Lameloise, Troisgros, Boyer "Les Crayeres," La Côte Saint Jacques, L'Espérance, Le Côte d'Or.

I read the scribbled list to Rat and Carl when they came down for breakfast. We were staying in a small, modern hotel that seemed to be full of stylishly dressed salesmen. I immediately assumed they were connected to the fashion industry of Milan but later discovered that they worked for a large automobile-parts chain.

Rat and Carl groaned in unison—which was surprisingly cute—as each restaurant name rolled off the list.

"Did you practice this?" I asked. "This groaning stuff."

"Our souls are enjoying a harmonic convergence," Carl said. I stared at him. *Harmonic convergence?*

"A harmonic gustatory convergence," Rat repeated, and they both started laughing.

"That's the galaxy," Carl said.

"Galaxy?" I asked, thinking clearly these two were losing their minds. "Can we start chanting here in a minute?"

"The stars," Carl insisted.

"Right," I said.

"Bocuse, Pic, Troisgros, that new guy Gagnaire. Those are the heavyweights."

"No question."

"Georges Blanc. Bernard Loiseau," Rat added.

We sat in silence for a little while, watching the salesmen table-hop, as if at the Four Seasons. A power breakfast enacted here on the bleak outskirts of Milan in a Holiday Inn–styled breakfast room.

"We have to do it," Rat finally declared. "It'll only take twelve days, and we'll remember it the rest of our lives."

Carl looked at me and I shrugged.

"Like Gary Gilmore said," Carl announced. "Let's do it."


Later, of course, we argued about what was the greatest moment of the next crazed twelve days. Rat loved the anti-chic of Pic, its solid feel, and the earnest charm of the young brother and sister who were striving to carry on the greatness of their father after his death.

Carl, who Rat accused of having a chicken fetish, could have spent months at Georges Blanc, eating his way through the menu of Bresse chickens. He liked Blanc's cocky showmanship, the helicopter pad, and the topless women by the pool, all set in a simple village. Georges Blanc had created a character called Georges Blanc, and there was something about this self-invention that Carl immensely enjoyed.

For me, it was simple. In the unlikely, very unspectacular, solidly working-class town of Saint-Étienne, we encountered a chef I wouldn't hesitate to call a genius: Pierre Gagnaire.

"The problem with this guy Gagnaire," Rat said, "is he wants you to think he's a genius. It's too New York for me. Too downtown."

She said this as if she hadn't been living at the heart of the downtown New York scene for the last five years and giving a very good imitation of liking it a great deal. But she was right. Gagnaire *did* want you to believe he was a genius. He had all the makings of a splendid caricature: self-centered, self-aggrandizing, a decided tendency to manufacture myth about himself, an over-dramatic quality . . . well, the list wasn't a short one.

But none of that mattered, not in any kind of important way, if you believed the man had a vision and was obsessed with executing it. And, of course, if he did it with an inventive talent that was overwhelming. All of which, for my money, he did. Call me a sucker for the entire Pierre Gagnaire Act. I bought it all.


It was late in the afternoon and hot. I was driving, Carl was in the front seat, Rat in the rear with Henry. Carl was telling me about the time his Special Forces camp had been overrun in Vietnam.

"I was lying stark naked in a pool of sweat."

"That's a good opening," Rat said from the back seat. "Very lurid."

"Then I hear this *whomp, whomp* of mortars going off. I'm half asleep and I'm thinking, 'Please, God, let that be some nervous kid shooting at shadows. Some kid *inside our wire shooting out of the wire.* I am too tired to move.' But then these suckers start landing all around us. *Ka-boom! Ka-boom!* Everybody starts shooting—*pow, pow, pow*—and all I want to do is go to sleep.

"I hear this light thump and look over my shoulder and this satchel charge comes hurtling through the tent door. I wrap that mattress around me like a big baby and *boom*, I'm hurtling through the air."

Carl was laughing and slapping the side of the Mustang. We crested a rise and Saint-Étienne was before us in all its glory, an industrial town sprinkled over hills.

"What's that?" Rat asked, pointing to a massive mound of broken earth.

"Slag heap," Carl said. "You know what this looks like? Western Pennsylvania." There was a comfortable tiredness to the town. It didn't seem like a place hurrying anywhere or trying to impress. Just an overgrown small town where people used to make things with steel and mostly don't anymore.

In this gray town that the Blue Guide called "important but unattractive," Pierre Gagnaire had created a Technicolor fantasy. It really was a preposterous notion: taking an abandoned pharmacy, gutting it, and erecting not a restaurant so much as an art gallery or an *art space*, as they said downtown, where Rat lived, that served food.

"*Fête, fête, fête*," Gagnaire told us the next morning, after we'd talked him into showing us around his creation. "This town needs *fête* to breath!" He was a lopsided, oversized fellow with an uncanny resemblance to Gérard Depardieu. With a quizzical, half-mad look to his eyes, he radiated an aura of impetuous restlessness. He was the kinetic, brilliant kid who never did well on tests but who the teachers always thought would end up either in jail or doing something very unusual.

He'd avoided jail and brought three-star celebrity status to his hometown, a feat no less remarkable then, say, Tunisia winning a gold medal in Olympic skiing. No one came to Saint-Étienne to eat. Indeed, no one in Saint-Étienne *ate*, as far as the rest of France was concerned. Maybe they consumed food, but *eat?* And now the Gods of Michelin were telling us that one of the best restaurants *in the world* was just a few miles down from the slag heaps in the old pharmacy?

It started with the building itself: a contemporary fantasy housed within a solid town house shouting bourgeois stability.

"The structure is like the plate: a bare surface on which to create. The food must look like the surroundings for the total experience," Gagnaire insisted. "That is why we have white walls and we have white plates."

Let's face it, this really does sound like a bunch of foodie babble at its worse, but I am here to tell you that Gagnaire, like that rare person who can actually wear a cape and not look ridiculous, pulled it off. From the moment you walked inside the restaurant, Gagnaire was trying to deliver a message, telling you to put aside normal expectations and keep an open mind for a different sort of experience. Gagnaire versus a traditional restaurant was like the difference between experimental theater and classic drama. And just as experimental theater troupes gravitate toward unconventional spaces, Gagnaire had erected an environment that reflected what he was trying to do in the kitchen and on the plate.

The menu read like no other three-star's: *Le queue de homard poêlée aux gnocchis, infusion de thym citron au jus de pomme poivre, quelques cèpes d'été* or *Langoustines Bretonnes, dorade marbrée et céteaux Madeleine en Tempura, feuilles de choux "coeur de boeuf" craquantes, chutney de petits patissons à la badiane;* or how about *Marinade de tous petits encornets aux gousses d'ail nouvelles, poitrine de veau de lait confite à la mélisse citronnelle, en terrine?*

It's hopeless, of course, to read this and really have a sense of what you might be eating if you ordered. Which is the point. In its own terribly hip way, Gagnaire's menu was a reversion to the old, pre-nouvelle days when menus would be filled with portentous but inexplicable items like Veal Orlov or Pigeon

Prince Rainier. One of the nouvelle tenets was not only to let ingredients taste like what they really were, but to write menu descriptions that would actually inform rather than dazzle or obfuscate.

To Pierre Gagnaire, his vague descriptions were important. "I want to suggest to the diner what I'm about to do but not be tied down to a recipe or some predictable formula. Every time I cook a dish it is different, never the same. Or why should I cook?"

The restaurant had a very L.A. feel that was easy to mock: lots of good-looking guys, none over thirty, dressed in black in a stark, white space highlighted with bursts of color; and, yes, the room did look like the food, bold slashes of color on a white background.

And about the food. While we were puzzling over the menu, Gagnaire appeared before us and asked if "it would be your pleasure that I simply cook for you?" It was such a charming, old-fashioned turn of phrase, all the more affecting when surrounded by the white and glass Gagnaire loved, that it was impossible to resist. And, truth was, we had no idea what anything on the menu would taste like. So we did what seemed easiest and accepted.

It came in nine or ten courses, I lost track somewhere along the way. What did Gagnaire call each course? I have no idea. But we ate, in order, more or less:

1. Sautéed perch with pine nuts, served warm.
2. Clams with carrots and assorted vegetables, minced finely, with a slice of very creamy regional chèvre.
3. Toast with a thick anchovy paste, warmed.
4. Clear tomato gelée with pureed artichoke, served cool.
5. Cool cannelloni stuffed with spinach, with a tomato confit on the side and a red curry sauce.

6. Mille-feuille shell with shredded radishes with an onion confit.
7. Gnocchi with crabmeat and scallops over a layer of white truffles.
8. Omble, a fish from Lake Leman, with frogs legs in a rich brown sauce (of cream, fish stock, and chives), along with a pea sauce with shelled peas and cream splattered around.
9. A baked tomato with girolles, carrots, and a beet-juice sauce.
10. Dorade royale with cracked wheat, shredded cabbage with *beurre montée*, a fried cabbage leaf on top.
11. And for dessert, peach juice with rose-petal liqueur.

Of course, reading a laundry list of the dishes that merely details their ingredients is a bit like describing a van Gogh by saying "a bunch of big sunflowers in a field." Gagnaire's food had an attitude, a certain in-your-face brashness that was irresistible. It was Food as Personality. To come to Gagnaire's restaurant was to be overwhelmed with the essence of Gagnaire, or at least the public character that Gagnaire had created. For all its trendy hipness, it was really a logical extension of the Personality Cult cooking perfected by Paul Bocuse.

"All my life I've wanted to go to Bocuse," Carl said as we pulled up the next day at the surprisingly small restaurant just off the Saône river on the outskirts of Lyons in Collonges-au-Mont-d'Or. While Gagnaire confronted your senses on all fronts with his particular quirky style—the slashing colors, the post-modern design, the black-turtlenecked waiters—visiting Bocuse was like going to an unpretentious auberge, with one notable exception: Bocuse's name and image are everywhere. The flashing lights out front spelling BOCUSE, the large paintings of the Great Chef, the framed letters and magazine covers, the Bocuse logo—the name beneath a Rabelaisian drawing of the chef—on everything, from the napkin holders to the cookbooks and aprons for sale in the foyer gift shop.

The menu—a handsome affair with an impressionist style painting of the restaurant's exterior in bright red and green on the cover—lists honors bestowed upon Bocuse and the staff:

PAUL BOCUSE, MEILLEUR OUVRIER DE FRANCE, PARIS, 1961

ROGER JALOUX, CHEF DES CUISINES, MEILLEUR OUVRIER DE FRANCE, PARIS 1976, ASSISTÉ DE CHRISTIAN BOUVAREL

JEAN FLEURY, MEILLEUR OUVRIER DE FRANCE, PARIS 1979.

They are listed like credits in a film and appear at the bottom of three of the four pages of the menu. The back of the menu is dedicated to a bilingual biography: the humble family auberge transformed by the ambitious Bocuse to the "First Restaurant in the World" by the Rich and Famous World's Best, whatever that is, as well as Bocuse's acclamation as the "Chef of the Century" by Gault-Millau. And, of course, his rise from no stars to one star in 1961 and three stars in 1965, including the requisite apprenticeships, with la Mère Brazier at the Col de la Luère restaurant and, as was mandatory for his generation, with the legendary Fernand Point.

Bocuse himself was nowhere to be seen, but his wife, Raymonde, was in charge, directing the staff of over sixty members. The dining room seemed filled with foreigners, Germans, French-Canadians, Americans, Japanese, which is not surprising for the place that is arguably the most famous restaurant in the world. There was a quiet confidence to the service and menu, with none of the frenetic striving of Gagnaire. It's the difference between a long-running play—a hit, for sure, a great and glorious hit, but one many years past its initial raves—and the hottest show in town that just moved from Off Broadway, where it stunned everyone with its success.

Consider the *menu dégustation* for 710 francs:

*Foie gras frais maison cuit en terrine*
                    *ou*
*Soupe de grenouilles cressonnière*
*Fricassée de homard à l'américaine*
*Granité des vignerons du Beaujolais*
*Pigeon en feuilleté au chou nouveau et au foie gras*
*Selection de fromages frais et affinés "Mere Richard"*
*Crème brûlée à la cassonade Sirio*
*Délices et gourmandises*
*Petits fours et chocolats*

A food historian—there really are such things—would deem it a classic. Not surprising and certainly not trying to be daring, the sort of menu that requires superb execution. A *Salade d'artichauts et haricots verts au foie gras* is as good as imaginable, with a simple olive oil vinaigrette, the haricots presented with minced shallots, the foie gras a cold, incredibly creamy square.

The *Sandre grillé sur sa peau à la marinière* reeks of Provence, grilled crispy skin, olive oil, big hunks of garlic, tomatoes, and a fish mousse wrapped in zucchini flower. It has that satisfying combination of being both simple and complicated. I followed it with *Poulet de Bresse rôti à la broche*, which was the perfect thing to have after Gagnaire's concoctions. A chicken. Grilled. Thank you.

Flashbulbs seemed to be going off every few minutes as the crowd scrambled to document their presence at Bocuse. It was fitting, really, because Bocuse had willed himself to celebrity status by throwing himself into the media spotlight and now the world came to Bocuse to throw themselves into the light his stardom cast. More than anyone, Bocuse grasped the concept of marketing the aura bestowed upon him by Michelin. No matter how much you packed a dining room, it was impossible to make serious money without, in essence, franchising your name. Some flinched at this notion as crassly commercial, others simply saw themselves as chefs, not businessmen, but Bocuse embraced it with the passion for which he was famous. He would become not merely Paul Bocuse, the Great Chef, he would branch out to become Bocuse, Inc.

The Bocuse empire stretched from the banks of the Saône to include his own line of wines, champagnes, teas, and foie gras; boutiques in Japan; a Beaujolais vineyard; the Pavilion de France at Disney World's Epcot Center. He's won so many awards that now he's started giving out his own, the Bocuse d'Or.

"It's like coming to church," Carl announced toward the end of the meal.

"Carl goes to church," Rat told me, as if I had questioned him. "He goes almost every Sunday."

"Only in New York," Carl said, "would going to church be interpreted as eccentric behavior."

"A charming eccentricity," Rat insisted. "It's just one of those things I love about you."

Carl lit up like he had slipped his finger into a light socket. "Yeah?" he asked, clearly disbelieving. "Yeah?"

There were times when Carl resembled nothing so much as a big, love-struck palooka who'd follow his bombshell gal anywhere. It was strange to see so much vulnerability emanating from a millionaire corporate lawyer. The truth was that I really didn't have a good sense of what Rat thought of the guy. But it was clear he was drop-dead in love with her. I kept thinking about poor Buddy Ebsen in *Breakfast at Tiffany's* coming to claim his child bride from the clutches of New York City. "Lulamae? Lulamae? It's time for you to come home."

"You don't want a lot of surprises in church, but you want to come away feeling that all is right with the world. That there is a logical order to the world that has been reaffirmed."

"I don't know, guys," I said. "You come, you pay lots of money, you eat great food. But church? Church?!"

"You know the difference between God and Paul Bocuse?" Rat asked.

Carl and I both stared blankly. "God doesn't think he's Paul Bocuse."

# Chapter
# Eighteen

The final push through the last of the three-stars fell into a comfortable pattern. (Push? Was it really a push? Or more a frolic, or perhaps a roll? We *rolled* our way through France. Yes, that's more like it.)

It was a very physical, focused life without a hint of redeeming purpose. Every morning I rose early and went for a long run, sometimes with Henry, for whom I'd developed a troubling fondness. Rat and Carl would be getting up when I came back, and by eleven o'clock or so we'd be on the road to the next restaurant.

Except for Bocuse and Gagnaire, every one of the remaining three-stars still offered rooms, as befitted their roots as provincial inns, and we always stayed at the restaurants. It made crawling upstairs after dinner easier, of course, but it was also intriguing to run into the chefs or members of the staff the next morning as they prepared for the daily onslaught.

That's how I encountered Bernard Loiseau, when I was stumbling around the dining room of La Côte d'Or, looking for a cup of coffee. Without thinking too clearly, I had this idea that I could just wander into the kitchen and find a coffeepot; it was the kind of thing you'd do at summer camp, or maybe at a big house party after a long night of drinking. I hadn't really focused on the notion that I was invading the domain of a three-star perfectionist.

With cup in hand, I was making my way through the deserted dining room toward the kitchen doors when I heard a bemused chuckle that was really almost a giggle erupt behind me.

"It is possible to have breakfast in your room, you know," Bernard Loiseau said to me. I turned around and saw a grinning, mostly bald fellow dressed in white. He had a face you took seriously, the mature, friendly face of a small-town doctor, an effect enhanced by his white garb.

"But I'm going running," I explained, and he was kind enough to nod at my nonsensical response. I was wearing shorts, a torn tee shirt from a ski race, and running shoes.

"Me, I like to shoot things," Bernard said.

"Like people stealing coffee from the kitchen?"

"You have stolen nothing," he insisted good-naturedly.

"Okay, people *trying* to steal coffee?"

"That is different," he agreed. "Let's have coffee and talk about the chicken," he said, suddenly more serious.

The chicken was the dinner we'd ordered the night before that had been, well, something of a disaster. If anything that happens at a wonderful restaurant like Côte d'Or could be called a disaster.

"So," Bernard said when we sat down over the coffee that one of his assistants had suddenly produced, "not our best night, huh?"

It had been a perfectly delightful night, actually. But the chicken had been, well, off.

This dish had intrigued me as soon as I'd seen it on the menu that was waiting in the rooms when we checked in. Who wouldn't be curious: *La poularde truffée à la vapeur "Alexandre Dumaine" au riz basmati truffé*. This was great stuff, all the more so when the menu noted that it took an hour and a half to prepare.

It was not the sort of dish that had made Loiseau famous or, in some circles, notorious. Back when he had but two stars and was striving mightily for his third, Loiseau had hit upon a technique he called *cuisine à l'eau*—water cooking. It was, in its simplest form, nouvelle cuisine taken to a new level. No butter, cream, or egg yolks. As William Echikson describes in his fascinating book about Loiseau, *Burgundy Stars*, "Bernard even refused the elemental trick of deglazing a pan with wine or liquor. . . . He employed a nonstick pan and even then he patted the food dry with a paper towel."

It was radical cooking, even in the post-nouvelle world. "Part of Bernard's intention," Echikson notes, "was to draw attention to himself. He succeeded, without a doubt. His inventions created a great and acrimonious debate within French gastronomic circles." They also gave rise to the classic wisecrack attributed to Bocuse "when he was strolling along the banks of the river Saône. 'What a pity,' Bocuse said. 'If only Bernard could see all that sauce going to waste.'"

As I wound my way through the three-star world, I was coming to realize that it wasn't so much their food that distinguished the chefs one from another, but more their ambition. What did three stars mean to each of them? Was it a climax to a long-held dream or just a launching pad for the Next Step, whatever that might be? Did they see themselves as chef or celebrity?

By all accounts, including his own, none lusted for fame more ardently than Bernard Loiseau. The flamboyant Loiseau—Bernard the Bird, everyone seemed to call him—wanted to be the most famous chef of his generation and didn't apologize for a second. Three stars was part of that, but it wasn't enough by itself. Bernard, it seemed, wanted to be the Fourth Star that would be illuminated by his three stars but a star that shown more brightly than any other.

"It's how we go about reducing the sauce," Bernard said, as I sipped coffee and tried to wake up.

The dish in question was basically a boiled chicken in the pot, a classic peasant dish. But Loiseau slipped black truffles under the skin of the bird, stuffed it with leeks, carrots, and chicken liver, and steamed it in a mixture of port and brandy, chicken and beef stock. When I'd asked about it before ordering—asked over the phone from my room, because it was suggested that one order the dish in advance—I was given an irresistible description of the moment when the covered dish was brought to the table and unveiled in an explosion of aroma.

Which came to pass pretty much as promised. The recently renovated dining room overlooking the gardens—part of Loiseau's successful three-star push—was pleasantly half full. We'd just had two trademark Loiseau dishes, his *jambonnettes de grenouilles à la purée d'ail et au jus de persil* and his *escargots*. He seemed to take special pleasure in putting his own touch to classic Burgundy dishes, like an ice skater or gymnast adding a personalized style to the mandatory exercises required for competition.

So instead of snails swimming in butter and garlic, Loiseau cooked snails still in the shell and served them wrapped in green nettles and he rejected frying frogs legs in butter. As Echikson writes, "Bernard lightened the dish by simmering fresh garlic cloves for half an hour—and then changing the water ten times to eliminate their overpowering taste. He blended the garlic with milk to the consistency of mashed potatoes. Then he made a thick green parsley puree. The frogs legs were fried, and at the last possible moment all the elements were put on the plate."

To Loiseau, it was a way to preserve the true flavors of the food. "You have the garlic taste without the force," he recounts in *Burgundy Stars*, "you have the natural juice of parsley without the butter. Each element is put together at the last moment, when it adds to the other. Not too many different elements, either, just two or three. You can't have too many tastes in the mouth at the same time."

The snails and the frogs legs had been so good, we'd actually ordered another round as soon as we had tasted them. "My

Lord," Carl murmured. "This is the best thing I've ever had," he said, savoring the juicy meat of the leg. "It actually tastes like frog. I always figured it would be a nasty taste, or why else did you throw all that garlic and crap on it?" He was joking—sort of— in response to the description from our waiter that the actual taste of the frog came through in Loiseau's treatment, but it was true that it was a strong but subtle flavor that was truly intoxicating.

It was the ordering of the second round that I thought must have thrown their timing off, a stutter step for the kitchen, forcing them to delay the preparation of the *poularde truffée à la vapeur "Alexandre Dumaine."* It seemed an easy explanation because when the dish did arrive and was unveiled, the sufficient *ohhhs* and *ahhhs* issued, the first bite revealed that something was simply off.

It was as clear as wine that had turned to vinegar. Or broth that had turned to salt, to be more precise. Salty broth over hard kernels of basmati rice. Rat and I, who were sharing the dish, took a bite and looked at each other. Then we took another, larger bite. It wasn't that the dish was disappointing, it was simply . . . wrong.

So we did something that we had never done at one of the three-stars—sent the dish back. The usual flurry ensued, apologies, the maître d'hôtel (whom I later learned, by reading *Burgundy Stars*, was named Hubert Couilloud) appeared and charmed us to the quick. A *bar rôti* was substituted and was delicious. It was, all in all, no big deal.

But the next morning Bernard Loiseau was concerned. "At most places," he said, with a shrug, "one dish, maybe it's not perfect, it's okay. But a three-star . . ."

Loiseau was impossible not to like, a man whose emotions played across his broad face like it was a television. He made much of his poor roots—I started with only a toothbrush, no showers or toilets in my parents' house, he confided over coffee, an oft-told tale, it seemed according to William Echikson—and didn't try to disguise his sweeping ambition. He saw fame as noble, a just reward for the risks and the impossibly long hours he worked, the years without a vacation.

As a teenage apprentice at Troisgros, he'd had an epiphany the day they received their third star. This was what he wanted in life. Three stars. More apprenticeships followed, stints at Paris, and finally a chance to take over La Côte d'Or in Saulieu. Though it had two stars, it was a restaurant on the way down in a town that seemed to be dying, thanks to the construction of the A6 highway fifteen miles to the east. In its glory, La Côte d'Or had been one of France's great restaurants, run by the legendary Alexandre Dumaine. But Dumaine had died, the A6 had opened up, and La Côte d'Or seemed to be a punishment more than a job for a young, passionately ambitious chef like Bernard Loiseau.

But living alone above the dining room in a shack of a room, Loiseau saw La Côte d'Or as his path to greatness. By sheer force of his personality as much as anything, he was able to convince banks to back him in first purchasing the restaurant and later pouring three million dollars into the renovations Loiseau felt were essential to compete for a third star.

"You know what I'm going to do before we leave France," Rat said, as we were wandering around La Côte d'Or. "I'm gonna find that Michelin fellow who makes them consider the *damn buildings* and not just the food and then I'm gonna tie him up with dental floss and do nasty things to him until they drop that nonsense forever."

She had a point. We were learning that grandiose architectural disasters had been wrought in the pursuit of Michelin approval. The Côte d'Or renovations had been criticized by one architecture professor as "kitsch," with a main dining room that lacked intimacy and empty hallways of "wasted space." But the mere fact that Loiseau was willing to back his cuisine with a $3 million renovation was said to impress Michelin. After the third star was awarded, *Le Monde* wrote, "Loiseau's cooking is not better this year—one doesn't know how to do better—but the ambience, thanks to the costly renovation, is magnificent. The third star last year would have crowned the cook; this year it seems to award the architect."

"These people, they know how to cook," Rat said as we were taking one last turn around La Côte d'Or, "but I swear to God, my little sister has got better taste than most of them."

"That the one who lives in the trailer?" Carl said.

"*Used to.* Then she married that rich doctor who moved to Cody from Dallas. Built a house kind of like this."

When he was contemplating expanding, Loiseau was well aware that his Burgundy competition, Marc Meneau, had spent a fortune renovating L'Espérance in Saint-Père-sous-Vézelay, had been rewarded with a third star, and had seen his sales jump 30 percent the next year. Georges Blanc had taken a simple eight-room country inn and transformed it into a resort with boutiques and a helicopter pad. At La Côte St. Jacques in Joigny, the father-son team of Michel and Jean-Michel Lorain had erected a miniature Versailles, complete with an underground tunnel linking the original inn with additions across the street. Even the Troisgros brothers had been compelled to turn their hotel-restaurant across from the train station in Roanne into a glass-and-chrome modern concoction.

There was something about it that was both ludicrous and depressing. Most of the renovations had a fun-house, amusement-park quality mixed with a heavy dose of Arab brothel. Like L'Espérance, Marc Meneau's creation.

"Glassed-in dining rooms that don't really go with the style of the nineteenth-century buildings," Rat read from Gault-Millau as we pulled up at L'Espérance. As if in reaction to the quiet

French countryside, the Mustang had become even louder, so that it took hours to recover from its throttled roar. We had become accustomed to people staring at us while we shouted at each other like a traveling troupe of half-mad, food-obsessed homeless people—with dog—wandering across the landscape, disrupting everything wherever we went.

Merely noting that the glass dining rooms "don't really go with the style of the nineteenth-century buildings" was a preposterous understatement, like observing that a football player showing up for the big game in a pink tutu "didn't really match the other uniforms." The Blue Guide describes Vézelay as a "small fortified hill-top village" with a tenth-century abbey- church, La Madeleine, of note, with a "terrace commanding attractive views." From which, the Blue Guide most definitely does not note, one can see what appears to be a spaceship trying to dock with a nineteenth-century manor house. That's L'Espérance.

Glass. These three-star chefs had a very unfortunate fetish for big, bulging glass edifices, glass in the bedrooms, glass everywhere. "Either they feel bad about these hideous additions," Carl said, in a little insight that surprised me, "and they figure if they throw a bunch of glass up it'll make it less like they are mutilating nature, or they have these architects who still don't understand that structures like the Pompidou Center are ruining France."

Later, when I learned that Meneau had hired Pierre Parat, the same architect who'd designed Paris's Bercy sports complex, I wasn't in the least surprised. The design purposes would have been dismally similar: erect some big impressive thing that will get a lot of attention and draw a big crowd. But what in God's name did this even remotely have to do with enjoying some of the best food you'll ever put in your mouth? Does it come as a shock that superb French chefs have a lousy design sense? Would you ask a bunch of architects to prepare a great meal? Or would you require architects to cook as part of a competition for the Ten Greatest Architects in the World?

But did all this theme-park ugliness matter? Of course. This is the same generation of chefs who rebelled against the overdone artifice of classical French cuisine, the chefs who challenged the French gastronomic establishment so that they could capture more of the essence of food, the chefs who championed regional distinctions. Why didn't they realize that by pouring millions of dollars into overblown glass greenhouses and sunken tubs with mirrored ceilings they were throwing themselves into massive debt to create an environment that stood for everything they were against?

Maybe that's why it was so good to step into Pic.

Right on the Avenue Victor-Hugo in the solid provincial town of Valence, it still felt like a restaurant, not a theme park. The clientele actually seemed local, with not an American or Japanese to be seen, and the dining room had a distinct fifties feel with plush, floral rugs, pink walls, chairs done in a flame tapestry, and simple, quite elegant tablecloths of a faint pink. It wasn't particularly attractive but comfortable and solid, like a prosperous, middle-class country club.

Perhaps Pic was saved because it never tried to expand into a fancy hotel as well as a three-star. It had only four rooms, and all had been booked. Which brought us to a more or less modern motel on the outskirts of Valence.

It sat not far from the highway in a field of sunflowers, a simple two-story affair that would have looked at home next to a Dairy Queen in Sioux Falls, South Dakota, or a lobster-roll stand in Auburn, Maine. Carl groaned when we pulled up, but Rat and I liked it right away. "This is just like a place outside of Cody where the rich boys in town always tried to take their girlfriends."

"Cody," Carl said. He was learning an impressive amount about Cody. We both were, for that matter.

"Oh, you'll like it so much when we move there, honey. Really, you will."

"I think I would like Cody, actually," Carl said. "Get a big place, run around and shoot things all the time, *see your parents every weekend.*"

Rat shuddered.

In the best American roadside tradition, a small pool was positioned behind the motel—*an in-ground pool*, as they would have advertised where I grew up. It shimmered on the edge of the sunflower field like a small, kidney-shaped watering hole.

"Love that pool," Rat said as we checked in. The man behind the Formica counter was in his late fifties, with the rough good looks of a soap opera leading man: a chiseled face, thick eyebrows, sweeping black hair flecked with gray. His manner was gruff, as if he vaguely resented the fact that we were checking into his hotel.

He rolled his eyes at Rat's comment. "It was her idea, you know. As if we need a pool. Who comes to Valence to sit by the pool, huh? Salesmen, businesspeople, that's who stays here."

"We came to eat," I said, rather melodramatically. In my mind I kept trying to formulate some higher purpose to our venture, as if we were gastronomic knights roaming the countryside, challenging the forces of evil to do battle. This was a much improved self-image than the reality of three transplanted food-crazed friends sinking into an orgy of overindulgence.

"Pic, huh?" he said, sizable eyebrows shooting upward. "It is the best thing we have in this town, and I have lived here all my life. Too bad about the old man, huh? His food was from the gods."

The "old man" was Jacques Pic, who had recently died, leaving his son, Alain Pic, to run the kitchen while his daughter took care of the front of the house.

"My wedding reception was there. She would have it no other way," he said, shaking his head but smiling. "Cost a fortune."

The "she" that he was talking about soon materialized by the pool. I found her there when I returned from a long run. The three of them—Carl, Rat, and Suzanne—seemed intent on re-enacting a bit of the Riviera in the middle of the sunflower field. They were drinking Ruinart champagne, the women in bikinis and Carl squeezed into one of those preposterous thong-type bathing suits that only professional lounge-lizard Italians or Greek shipping tycoons should ever attempt to wear.

Suzanne looked to be in her late twenties, a good thirty years younger than her husband, a very pretty brunette with a quick laugh and bright blue eyes. "You are selling something, no?" she asked, extending her hand. I took it, dripping wet from my run, puzzled.

"You have heard the lecture, no? Of why build a pool for salesmen?"

"You are from Valence?" I asked, not really knowing what to say to this charming woman lounging by a strip of water in a sunflower field.

"We are all from Valence, of course. No one moves to Valence. Me, I married the most handsome man in town." She looked at Rat and said adamantly, "You will see. Marc is the best-looking man for fifty kilometers!"

"I'm sure," Rat answered. Behind her sixties-styled aviator glasses she might have been thinking anything. Was she enjoying Suzanne?

"No, but *I* am!" Suzanne swore. "I have looked, I promise!"

"What's a girl to do?" Rat asked in sudden solidarity.

On this note, I jumped into the pool. It was warm and very clear but without a hint of chlorine.

"What do you use to clean the pool?" I asked Suzanne on surfacing.

She laughed. "This is important? I know, I know everything about the pool. It's my baby."

"What else do you do?" Carl asked. He had been lying motionless in his tiny bathing suit and I figured he was either asleep or pretending to be asleep so that he wouldn't have to take responsibility for the trunks.

"I am an accountant!" she announced, improbably.

"Do you want to have dinner with us?" Rat asked.

"Americans!" she exclaimed.

"Maybe you and your husband," I suggested. Rat glared at me.

"He plays cards tonight. It is Wednesday, you see."

I nodded. It *was* Wednesday.

"Come on," Rat insisted. "It'll be fun. If I don't have some foie gras tonight I'm just going to die."


Maybe the place felt so comfortable because we were with Suzanne, who knew everyone, of course, but I think it was really a question of Pic's style. They were out to please, not to impress.

And I was very hungry, which is always a good thing.

Hunger drove me to start with grilled John Dory with basil and *girolle* mushrooms. It was smoky and superb, served in a fumet sauce of shellfish reduction. Then *Poêlée de langoustines à l'huile d'olives et truffes*, warm shrimp in an oil-based sauce, served on a cool base of radicchio and minced olives. Finally, I had a *Cassolette d'écrevisses et truffes de la Saint Jean*, which was basically a wild rice risotto with a wild crawfish that wasn't farmed and had a very short season. It was shockingly light, without cream or butter.

"This man," Suzanne said, nodding toward me, "he likes his crustaceans."

"A dangerous man with a knife and fork, that's God's gospel," Rat assured her.

We'd been drinking a lot, probably too much. I blamed it on Rat and Carl, who had felt it necessary to start drinking champagne in the afternoon.

I felt awkward with Rat and Suzanne talking about me, as if I were either not present or deaf and dumb. So I reached across the table and speared a piece of Rat's dish. It was slivers of beef sandwiched between foie gras. The tastes and textures were extraordinary: rare filet mignon with creamy foie gras in a light red-wine sauce.

We'd dropped our pretentious Margaux-only rule to work our way through several bottles of Paul Jaboulet's Crozes-Hermitage.

"You think they will let me take some of these with us?" Carl asked, holding up a bottle.

"Some of these?" Rat laughed. "Like a wine doggy bag. We could tell them that Henry needed a drink."

"Terribly unfair of us not to bring a spot of Crozes-Hermitage to Henry," Carl agreed, switching, inexplicably, to an English accent.

"No, no, no!" Suzanne yelled. "We have a cellar! We have a restaurant! We go to the pool and drink!"

No one argued.

It was later, much later, though I'm not exactly sure of the hour, when Rat, Carl, and Suzanne decided it was very important that they see who could swim the fastest. This presented certain logistical problems, as the pool was not very large and was kidney-shaped as well. A six-lap format was settled upon after serious discussion. As I was declining to compete, I became the designated starter. I thought I could handle the challenge.

"Un, deux, trois—"

A loud explosion completed my count. The swimmers dove into the pool, as if they had heard the starter's shot. Ears ringing, I looked over to my immediate right and saw our hotel proprietor with a strange grin on his face and a shotgun in his arms.

"So," he said, "we see who is the fastest, no?"

# Chapter
# Nineteen

He was wearing an English hunting jacket over his chef's whites. While we talked, he was constantly drawing—figures, numbers, funny faces.

I was sitting in Pierre Troisgros's office, a small, cluttered space attached to the lobby of his hotel-restaurant in Roanne. He was an old friend of Hubert's and had invited me in for a drink and a chat. The night before we'd enjoyed one of his quietly spectacular meals.

His mood seemed to be nostalgic and a touch melancholy. Next year he was publishing a book that would be the history of the three generations of the Troisgros family, the story of how they had taken the unassuming station-house restaurant in Roanne and transformed it into one of the most famous destinations in France.

The story began with the *cuisine du terroir* of his parents, whose clientele were local businessmen and factory workers. They served a *table d'hôte* with a table large enough for forty-five people. This was the kitchen in which he and his brother were raised.

"For those travellers who had the good luck to know Le Restaurant Troisgros in the sixties and early seventies," writes Rudolph Chelminski in *The French at Table*, "there are two images that stick in the memory vividly . . . the little old kitchen and the little old father. . . . Jean and Pierre and their growing army of assistants tended their pots and pans in the modest galley which had served their mother. . . . It was both comical and impressive to realize that so much food of such incredible quality came from the overheated, overcrowded back room, where the cooks had to walk with their elbows in, lest they bonk into a passing *entrecôte*."

The second phase of the Troisgrois legend begins in the years Pierre and his brother were helping to create nouvelle cuisine, inspired by their apprenticeship with Monsieur Point at La Pyramide and their close friendship and rivalry with Bocuse and Guérard. "It was when we *unconsciously* changed cuisine," Pierre said, with a skeptical raise of his eyebrow. Though he is as famous as any chef in the world, Troisgros radiates a certain amiable skepticism for the publicity-mad hunger of a Bocuse, who once said, "You have to beat the drum in life. God is already famous, but that doesn't stop *Monsieur le Curé* from ringing the church bell."

The third phase was being led by his son Michel. "There is today," he said, with a smile that could only be called sweet, "a nostalgia for the *cuisine classique* and *cuisine du terroir*. Now they make subtle but critical changes to the old dishes by the addition of a fresh herb, using olive oil instead of butter, adding a vinegar—we use eighteen different types—or some emendation to give the dish a new slant. Like cod. It's not classic haute cuisine, not lobster or *écrevisses*, which have such a short season, but it can be three-star quality."

And then, surprisingly, this big, most old-fashioned-looking gentleman, who seemed out of place even among his own sleekly modern renovations, began to talk about the improvements technology in the kitchen had brought. Not just convenience, he insisted; technology let them do more. Like—and I couldn't believe he was saying this—electric knives. *Electric knives?* Those things they sold on late-night television to go with fondue pots? But Pierre Troisgros explained how electric knives had made it much easier to prepare fish or vegetable terrines that were difficult to cut by hand. And the ovens—now they had four, including steam ovens.

I'd seen the kitchens—sleek and chrome-infested, like the hotel, really. It was impossible not to feel—as I suspect Pierre Troisgros did—that a certain magic of discovery had been lost in the renovations. I tried to imagine what it must have been like to wander off the train at Roanne, drift across the street, and sit down in an unassuming little restaurant and have the best food of your life. Dazzling, astounding food.

But Troisgros was adamant. Change was good. They had learned more, had grown in their art. Take their famous *saumon à l'oseille*. It was a signature dish, one that had been on the menu for over two decades. "Pierre Troisgros's invention of *saumon à l'oseille* typifies what Gault and Millau called nouvelle cuisine," writes William Echikson in *Burgundy Stars*. "Until Troisgros, the accepted way of cooking fish was to take thick chunks and coat them in flour and bake them in butter. Troisgros threw out the coating, cut the fish in thin scallopini, and cooked them in white wine until they were just rose. In his garden, sorrel sprouted, so he threw it over the fish."

But now they offered several versions of it. Both still used cream sauce, but one was served with the sorrel crispy from the pan and layered on top of the salmon. Another version was prepared with whole sorrel leaves surrounding a more rare salmon that had been steamed.

He held up the menu he had been drawing on: there were two happy-looking pieces of salmon with bright eyes and smiles, one with crispy sorrel, the other surrounded by sorrel. "Like this, no?" he smiled, then grew more serious.

"I really think," he said, "that we pass on knowledge from generation to generation and it is up to each generation to throw out much of what they have learned. But they couldn't throw it out unless they had learned it. You understand, no? I believe French cooking is *the* cooking for our civilization."

I left Pierre Troisgros in his office, looking over designs for the labels of his wine bottles.

"A passion for wine is an inherited trait," Troisgros wrote in the latest edition of Larousse's *Wines and Vineyards of France*, "and I have been careful not to rid myself of it."

Across the street from Troisgros, Rat and Carl were sitting at a table in the little railway station café. Rat was reading a French soccer magazine—she was a great fan—and Carl was working his way through a stack of the violent, erotic comic books the French adore. They looked comfortable together, and for perhaps the first time, I began to see them as a couple. Away from his law office, Carl had grown a goatee, and it gave him an aging hipster cast, an effect increased by the leather sandals he'd bought at the market in Florence and the worn pair of khakis that seemed to be the only non-suit pants he'd brought to Europe. The loud, suspendered figure I vaguely remembered from a New York party seemed very far away indeed. Henry lounged at his feet, looking most content.

It was not a long drive from Roanne to Vonnas, the town Georges Blanc had transformed. I drove while Rat and Carl read and napped. They still seemed to be recovering from the long night of poolside drinking in Valence. Suzanne's shotgun-wielding husband had turned out to be a delightful fellow and one of the most impressive drinkers I'd ever encountered. He was quite modest about his cellar, but at some five thousand bottles, it had many hidden delights.

Sitting by the pool with a half dozen different wines open around us, he and I had talked about bird hunting until the sun came up. Carl mostly dozed in the grass, reviving whenever a new bottle was opened. "Fabulous," he'd say, "just fabulous," concentrating intensely on his glass, then, when it was empty, putting it down gently and falling back to sleep. Rat and Suzanne talked quietly by themselves.

Around dawn, Denis—that was the hotel's proprietor's name—nodded toward his wife and said, simply, "She will leave me soon."

I'd laughed, trying to shake his mood, but he'd reiterated very matter-of-factly, "It is true. My hope is that she will take lovers and stay with me. Do you think that is possible?"

He seemed to want yes for an answer, but I was hesitant to rush in and reassure him not to worry, that his young wife would soon be taking lovers, no doubt about it.

"You think no?" he asked glumly.

"Well . . ."

"My friends all thought I was crazy when we married." He shrugged. "'Just you wait,' they said. But I told them, 'Better to seize life by the throat and choke it then wait for it to kick you in the teeth, huh?'"

I thought about this, watching the sky begin to lighten. It suddenly seemed very cool by the little pool just before dawn. "That's why we came to France," I finally said, and I think I meant it and I think it might even have made some sense.

The drive from Roanne to Vonnas was quietly spectacular, a pastiche of the richness of French agricultural life. Haywagons topped with heavy loads. Huge Charolais cattle roamed through fields squared neatly by hedgerows. An hour from Roanne, we passed through the heart of the Beaujolais district, the rolling hills crowded with vineyards of gamay grapes, low and pruned short. Stretching along the Saône for fifty-five kilometers, the region held over seven thousand wine-growing estates.

On the eastern bank of the Saône, the land leveled, hay fields stretching out toward the horizon. Queen Anne's lace wildflowers lined the road, the sky bright blue, with big, puffy clouds.

I was suddenly struck by how much I would miss France. It was a curiously nostalgic feeling for a place I hadn't left, but the list of three-stars was down to three, and I was already thinking of what life would bring back in New York.

Rat woke up.

"What's that smell?"

"Smell?"

But then I caught it. A rubbery, burning smell. Not a good smell at all.

"I think," Rat said most calmly, "I think we might be on fire."

"That's crazy," I snorted, just as smoke began billowing up under the red hood of the car.

Carl woke up, took a deep breath, and shouted, "Fire!"

Henry, not to be left out, started barking.

A tiny Citroën Deux Cheveaux passed us, horn honking wildly.

"All right, all right," I mumbled. "Give me a break."

Through a rising cloud of thick smoke, I pulled the car over, crushing a long line of the wildflowers I'd been admiring.

"Where's your fire extinguisher?" Carl demanded, reverting to his years of military training.

"I don't have a damn fire extinguisher," I shot back. "Who carries a fire extinguisher, for cryin' out loud?"

"People who don't want their old Mustangs to burn," Carl said.

If I'd had a fire extinguisher, I would have definitely used it to slide the nozzle down his throat. Then a little squeeze of the handle. . . . It was a delicious notion.

We were out of the car now, standing around, staring at it, as if our concentrated looks of concern might extinguish the flames.

"Only one thing to do," Carl announced.

"Run?" Rat suggested.

Carl reached into the back seat and grabbed the case of Ruinart champagne that I was planning on taking back to the States.

"Carl!" I shouted.

But it was no use. He uncorked a bottle in record time and, with a quick shake, was soon spewing my favorite champagne in the world all over the hood of the smoldering Mustang. Great white clouds of steam joined the black smoke.

By now, a half dozen cars had stopped, the crowd drawn by the hope of something truly disastrous unfolding.

"Ahhh, the *champagne!*" shouted a wizened old fellow in a beret. Then he quickly reached into the cardboard case and brought out a bottle and started to uncork it.

"Wait!" I shouted, but now Rat was grabbing a bottle and then the teenager with the shoulder-length hair who'd gotten off his motorcycle to watch the fun.

"*Zee Mustang!*" the man in the beret cried. "We must save zee Mustang!"

"Forget the car!" I yelled. "It's insured! Save the champagne!"

But it was no use. The hood was lifted and a dozen bottles of my precious Ruinart champagne spewed over the engine.

The older Frenchman peered into the steamy mess of the engine and declared, "*Bon!* Nothing too bad, I think."

*Oh?* I wanted to scream. *So you're a Mustang expert, are you?*

"Now what?" Rat asked.

"There is a telephone in the café just two kilometers down the road," the long-haired fellow with the motorcycle said. "You can call the automobile club."

"If it's the transmission, we've got plenty of fluid," Rat said drily. "*Plenty* of fluid."

This puzzled everyone.

"Zee fluid?" the beret started to ask.

"Well, we were in Brussels and—"

"Can someone give us a ride to the bar?" I interrupted before I was forced to open up a few of the cans and drown Rat in transmission fluid.

This unleashed a great discussion among everyone of how we could get to the bar. Of course no one had a large enough car, this being rural France, to take the three of us, none of us exactly small, plus Henry, who wasn't so tiny himself, in one car. The transportation conference raged, while I sat down along the road and drank what little was left in the converted fire-extinguisher bottles of Ruinart.

Finally it was decided. Rat would go with the motorcyclist—both seemed to like this idea; Carl would ride in the small Peugeot that the kindly schoolteacher from Bellevue was driving; and Henry and I would squeeze into the Citroën Deux Cheveaux. And so we went, this odd little caravan, leaving the Mustang, hood open, looking like a very tired, fire-breathing dragon taking a nap by the side of the road.

"The fluid of the transmission, this is difficult to find in America, no?" asked my driver, Monsieur Ducloux. He had introduced himself very formally, as if in a diplomatic receiving line.

When we walked into the café, the regulars looked up from their glasses of *vin rouge* and unapologetically stared. *What is this?* We were smudged with smoke and champagne and looked like we'd been in a nasty fight. Henry trailed, tail wagging happily.

The café smelled wonderful and now very familiar: thick tobacco mixed with onions and the hint of a grilled steak and red wine. Suddenly I was ferociously hungry.

"Let's eat," Rat said.

"God, yes," Carl agreed.

Madame Vadot, the proprietor, recommended her nephew, a *mécanicien extraordinaire*, and a very hard worker since he'd recovered from that spot of trouble he had with the *gendarmes* over that borrowed car. She rolled her eyes. He had to borrow the *mayor's* car?!

We reached the nephew by phone and he was very excited. "A Mustang? A Mustang? This is true?" Then we invited the motorcyclist, the schoolteacher, and Monsieur Ducloux, who was a farmer with a little business on the side—very quiet, no need for the tax authorities to know everything—to join us for lunch.

Soon the table was crowded with *charcuterie*, *saucissons en brioche*, *pain d'épices*, and a very good bottle of Beaujolais. Several bottles, actually.

The nephew joined us at some point. He was in his early twenties and wore a blue smock and bright green sneakers.

"Have some *jambon persillé*," Rat insisted, pushing a plate toward him. He dove right in.

"So!" he announced, enjoying the audience, "it was a simple correction. Did you know that someone had *taped* your transmission line?"

"So we can drive it?" Rat asked, brightening.

"It is like new!" he declared, a bit overenthusiastically for my money.

"Thank God," Rat said. "It would kill me to miss dinner."

Madame Vadot, a bit miffed that we were contemplating dinner somewhere else, asked of our plans.

When we told her we were heading for Georges Blanc, Madame smiled broadly and produced a worn menu from Blanc. It was from a dinner celebrating the marriage of her niece to a rich stockbroker from Paris.

"Oh, monsieur," she said, "how we ate! Like kings, we ate!"

What did she have? I asked.

"*Poulet de Bresse à la Crème!* In your mouth it was a visit from God!"

Monsieur Ducloux disagreed. The *Canard Rôti aux Épices*, he insisted, pointing at the menu, that was even better.

"You are an inspector for Michelin now, huh?" Madame demanded.

The nephew thought *Pigeon au Foie Gras* looked the best.

The schoolteacher was convinced the *Homard Breton à la Coque* would be the only thing to order. *Homard! Homard!* It is the best, no?

Carl stood up and announced there was only one way to know.

"We call Monsieur Blanc and ask him, no?" laughed Madame.

Carl raised a glass of the house *rouge*. He'd had quite a few of these over lunch. Tonight, he declared, we all eat at Georges Blanc!

*But monsieur—*

"You will all be my guests! To celebrate the rescue of the *voiture extraordinaire Mustang* and—"

He paused, raising his tumbler of *rouge* higher . . .

"My engagement to the *mademoiselle*!"

Great cheers and clapping followed. Rat looked stunned and then began to cry. In the corner, Henry perked up. *What was this?*

Madame Vadot rose to offer a toast. What was the intended mademoiselle's name? she asked. Her *maiden* name she stressed, and everyone laughed.

"Rat," Carl said.

A confused moment ensued. *Rat? Rat?* And then a toast to the Rat was raised and she and Carl were kissing and then Rat asked Madame if she would mind—

Of course not, anything for the bride!

If she would mind describing once more the *Poulet de Bresse à la Crème?*

I was starting to get very hungry.

© Nancy Cohn

## ABOUT THE AUTHOR

STUART STEVENS has established himself as a popular and highly regarded travel writer with *Night Train to Turkistan* and *Malaria Dreams*. He has published stories and articles in *Esquire*, *The New Republic*, *Outside*, and other magazines and has written for the Emmy Award–winning television series *Northern Exposure* and *I'll Fly Away*. His novel *Scorched Earth* has been optioned by Warner Bros. The Stuart Stevens Group political consulting firm has produced media for presidential, senatorial, congressional, and gubernatorial races both in the United States and abroad. Stuart Stevens was born in Mississippi and lives in New York City.